101 Railway Stations

A JOURNEY OF VARIETY

101 Railway Stations

A JOURNEY OF VARIETY

Jeffery Grayer

crecy.co.uk

First published 2018

© Jeffery Grayer 2018

ISBN 9780860936923

Printed in Bulgaria by MultiPrint

Crécy Publishing Ltd
1a Ringway Trading Estate, Shadowmoss Rd,
Manchester M22 5LH
www.crecy.co.uk

Front cover: Two of the selection of the stations featured in this book: Poyle Estate Halt (upper) and Leeds Central. *Colour-Rail/Rail Photoprints*

Rear Cover:
Main image: Post closure view of Otterham station.
Inset top: Hull departure from Withernsea.
Inset middle: Paddington express at Birmingham Snow Hill.
Inset lower: Map of Knockando on the Strathspey 'Whisky route'.

Picture credits
Every effort has been made to identify and correctly attribute photographic credits. Should any error have occurred this is entirely unintentional.

Contents

Introduction

In the 1880s it was estimated that there were some 9,000 railway stations on the network in Britain. By 1948, at the time of nationalisation, this figure was down to a little over six and a half thousand and by 2015 the number had reduced to just over two and a half thousand on the Network Rail system – a reduction of nearly 75%. This book showcases a small sample, illustrating the wide variety of stations that once served, or continue to serve, the network.

In choosing a representative selection I have been guided by the observation that there have been a great many different types of station from the humblest halt to the largest metropolitan terminus, and their provision has been prompted by a wide variety of factors. Some were provided at the request of landowners through whose property the railway passed, while the sole purpose of others was to provide junctions for the numerous branch lines that once criss-crossed the country. Extraction of a variety of minerals led to the creation of others, while many grew up to service the increasingly popular seaside resorts. Additionally some were strategically inspired, deliberately cutting deep into the territory of rival companies. Local feelings ran high in the rush to provide lines and many were built that defied economic logic and consequently had relatively short working lives. Light railways had their own particularly quirky style of architecture, while the major companies sought to make monolithic statements in the major cities where competing lines vied with each other for traffic. Although the origins of many of today's stations lie in the Victorian age, Britain boasts a tremendous variety of styles from the ornate to the starkly modern. In the railway revival of the 21st century stations are again being opened, or occasionally reopened, in a style often drastically different from that of the original.

Using examples from all the former regions of BR, this is a highly selective look at the railway station, one of the key elements that has gone to make up the fabric of British society from the 19th century through to the resurgence of passenger usage being experienced in the present day. It is true that a station is often more than just a sum of its parts, and the reasons for its construction, its location, the customers who used it, the goods that were carried and the communities served all contribute to the diverse range of facilities that once graced this island. Sometimes unexpected events thrust a station into the limelight while changing circumstances over their lifetime rendered others with changed priorities or sometimes no purpose at all. These are elements that go to make up the unique character of the British railway station. In researching these locations, not only the fabric of the buildings and their history are covered, but also some quirkier elements in their stories have emerged and these are enlarged upon here.

My thanks go to the numerous photographic contributors to this volume including Martin Boddy, the late Ben Brooksbank, John Chalcraft of Railphotoprints, Roger Holmes, George Woods, Roger Joanes, Derek Fear, Kevin Robertson, Ron Fisher, the RCTS, John Evans, Nick Catford, Colour-Rail, David Pearson, the SLS, the South Western Circle, Mrs Margaret Warburton and Alan Sainty, whose images have complemented those from my own collection. Images from Wikipedia are licensed under the Creative Commons Share alike licence. Thanks are also due to the many contributors to the former Ian Allan library, now known as the Crécy Heritage Library, over the years, the files of which have been plundered to provide many of the illustrations contained herein. Map extracts are reproduced by kind permission of the Ordnance Survey.

Jeffery Grayer
Devon, 2018

(See Station No. 38) A delightful image of the railway infrastructure of Brecon seen on 15 June 1960, comprising an attractive station building, signal box and small turntable, which can be seen on the right. All this was to be swept away following closure to passengers some 18 months later, with goods services following in 1964. *Ben Brooksbank*

101 RAILWAY STATIONS
A journey of variety

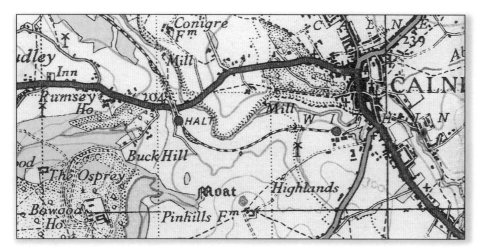

1 BLACK DOG HALT
Churchill's depression?

Winston Churchill experienced what he called his 'Black Dog', a phrase that the great wartime leader used to describe his periodic fits of depression. One might well feel depressed indeed at the closure of so many rural lines in the countryside. One such was the 5¼-mile branch from the main line at Chippenham to the market town of Calne in Wiltshire. It was closed in 1965 after having the usual 'basic railway' treatment meted out to it, i.e. destaffing and ripping up of all but the bare necessity of track, giving rise to that general air of desolation that hung about so many stations in the 1960s. Cited in the Beeching Report as one of the detailed costing examples given to support closure, it apparently would result in a net financial saving of £24,000 per annum if closed. Taking commuters into Chippenham for London and Bristol connections and locals for shopping, etc, was not enough to stave off closure. What might have saved its bacon was the local Harris sausage factory, but that stopped sending its products by rail.

Although only a siding for the occasional transport of racehorses, kept on the estate and destined for various race meetings across the country, was stipulated by the local landowner, the Marquess of Lansdowne domiciled at nearby Bowood House and through whose land the line passed, the railway company went one better and decided to construct Black Dog Halt for his lordship's personal use. He was also entitled to a special reserved compartment in one of the line's autocoaches. The company also provided an additional siding for the loading of his silverware when he wished to transport it to and from his London residence. In return for his own station he agreed to provide a house rent-free for the man in charge of the stopping place, together with firewood and coal free of charge, and a contribution of 50% towards the staff wages. However, this generosity did not come without strings in that he personally vetted any staff appointed.

Initially there were no intermediate stations on the branch, but the private station was opened at Black Dog Siding in November 1863. It took its name from the adjacent Black Dog Hill, an Inn of that name having closed around 1850. The inn building still stands, now a private house, part way up the hill on the south side. There were no restrictions on the use of the station by the public but it did not appear in a public timetable until 15 September 1952, and a station nameboard was finally fixed to the building at the end of that year. In 1898 the GWR had requested that Lord Lansdowne should allow a nameboard showing Black Dog Station to be mounted on the platform, but permission was refused. Prior to that date anyone wishing to travel to the station had to buy a

Above: Black Dog Halt is seen on 25 July 1965, a couple of months before closure of the branch. *Colour-Rail*

Right: A repositioned nameboard still survives on the former platform at this unique halt, opened to serve the nearby estate of Lord Lansdowne at Bowood. A sign was not provided until 1952 when the halt appeared in public timetables for the first time, and staffing, in the form of a Grade 1 Porter, did not cease until 1960.

ticket to Calne or to Stanley Bridge Halt in the opposite direction. Even after that date the lower classes were discouraged from travelling, access being segregated with carriages from the estate using a surfaced road while pedestrians had to use a muddy track. An ivy-covered notice on a post curtly informed the would-be traveller – 'Carriage approach to the station. Foot passengers under the bridge' – a metal finger pointing the way. Access to a long goods platform served by sidings was by a ground frame. During the First World War a top-level war cabinet meeting took place in a carriage berthed in the siding; at the time a military unit was stationed in outbuildings opposite the station.

Black Dog had a stationmaster until 1930, after which the Marquis was persuaded that a leading porter would suffice with the proviso that he was not to air any political views when dealing with the nobility and that he must keep clear of the local court where Lord Lansdowne was chairman of the magistrates! In 1950 the station house was sold and was later converted into a modern bungalow. On 8 June 1953 the station was renamed Black

Dog Halt, and on 1 February 1960 it became an unstaffed halt, the siding being last used by a local coal merchant on 1 November 1963; it was lifted shortly afterwards.

The short passenger platform was on the west side of the line and was provided with a substantial timber building incorporating rooms at either end and a waiting shelter; this survived closure on 20 September 1965 until 1967 when the track was lifted. The platform survives, as does part of the back wall of the platform building. The station nameboard has been returned to the platform although naturally not mounted in its original position due to the removal of the building. The goods platform is also extant, as is the stationmaster's house, which continues in its role as a private residence. The rail overbridge crossing the A4 road to the north of the station has been replaced by a modern footbridge. The last full-time railway employee to be based here was Douglas Lovelock, who lived in Station House and had worked at Black Dog since 1930 when, as was mentioned above, a leading porter was considered sufficient. Douglas was also involved in the demolition of the station. Bowood House survives in its Capability Brown-designed landscape, although now with the commercial expedient of opening its doors to the public and the addition of an adventure playground, golf course and boutique hotel.

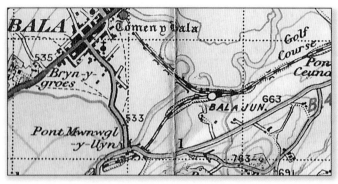

2 BALA JUNCTION
No public access

Together with other junction stations situated in the wilds, such as Dovey Junction and Killin Junction, that at Bala Junction was intended purely as an interchange point for rail passengers and was not designed for anyone wishing to join a train here. BR did not even mention it in its index to stations within the public timetable, although it did feature in the relevant timetable page with a footnote 'Passengers to and from Bala change at Bala Junction by most of the trains'. After the 1920s it was possible for the intrepid traveller to reach the station on foot using what was described as 'a bullock infested and ill defined path' across fields, but as there was little in the way of local habitation in the immediate vicinity, few probably availed themselves of this opportunity.

The station, which had no traditional 'forecourt', boasted three platform faces – the Bala branch used the northerly face of the island platform – a lattice footbridge and a signal box that contained a large 53-lever frame. A 'pagoda' shelter was provided on the down platform and a more substantial brick-built double-sided waiting room with canopies on the island platform. A cast-iron water tank and water cranes completed the ensemble. Not only was this a junction – the large running-in board proclaimed

Bala Junction, situated as it was in the middle of nowhere, only came alive when trains passed on this long single-line route and when a few passengers changed trains for the branch service to Bala and Blaenau Festiniog. *Ben Brooksbank*

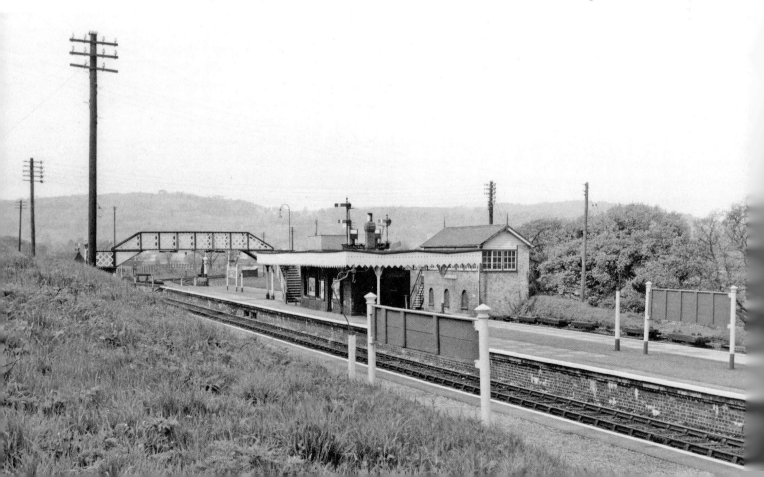

BR Standard Class 4 4-6-0 No 75028 enters Bala Junction station with a service to Ruabon. As the station nameboard testifies, this photograph was taken before the closure of the route from Bala to Blaenau Festiniog, which occurred from 4 January 1960. The line to Bala, which survived for another five years, can be seen curving away to the right. *Ben Brooksbank*

Looking east, the multi-lingual sign informs the passenger that only the bridge may be used to cross the line. *Ben Brooksbank*

Table 83— *continued*

BARMOUTH, DOLGELLAU, BALA, CORWEN AND RUABON
WEEKDAYS ONLY

Miles		am TC Bala to Birkenhead	am TC Barmouth to Wrexham		② am		am TC Barmouth to Birkenhead		pm TC Pwllheli to Birkenhead		② pm		pm TC Bala to Wrexham	② pm		pm TC Pwllheli to Chester		② SX pm	② SO pm		
	Pwllheli .. dep	..	5 50	..	8 20	..	8 20	..	12 45	..	..	..	..	4 5	..	5 30	..	6 30	6 30	..	..
0	**Barmouth** .... dep		**7 18**		**9 45**		**10 20**		**2 35**		**4 5**			**5 48**		**7 15**		**9 10**	**9 40**		
1½	Morfa Mawddach		7 24		9 54		10 26		2 42		4 10			5 54		7 21		9 17	9 46		
2½	Arthog		7 27		9 57		10 29		2 44		4 14			5 56		7 24		9 20	9 48		
7¼	Penmaenpool		7 39		10 10		10 41		2 57		4 28			6 9		7 37		9 33	10 1		
9¼	**Dolgellau** .... arr		**7 43**		**10 15**		**10 46**		**3 2**		**4 32**			**6 14**		**7 42**		**9 38**	**10 6**		
	dep		**7 44**				**10 48**		**3 4**							**7 44**					
12½	Bontnewydd		7 50				10 55		3 11							7 51					
14	Wnion Halt		7 56				..		3 17							7 58					
16	Drws-y-Nant		8 2				11 12		3 24							8 4					
19½	Garneddwen Halt		nn				..		nn							nn					
20¾	Llys Halt		8 11				..		3 40							8 14					
22¼	Llanuwchllyn		8 16				11 25		3 44							8 19					
23¾	Glan Llyn Halt		8 20				..		3 48							8 23					
24¼	Llangower Halt		8 23				vv		3 51							8 26					
26½	**Bala G** .... arr		**8 45**				**11 42**		**4 7**							**8 42**					
	dep	**7 12**	**8 30**				**11 25**		**3 50**				**5 40**			**8 30**					
30¾	Llandderfel	7 20	8 39				X		4 9				5 48			8 44					
33½	Llandrillo	7 26	8 45				X		4 15				5 54			8 50					
36	Cynwyd	7 31	8 50				11 54		4 22				6 0			8 55					
38½	**Corwen**	**7 37**	**8 55**				**12 1**		**4 27**				**6 10**			**9 3**					
39¾	Bonwm Halt	7 40	tt				..		4 30				6 12			9 7					
41	Carrog	7 45	9 0				12 7		4 36				6 16			9 11					
43	Glyndyfrdwy	7 53	9 6				12 12		4 41				6 20			9 15					
46¾	Berwyn Halt	8 3	9 15				..		4 50				6 30			bb					
48¼	**Llangollen**	**8 12**	**9 22**				**12 26**		**4 58**				**6 37**			**9 30**					
52	Trevor	8 21	..				..		..				..			..					
53	Acrefair	8 25	..				..		5E10				..			..					
54½	**Ruabon** .... arr	**8 30**	**9 35**				**12 41**		**5 17**				**6 54**			**9 46**					
71½	65 Chester (General) .... arr	9 12	11 9				1 20		6 2				8 58			10 33					
86½	65 Birkenhead (Woodside) „	9 55	11 58				2 7		6 48				9 43			11g44					
80	65 Shrewsbury „	9 30	10 35				1 36		6 27				7 45			10 59					
109¾	65 Wolverhampton (L.L.) „	10 26	11 26				2 26		7 24				9 8			11 55					
122¼	65 Birmingham (Snow Hill) „	10 55	11 55				2 55		7 51				9 41			12a30					
232¾	65 **London** (Paddington) „	**1 5**	**2B 5**				**5 0**		**10 8**				..			**5a 5**					

a am
B On Saturdays arrive 2 10 pm
bb Calls to set down from Corwen and beyond on notice being given to the Guard at Corwen
G Passengers to and from Bala change at Bala Junction by most of the trains
g On Saturdays arr 11 48 pm
nn Calls to take up or set down passengers during hours of daylight only. Passengers wishing to alight must give notice to the Guard at previous *stopping* station, and those desiring to join should give the necessary hand signal to the Driver
SO Saturdays only
SX or E Saturdays excepted
TC Through Carriages
tt Calls to take up on notice being given before 8 45 am to the Station Master at Corwen
vv Calls to take up only. Passengers desiring to join should give the necessary hand signal to the Driver
X Calls when required to take up for Corwen and Llangollen and beyond Ruabon on notice being given at the station; also to set down from Dolgellau and beyond on notice being given to the Guard at Dolgellau
② Second class only

'Bala Junction for Bala and Blaenau Festiniog' – but it also acted as a passing place on the long single-line route from Ruabon to Barmouth Junction. The passing loop was also used for run-round purposes by the Bala Town and Blaenau branch engine, as there was no turntable provided. White posts indicated the position of the set-down and pick-up points where the single line token could be collected by passing train crews. The station was sited near the River Dee, which the line followed for much of its length. There was no goods yard here, any wagons for Bala being detached and taken forward by the branch train.

The service beyond Bala Town was withdrawn from January 1960 but a shuttle continued to the more conveniently located Town station. This shuttle was amplified by some through workings from Bala Town to such places as Wrexham and Birkenhead. In January 1965 the main line was officially closed, although flooding had cut the line prematurely in December 1964 and a bus had to be substituted between Llangollen and Bala Town, with trains running from Bala Town to Barmouth reversing at the Junction. A three-year moratorium was placed on the line but no rescue came and in 1968 the S&T Department of the Festiniog Railway descended on the virtually untouched station and removed items of signalling equipment for re-use on the narrow-gauge line. Platform edging stones were also removed for re-use at the restored Carrog station further up the line.

The rail replacement bus service, Crosville D94 Wrexham to Barmouth, soon became one of the largest loss-making rural bus services in Wales, as is often the case with rail replacement services. Little remains today at the site of Bala Junction other than platform faces and barren trackbeds, but if the ever-expanding Llangollen Railway reaches further westwards then perhaps one day one might see trains again running through to Bala via the junction.

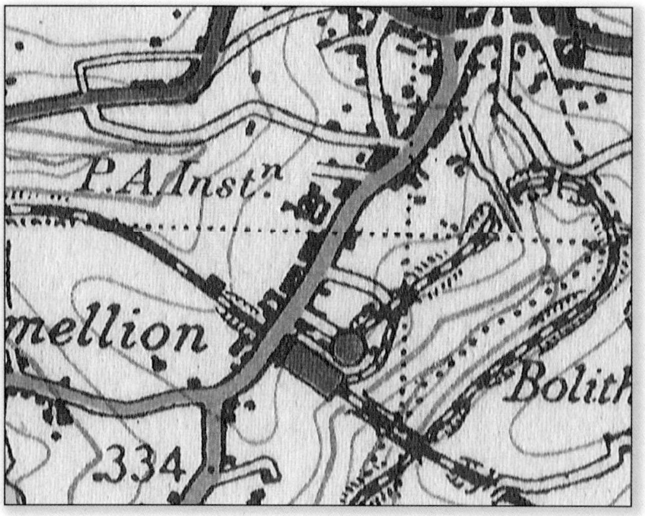

3 LISKEARD
A bit of a funny angle

Passengers arriving at Liskeard intending to take the branch train to Looe find themselves directed not to a bay platform parallel to the main platforms but to one remote from the main line and set at a 90-degree angle to it. This unusual arrangement dates from the turn of the 20th century when a connecting line was built from the GWR main line at Liskeard to the Liskeard & Looe Railway, which ran from the seaside resort to Moorswater, situated beneath the main-line viaduct that carried the GWR high above the valley beneath, and forming a junction there with the Liskeard & Caradon Mineral Railway. To connect the Looe line

Set at right-angles to the main line, the platform used by the Looe branch train is seen here in the late 1960s. Notice just the 'W' of the former GWR monogram picked out in white on the seat ends. *George Woods*

with the GWR was no mean feat, for although the lines are only some quarter of a mile apart as the crow flies, there is a difference of 150 vertical feet involved. A line 2 miles and 5 chains in length describing an almost complete circle was required to raise the line up to the required level and even then arrival at Liskeard was at right angles to the main line. Neither junction was satisfactory; that at Coombe south of Moorswater faced north, requiring Looe trains to reverse to head south, while that at Liskeard as already mentioned was far from ideal, necessitating access to the main line through a siding that was not particularly easy. Opening in 1901 the connection still serves the Looe branch today in spite of the operational difficulties.

Back in the 1930s it was planned that these awkward junctions, which precluded the speedy transfer of freight and prevented through running of excursions to Looe, could be superseded when a Government scheme of November 1935 made available £30 million to the various railway companies for such things as electrification, new works and improvements. The GWR aimed to provide a completely new branch to Looe, leaving the main line 1½ miles west of St Germans, proceeding down the Hessenford valley to Seaton Beach, then continuing 3 miles along the coast to terminate on high ground at East Looe. This scheme involved some very heavy engineering works including two viaducts and two tunnels with a combined length of some 3,000 yards. It was planned that the journey from Plymouth

'Western' diesel-hydraulic No D1010 *Western Campaigner*, now preserved, departs from Liskeard with a parcels service for Plymouth. A DMU stands at the down platform, while the Looe branch-line platform can be seen at right angles to the main line in the right background. *George Woods*

Illustrating the tortuous nature of the connection between the main line and the Looe branch, a DMU enters the down platform at Liskeard with the 'Mayflower' rail tour run by Railway Pictorial Publications Railtours (RPPR) on 12 October 1980. The special had visited Moorswater sidings, accessed from the Looe branch. *CH Library, D. E. Canning*

to Looe would be done in 35 minutes, some 30 minutes less than the time taken via Liskeard, utilising streamlined diesel railcars. Although work was started in 1937, the outbreak of war deferred matters and in the post-war world conditions were not so conducive to such a scheme and it was abandoned shortly after nationalisation.

Dieselisation in September 1961 eased some of the problems of reversal at Combe Junction and one unit could now operate the branch service. Threatened with closure at various times during the last 50 years the difficulty of providing alternative bus services has ensured the continuance of the branch into the 21st century, and today one can still turn sharp left on the main-line platforms at Liskeard to find the branch train waiting at its separate platform at what remains 'a bit of a funny angle'. There are currently some dozen or so departures per weekday for Looe plus a Sunday service in the summer.

4 BROAD STREET
Give my regards to Broad Street

The number of London termini that have closed can be counted on the fingers of one hand. An early casualty was Nine Elms, being replaced by Waterloo in 1848. Holborn Viaduct closed in 1990, being effectively replaced by City Thameslink station, and a more recent closure was Waterloo International in 2007, upon transference of Eurostar services to St Pancras. Broad Street was another of this small band, meeting its end in 1986 after a long period of decline.

Opened in 1865 by the North London Railway, the line proved an immediate success with quadrupling of the tracks taking place in 1874 and nine platforms being eventually provided to cater for the considerable

Above: By the end of services in June 1986 the frontage of the formerly elegant Broad Street terminus had become something of a jumbled architectural mess as witnessed in this 1983 view.
Ben Brooksbank

Right: The platforms crowded with enthusiasts bear witness to the fact that unusual motive power in the shape of SR Hastings line DMU No 1007 has been provided for this London Termini rail tour on 12 September 1970. The run-down nature of the station is evident even in this view taken 16 years before actual closure.
George Woods

commuter traffic. At its peak it was the third busiest station in London after Liverpool Street and Victoria, with some 27 million people passing through its doors in 1902.

The striking terminus was constructed in a rather mixed fashion incorporating Italian, oriental and municipal styles with a clock tower and almost Venetian side staircases with marble columns. Over the years the building acquired various accretions often rendered in different materials such as Portland stone markedly out of line with the design and texture of the original building. A very plain entrance facade detracted significantly from the building's aesthetic appeal and adversely affected the impact of the twin staircases that emanated from either side of the main building, each staircase dividing into two parts. Unrepaired war damage and an increasingly shabby and unkempt appearance did little to enhance the traveller's experience. A crude cutting back of the train sheds, which had become unsafe, and an unsympathetic treatment of the platform entrances and concourse facilities rendered the whole station 'a bit of a mess'. In 1956 the main terminal building was closed, passengers being redirected to a new concourse building at platform level. Although proposed for closure as part of the Beeching Plan, Broad Street did manage to survive for a further 23 years.

Trade fell and latterly only three platforms were in regular use, serving just 6,000 passengers daily, until finally just one temporary platform sufficed for the remaining shuttle to Dalston Junction, enabling the station building to be demolished before final closure of the route. The site was obviously a prime one, situated as it was adjacent to Liverpool Street station in the heart of the financial district, and BR wasted no time in clearing it to enable the 32-acre Broadgate office, shopping and restaurant complex development to take place. Paul McCartney's 1984 film and album *Give my Regards to Broad Street* features the former Beatle walking into the decrepit station and sitting alone on one of the station benches filmed on a suitably wet evening, the overall gloom reflecting the fortunes of the station itself.

5 ALSTON
England's highest market town?

Railway lines were often promoted to tap deposits of minerals, with passenger traffic very much an adjunct to the primary business of carrying freight. It is perhaps surprising to find that in many cases the promotion of a line and its subsequent construction was often followed only a short time later by either the exhaustion of the mineral deposit or changing economic circumstances that rendered the extraction of the item economically unattractive. Such was the case with an area of the North Pennines around Alston. There were lucrative lead ore deposits near Alston and Nenthead, with more than 100 mines operating towards the end of the 18th century, but in the pre-railway age transport to market was expensive and slow. The opening of the Newcastle & Carlisle Railway in 1837 provided a railhead for the ore at Haltwhistle, then a branch line to Alston and Nenthead was subsequently considered change to Following which a branch line to Alston and Nenthead was considered and subsequently authorised by Parliament in 1846. A considerable climb of 500 feet was required to Alston, which today claims to be the highest market town in England, although this distinction is shared with Buxton in Derbyshire. Further severe climbing would have been required to continue the line from Alston to Nenthead, but due to landowner opposition the original route was amended and the planned final 4 miles to Nenthead was abandoned as it was felt that a railhead at Alston would be sufficient.

The branch opened fully in 1852 and as its main purpose was mineral traffic just two passenger services daily were initially provided. From the 1870s onwards the fortunes of the lead industry in the area declined sharply with an accompanying reduction in the local population, which fell from more than 6,000 in 1851 to just under 2,000 in 1971. Although there was some trade associated with zinc mining and the carriage of coal and lime, thereafter goods traffic was rather meagre. Alston's facilities included a single 106-yard passenger platform, a goods shed, a carriage siding, and several sidings on either side of the platform. Unusually the southern end of the platform had steps rather than a ramp. There was also a turntable, although this became disused by 1951.

The station building, which has a Grade II listing, was an imposing Tudor-style structure with random stone courses, mullioned windows, moulded door and window hoods, ball finials, and lofty coupled chimney stacks. Subsequent rendering marred the overall appearance and a single-

The terminus at Alston is seen on 22 March 1976 with diesel units Nos 51212/56373 forming the branch service to Haltwhistle. The service was withdrawn a few weeks later. In the 1970s the station took on a new lease of life as the headquarters of a preserved narrow-gauge railway. The South Tynedale Railway Preservation Society took over from this earlier group in 1983 and has since restored services over 3½ miles with plans to reach Slaggyford and ultimately to restore services back to the junction at Haltwhistle.

storey extension was added in 1904/05. A trainshed, which was originally curved, covered the platform and two tracks, and on its west side adjoined an engine shed, which closed in 1959, and water tower. The trainshed roof was later extended and rebuilt, but was dismantled in the mid-1960s as an economy measure, adversely affecting the overall aesthetics of the building. However, some attractive features remained until the end, including gas lighting together with the original LNER nameboard painted in the NE Regional colour scheme of tangerine. Goods services ceased in 1965 and the station became unstaffed from January 1969. The final timetable recorded six weekday and seven Saturday return journeys on the branch.

As far back as 1929 the LNER had considered closing the line to passengers and it was no surprise when it was listed in the Beeching Report as 'already under consideration for closure'. Although passenger revenue on the branch was a paltry £4,000 per annum, the lack of a direct road link prolonged its life. However, following completion of a new road, closure was again proposed in 1973, although it was to be a further three years before it was enacted, making it one of the last of the Beeching cuts to be implemented. After closure the site was reborn as the terminus of the South Tynedale Railway Preservation Society narrow-gauge line, which has hopes one day of reopening the whole branch.

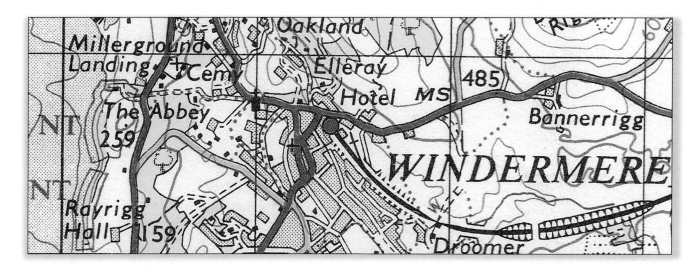

6 WINDERMERE
No rash assault!

'Is then no nook of English ground secure from rash assault?'

In the early 1840s William Wordsworth's popularity was at its height, having been confirmed as Poet Laureate to succeed Robert Southey who had died in 1843. His words above are taken from his poem 'Suggested by the Proposed Kendal and Windermere Railway' (1844). His wife Mary had earlier suggested that they would have to evacuate their home at Rydal Mount in Grasmere once the West Coast route had reached Lancaster because the Lake District would be invaded by visitors. The Windermere branch, which, in response to protests, terminated short of the lake in the parish of Birthwaite, opened in 1847. In response to a plan to build a line through Ambleside to Keswick, which was in fact never constructed, John Ruskin, painter, art critic and social historian who had moved to Brantwood near Coniston in 1871, revealed his feelings

The original interior of the station at Windermere is seen here prior to truncation of the platforms and sale of the covered area to a retail outlet.

An exterior view of the original station with a veteran Bedford OB coach on the 'Mountain Goat' service, which began in 1972 taking tourists and hikers to the more remote areas of the Lake District. The Bedford, known affectionately as 'Li'l Billie', was later exported to Japan to undertake a similar role transporting tourists.

regarding the infringement by the iron road. Ruskin regarded the Lake District as a haven from the worst excesses of the Industrial Revolution and made no secret of the fact that he detested railways. He wrote:

'But the stupid herds of modern tourists let themselves be emptied, like coals from a sack, at Windermere and Keswick. Having got there, what the new railway has to do is to shovel those who have come to Keswick to Windermere, and to shovel those who have come to Windermere to Keswick. And what then? ...and all that your railroad company can do for them is only to open taverns and skittle grounds round Grasmere, which will soon, then, be nothing but a pool of drainage, with a beach of broken ginger beer bottles; and their minds will be no more improved by contemplating the scenery of such a lake than of Blackpool.'

Perhaps the line's most famous service was the 'Lakes Express', which ran from London Euston to Keswick and Workington with a portion for Windermere. Originated in 1927 by the LMS, it ran during the summer until the war years after which it was reintroduced in 1950 until the final summer of operation in 1964.

Today the only line in the Lakes still operated as part of the national network is that from Oxenholme to Windermere, trains to Coniston and Keswick having ceased to run many years ago. Just one platform suffices at the terminus, the original station having at one time boasted four platforms and an overall roof. Three tracks were taken out of use when the branch was reduced to a one-train-operated single line in 1973 as an economy measure. The single track was cut back to a new truncated station in 1986 following the demolition of the trainshed and the building of a supermarket, which incorporated the facade and canopy of the original station; the supermarket was designed to mimic the appearance of the original trainshed.

Currently services are operated by First TransPennine Express, which runs Class 185 DMUs on the line to the junction with the WCML at Oxenholme Lake District, with a couple of services daily running through to Manchester Airport while a few continue beyond Oxenholme but only as far as Lancaster or Preston. For the future, Network Rail is looking at the possibility of an infill electrification project to allow direct electric services to operate between Manchester and Windermere after electrification of the Deansgate-Bolton-Leyland line. Passenger usage has generally been increasing of recent years, rising from 252,000 in 2004/05 to 401,000 in 2013/14.

In the winter of 1958/59 Newhaven Docks plays host to a paddle-steamer, probably the PS *Freshwater*, which was used for excursions, and in the distance can be seen a ferry on the regular service to Dieppe. *Ben Brooksbank*

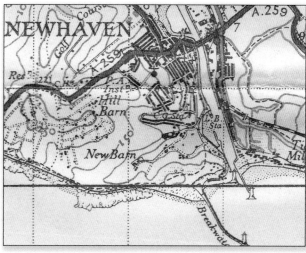

7 NEWHAVEN MARINE
Parliamentary privilege

Although Newhaven Marine would warrant inclusion as an example of a station constructed to serve a harbour, it is perhaps better known these days as one of the few examples of a station playing host to a 'parliamentary' or 'ghost' train. Originating from the

Railway Regulation Act of 1844, which set minimum standards for passenger accommodation, the term 'parliamentary train' has today come to mean a minimal service that often operates on just one day a week, perhaps in only one direction or, at its most extreme, as in case of Newhaven, a service that is not available to passengers. The running of such services is considered by the rail companies to be a way of fulfilling their franchise obligations and as a cheaper alternative to applying to Parliament for authority to close a station or abandon a line completely. Thus it is that once a day an empty train arrives at Newhaven Marine station, waits a few minutes, then departs for Brighton, not stopping at the seven intermediate stations.

In this late-1960s view a 4-CEP electric unit waits at the platform of the Marine station while one of the 'Booster' electric locomotives can be seen in the bay on the right. The last of this trio of Co-Cos, which had previously handled boat trains from London to the port, was withdrawn at the end of 1968, although one was reinstated briefly and worked into January 1969.

The French car ferry *Villandry* is seen alongside Newhaven quay on 12 September 1967 in this view taken from the footbridge of Newhaven Harbour station. The tracks branching off to the right past the level crossing lead to Marine station. *CH Library, H. A. Gamble*

All this is a long way from Newhaven's railway origins in 1847 when it was confidently predicted that it would, as described in a guidebook of 1852, become the 'Liverpool of the South'. The port was tidal and it was not until 1878 that the Newhaven Harbour Co was created to construct moles, a quay for cross-Channel packet boats and to provide a quayside station originally named Newhaven Harbour (Boat Station) in 1886. It was to be renamed Newhaven Marine in 1984. In 1928, for example, more than 320,000 tons of cargo and 258,000 passengers were handled, and in the 1960s the drive-on, drive-off car ferry and the Stirling Motorail service had increased traffic to 485,000 passengers by 1966. The single platform of Marine station could take twelve coaches and is just 16 chains (320 metres) to the south of Newhaven Harbour station. A run-round loop was provided and although the line from Lewes to Seaford was electrified in 1935 the section to Marine was not so treated due to the lack of flexibility that EMU stock displays when carrying boat passengers and their luggage. The post-war arrival of the three 'Booster' locomotives did see the section to Marine electrified in

1949. Booster locomotive No 20003 inaugurated the electric service although reliefs continued to be steam-hauled for some years. From 1959 Class 71 'E5xxx' locomotives assisted with these electric duties, followed in 1962 by the Class 73s. After October 1970 boat trains were worked by EMUs. The original customs shed adjoining the station was demolished and a new building erected near the site of the former London & Paris Hotel. The nearby level crossing was resited in 1978.

Marine station, which was rebuilt as recently as 1983, closed to passengers in 2006 following safety concerns after a roof was damaged. Today the station is in a very sorry state, overgrown with weeds and littered with discarded rubbish. The Southern TOC used to offer a complimentary taxi from Marine station for any passengers with a Marine ticket. This service was withdrawn when the station was removed from the fares database. In 2016 the station was re-added to the fares database on self-service machines; however, no fare pricing is displayed when the station is selected, so tantalisingly one is still unable to catch a train from Newhaven Marine.

The golfers have long gone, as have the little trains in this view of Caffyns Halt taken in the 1960s. The bridge still stands today although minus its approaches. If the long term aims of the Lynton & Barnstaple Society are realised then once again this spot will echo to the sound of narrow-gauge trains working hard.

8 CAFFYNS HALT
Anyone for golf?

There were a number of railway halts especially opened to cater for golf enthusiasts – one thinks of the former Golf Club Halt on the Hundred of Manhood & Selsey Tramway, Golf Club Halt on the Dyke branch, Golf Clubhouse on the Banff branch, and Denham Golf Club station, which remains open today on the Chiltern line. However, Caffyns Halt was located on the former narrow-gauge Lynton & Barnstaple Railway (L&BR), which opened for business in 1898, although the stopping place at Caffyns did not follow until December 1906. It was originally called New Mill Halt but changed its name when it began to cater primarily for golfers at the golf course that had been laid out on Caffyns Down. This was not the first

golf course in the area, as the promoter of Woody Bay had one laid out on Martinhoe Down in 1894. Unfortunately he went bankrupt in 1900 and his grandiose plans to turn Woody Bay into a holiday resort failed.

Trains on the L&BR stopped within a short walk of the course. Golfers were requested to contact the guard for the Caffyns Halt stop or to give a hand signal if they wished to board. In early 1909 land at the Valley of Rocks was surveyed with a view to laying out a more convenient course, as a great many visitors to the Lynton area had apparently complained that the course at Caffyns Down was too remote and that the train service too limited. It was thought that a course at the Valley of Rocks would

The scanty present-day remains of the decaying club house at the former Caffyns golf course.

prove a great attraction. Sir George Newnes, the great promoter of the L&BR, was not initially keen, but later changed his mind, although he was of opinion that it would kill off the Caffyns Links and therefore presumably take away some trade from Caffyns Halt. This scheme was never proceeded with and following closure of the railway in 1935 golfers from Lynton had to take the bus to the Caffyns Links – but there was a convenient stop some 200 yards from the course. The club's final year was 1940 when the nine-hole course had a membership of some 80 enthusiasts and visitors' fees were 2s 6d a round! The ruins of the clubhouse can still be seen on Caffyns Down as a testament to happier times. Today golfers from Lynton have to travel to Ilfracombe, Woolacombe or Barnstaple to indulge their passion.

The halt at Caffyns was not ideally situated from an operational point of view, being on a gradient of 1 in 50 leading to the summit of the line at 980 feet near Woody Bay; the train crew of up trains especially were no doubt pleased when no passengers appeared, meaning that they could continue on their way without interruption. The single platform was 132 feet in length and contained a small rendered block-built waiting shelter similar to that provided at Snapper Halt further down the line towards Barnstaple. The track here was single with no passing loop or sidings provided. A nameboard proclaimed 'Caffyns Halt (For Golf Links)' and a station lamp was provided for the hours of darkness, attached to the waiting shelter, which also housed a couple of advertising boards. The halt, the remains of which were not cleared away until the 1980s, was situated next to an overbridge, which is the only artefact remaining at the site today, and even that has lost its approach road banks. The trackbed was used as a farm track after closure.

So should Caffyns ever have been opened? During its existence it contributed very little revenue, and as it was situated only a mile or so from the rather inconveniently sited Lynton terminus it required very little additional effort, and certainly did not result in any great time saving, to walk from Lynton to the golf course as it did to get to Lynton station and travel one stop on the infrequent trains of the L&BR. Today trains recreating the L&BR operate from the next station along the old line at Woody Bay and there are exciting plans to extend the running line to Blackmoor Gate in the future, but an extension towards Lynton, which would see trains running through Caffyns again, is perhaps not so likely, at least in the medium term.

In happier times an example of the usual motive power for the branch, a Wainwright Class 'H' tank locomotive, in this case No 31512, awaits the right away with a special working on 24 September 1960. The rather bleak nature of the surroundings is evident in this view. *Alan Sainty collection*

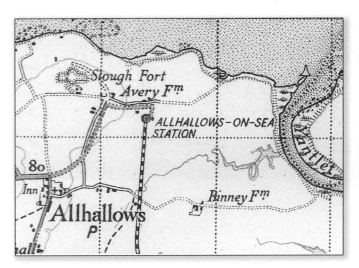

9 ALLHALLOWS-ON-SEA
Would you want to holiday here?

Would you really want to holiday here? Well the SR obviously thought so when it opened the 1¾-mile branch from Stoke Junction in May 1932, advertising it as 'A new seaside resort in the making – Facing Southend!' and 'Healthy Homes for Londoners – Only 37 miles from the City'. Situated as it was on the muddy banks of the Thames estuary, this was always going to be an unlikely spot to take off as a holiday resort and certainly one to justify being served by rail. The terminus was in an isolated spot some distance from the 'beach', which was more realistically designated 'Mud' on the OS map, and also just downstream from a sewer outfall. The suffix 'On Sea' is questionable as it was technically a mile within the boundary of the Port of London Authority.

The 400-yard trek to this 'beach' was facilitated prior to the Second World War by a miniature railway. In addition to attracting an influx of 'trippers', it was hoped that as it was only 37 miles to Charing Cross commuters would be attracted to live in Allhallows, taking the train to the city each morning. Although some lengthy trains operated in the 1930s and 1940s to bring in holidaymakers, the line from Stoke Junction being subsequently doubled, this was never enough to make the branch a paying proposition. Summer weekends in the immediate pre- and post-war years were the only times when the level of traffic was anything like that which had been expected. For example, in 1934 the August Bank Holiday on 5 August saw some 9,500 passengers arrive at their rather bleak destination.

The Allhallows-on-Sea Estate Company was incorporated with the intention of transforming the flat, featureless, windswept marshland in the area into a new holiday resort. The SR had a financial interest in the new

---

ALLHALLOWS-ON-SEA. *38¾ miles from London.* **SERVED BY FREQUENT SOUTHERN ELECTRIC TRAINS FROM LONDON (CHARING CROSS) WITH CHANGE OF TRAIN AT GRAVESEND CENTRAL. JOURNEY TIME FROM LONDON APPROX. 1½ HOURS.** Allhallows, although having its roots in antiquity, is in some respects, one of our newer resorts.

Situated on Kent's northern shore, where sea and countryside meet, the open fields, the views over the plainlands of the Isle of Grain, the sands and the safe bathing bring many visitors to its shore.

From the plateau reached by the road from the station, both the Thames and the Medway rivers can be seen at the same time, as well as all kinds of shipping en route for London, the Medway ports, or the open sea.

Allhallows has a bright future. Roads have been built and development into a pleasant rural resort is well on the way.

The sad remains of a dream unfulfilled. The platform has been cut back and soon all traces of the railway will disappear, apart from a water tank marooned in a sea of mobile homes.

company and worked closely with it in the construction of the line. The new company donated land for use by the railway and also contributed £20,000 towards the construction of the line.

With the decline of the British seaside holiday the branch was singled and eked out an uneventful existence until the not unexpected closure in December 1961. The existing single-sided platform had been converted into an island platform in 1933 to cater for the crowds and a longer full-width steel canopy provided. A small signal box was located on the platform. A block of flats, Albany Court, was constructed as part of the infrastructure of the planned new settlement, together with a public house and hotel, The Pilot, and a row of semi-detached houses in the cul-de-sac known as the Queens Way. However, the developers' dreams of another Southend-on-Sea burgeoning on the estuarine marshes were to be sadly dashed. A small goods yard with goods shed and turntable were provided but freight fared nearly as badly as passenger traffic. In the thirty years after 1930 the local population only increased by 250 to stand at less than 600 in 1960. After closure, a former tea room in front of the station building was used as a night club and the station building itself was used as a bakery until demolition in the 1970s. Ironically today there is a sizeable population, occupying homes on a large caravan site that was built on the site of the station, in the vicinity of the former railway. One remaining railway feature is the former balloon water tower, now surrounded by a sea of mobile homes.

The waiting shelter and seat at Campbell's Platform. *Chris Mckenna, licensed for reuse under the Wikipedia Creative Commons Licence*

Campbell's Platform is seen in 2004 with a passing Festiniog Railway service. *Jonathan Simkins, licensed for reuse under the Wikipedia Creative Commons Licence*

10 CAMPBELL'S PLATFORM
A station of one's own

A station of one's own – well, maybe if you were an important landowner or member of the aristocracy in Victorian Britain, but for the everyday railway enthusiast probably just a pipe dream. In the case of Colonel Andrew Campbell, a retired lawyer late of the Black Watch, this dream came true but very much out of necessity rather than through any wish to play trains or to be his own stationmaster. Buying a remote manor house, Plas Dduallt, parts of which date back to the 15th century, as a restoration project in 1962, he found that access was going to be a problem. At the time of purchase there was no road to the house and even tractors could not make it up the surrounding steep slopes. Thus the preserved Festiniog Railway (FR) narrow-gauge line, which ran a few hundred yards from the house, proved to be a lifeline.

A halt was established by Col Campbell in 1965 and he even had his own locomotive, a 20hp Simplex 4wDM purchased from St Albans Sand & Gravel Co Ltd. Fitted with an all-over cab, it arrived on FR metals in July 1966 for his personal use on the line. His daily journey began with checking that all was clear before moving the locomotive out of its siding and onto the line over which he had a 'running powers' agreement with the railway company to and from Tan-y-Bwlch, providing of course that his trips did not interfere with the normal operation of the line. His car was kept at Tan-y-Bwlch, whence he would travel to Dolgellau where he worked as a solicitor for the Council. Returning home with his shopping, he would wheel his provisions down from the platform in a wheelbarrow, but in later years this was superseded by an electric winch that hoisted the goods down to the house below. Although he benefited from his relationship with the FR – the railway even provided a removal train to bring in his furniture – it was very much a two-way affair as, being an explosives expert, Col Campbell was of great assistance when the FR attempted to cut its way through to Blaenau Festiniog via the deviation necessitated by the flooding of the old route. He also assisted the railway by providing dormitory accommodation for volunteers in old barns.

Today Campbell's Platform remains as a private unstaffed halt available for use by residents and visitors to Plas Ddault, which takes in visitors who are keen to experience its seclusion and idyllic setting amid the Welsh mountains. A little further down the line lies another private halt serving Coed-y-Bleiddiau cottage, a private residence that was built in about 1860 for the railway's line inspector. Being more than half a mile distant via a steep footpath from the nearest road, this too benefits from its proximity to the railway. In the 1930s the cottage was used as a holiday home by several families, including apparently that of Kim Philby, the notorious spy.

The Colonel died in 1982 but his platform, with its nameboard, seat and small slate shelter remains as a testament to him; a 30-minute documentary entitled 'The Campbells Came by Rail' made by the BBC details his story. Ownership of his locomotive, now appropriately named *The Colonel*, was transferred to the FR upon his death and it can usually be found at Glanypwll where it is used as a yard shunter by the Civil Engineering Department.

At Wingham Canterbury Road terminus a pile of sleepers, rather than the more usual buffer stop, marks the end of the track. Although it was the intention to extend to Canterbury, this was never achieved and the line ended here in the middle of a field. *Peter Harding collection*

11 WINGHAM
Overkill – the village with three stations

A small village such as Wingham in Kent might have considered itself lucky to have a railway station to serve its population, which numbered only 1,200 in 1935. Even today there are fewer than 2,000 inhabitants, so the eventual provision of no fewer than three stations for the village, courtesy of the East Kent Light Railway (EKLR), needs some explanation. A survey published in 1940 stated that 'Had it not three stations one would pass Wingham as a village, but town or village, the beauty of its solitary street and church can never be disputed.' The EKLR was developed to tap the Kent coalfield and formed part of the famous Colonel Stephens empire of rather decrepit rural light railways. The 'main line' ran from Shepherdswell ultimately to Wingham (Canterbury Road) station with a branch from Eastry to Richborough Port. Many spurs and branches were laid down to serve the mostly unsuccessful mines of the Kent coalfield and there were optimistic plans to construct several other lines, but these were never implemented. The success of Tilmanstone Colliery allowed a small 3-mile section of the route to continue operation until 1986 as it was only at Tilmanstone that hopes of substantial winnable coal deposits were realised.

Wingham gained its first station in about 1916 when services began in the expectation of traffic from Wingham Colliery. Unfortunately the mine was aborted without producing any coal. In 1920 a short extension to Wingham Town, where there was a short spur line to Wingham Engineering Works, which undertook some repair work on the EKLR's locomotives for a time, was completed, the original station being renamed Wingham Colliery. The year 1925 saw a further short extension to Wingham (Canterbury Road), and although there were hopes of extending the line all the way to Canterbury this was to be as far as the line ever reached, ending in the middle of a field at the Wingham parish boundary. A major stumbling block to completion to Canterbury was the fact that the City Council was opposed to the provision of a level crossing over the busy A28 at Sturry Road and there were also objections from the War Department and the Ecclesiastical Commissioners. Various alternative routes were then suggested and approved, culminating in

Another view of the spartan facilities provided at Canterbury Road station.
Peter Harding collection

approval of the initial direct route in 1931 – but by that time the impetus for further extension had faded, and Wingham (Canterbury Road) thus became an unlikely terminus. Hence the village of Wingham ended up with three stations within a mile of each other. The sparse passenger service, always considered secondary to the coal and freight traffic, limped on until the nationalisation of the railways, with the final passenger service of two trains each way on weekdays running on 30 October 1948. Freight continued to Wingham until 1951.

As might be expected, station facilities at all of Wingham's halts was of a very basic kind. The timber-faced platform on the up side of the line at the Colliery halt was 100 feet long and contained a seat, a wooden hut and a ticket office, which were subsequently moved to the Town station when that opened for business. Town station boasted a 125-foot brick-faced platform, containing the transferred buildings, which was also on the up side of the line, and initially a loop and a siding were laid in. With the opening of the extension to Canterbury Road, Town station was downgraded and the new station became the principal one for the village. The loop and siding were removed and the station building was moved once again, this time to the new terminus, replaced at Town station with a wooden hut. Canterbury Road station, which was one of the few to be staffed, had a 60-foot-long sleeper-faced platform on the down side of the line.

Each train terminating here stopped short of the station to allow the locomotive to be uncoupled from the passenger coaches, which would then run into the platform by gravity while the locomotive waited in a siding. The siding and goods yard, where there was a corrugated-iron goods shed, was on the south side of Canterbury Road. In 1946 the iron hut collapsed and was replaced with a grounded van body. With the increase in traffic at Canterbury Road it became common practice to allow passengers to alight in the goods yard, avoiding the need for the train to cross the road. Some 30 feet beyond the end of the platform the line terminated not with a buffer stop but with a sleeper chained to the end of the rails.

In connection with the hoped-for extension to Canterbury a cutting was dug for a further 200 yards beyond the station and some further land was acquired and fenced. Track was laid by the Royal Engineers for some 150 yards during the Second World War, possibly to allow more room for manoeuvre on the far side of the road crossing should the Army have wished to store munitions or supplies here. Gibson's Farmshop now stands on the site of the goods yard, although it was previously known as The Little Station Farmshop.

This September 1964 view shows a Hull DMU service waiting to depart from the attractive terminus of Withernsea. *RCTS*

12 WITHERNSEA
Whither Withernsea?

The creation of seaside resorts from scratch was greatly assisted if a railway link was planned to bring in the expected crowds. Such was the thinking behind the plans of one Anthony Bannister, a merchant from Kingston-upon-Hull, later to become Lord Mayor and Sheriff of that city. He felt that the plans of the Hull & Holderness Railway, with the twin objectives of linking the industrial port of Hull with the rich agricultural land of South Holderness and also developing a seaside resort on the North Sea coast to rival Whitby and Scarborough, which had been promoted by the York & North Midland Railway, were worthy of his sponsorship. The coast between Tunstall in the north and Easington south of Holderness was surveyed and Withernsea, a small coastal village of some 120 inhabitants, was chosen to be the terminus of the new line and thus, whether it liked it or not, to become the designated location for transformation into a new resort. The 20¾-mile line from Hull was duly opened in 1854 and traffic was expected to be two-way, the more important being trippers brought into the resort and, once it had developed, commuters and produce travelling into Hull. Bannister became

Chairman of the Withernsea Pier, Promenade, Gas & General Improvement Company.

There was little at Withernsea to tempt the holidaymaker at first, but the erection of a prestigious three-storey hotel, the Queens, right next to the station in 1855 was a bold statement of intent. Other attractions were added in the ensuing years such as the erection of beach groynes in 1871 to prevent coastal erosion and a pier, which was completed in 1877. The latter, stretching nearly 1,200 feet out to sea, cost £12,000 to construct and its entrance was graced with a large castellated gateway. Unfortunately many ships collided with the pier in later years until just 50 feet of it was left prior to total demolition in 1903.

Around the turn of the century one of the entrepreneurs behind the resort's development had his own private promenade built on the cliffs behind his residence, and in 1910 a Central Promenade was built. By 1960 some 2,200 yards of promenade existed, augmenting the delights of the Pleasure Ground with its Big Wheel, miniature railway operating the 'Withernsea Express', fairground rides and open-air bathing pool. A Grand Pavilion built in 1937 boasted the largest sprung dance floor in the North of England and special trains were laid on to bring in hundreds of terpsichoreans from Hull. The Queens Hotel, which never lived up to expectations, became the Station Hotel, then a hospital and ultimately a care home.

Withernsea terminus was basically an island with the main arrival platform on the north side with a recess at the outer end to form a second platform. A third platform was provided on the south side of the station. The inner end of the main platform road led to a turntable from which locomotives could be released via a run-round loop. On the south side were two lengthy sidings for the stabling of coaching stock. As late as 1962 there was still quite a reasonable service using modern diesel multiple units that had been introduced in 1957. Proposed for closure in the Beeching Report, the line carried its last passengers in October 1964, which saw the neighbouring Hornsea branch also shut. Goods services continued to Withernsea until 30 April 1965.

Following closure the trackbed area was used as the site for a market, with the station building and platform canopy remaining in place until the late 1990s, after which they were demolished. The only surviving building on the old station site is the stable block of the former Queens Hotel and a section of the former platform. Reading current reviews of accommodation available at Withernsea reveals the universal story of traditional seaside resort decline, the town being described as run-down. Although much of this is blamed locally on the closure of the railway, it is undoubtedly part of a wider malaise that has seen the ambitious dreams of Victorian resort developers in many cases crumble. Ironically Bannister was to spend his last day in Withernsea, the resort he helped to create, and having returned to his home at Hessle by train he expired during the night having caught a chill while participating in a regatta.

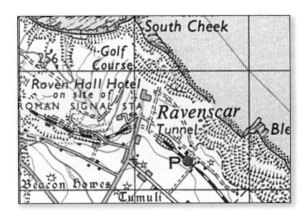

13 RAVENSCAR
A station for the town that never was

When a station on the Whitby-Scarborough route opened here in July 1885 it was simply known as 'Peak', lying as it did at the highest point of the line with steep climbs at 1 in 39 from both northerly and southerly directions. A single track with a platform on the up side and a goods siding and cattle dock on the down side comprised the facilities at that time. It was located in a very exposed position on the cliffs above the North Sea and on one occasion the wooden waiting shelter was blown away. The NER requested that a station house be constructed and when this was met with a refusal by the Scarborough & Whitby Railway Co the station was promptly closed in March 1893. Just over a year later, the company having relented by providing a station house, it was reopened. There was little or no habitation in the immediate vicinity.

In 1895 the village of Peak was bought by a consortium of four businessmen who formed the

Ravenscar Development Co, with the intention of turning the area into a Victorian seaside resort to rival the nearby towns of Whitby and Scarborough. In 1897 the local area and the station were renamed Ravenscar, the name apparently inspired by the raven flag carried by Viking invaders with the addition of 'scar' meaning 'cliffs' or 'rocky outcrop' in old Norse – or perhaps it was to avoid confusion with the Peak District. In any event, an NER poster trumpeted 'twixt moors and sea … magnificent undercliff and hanging gardens … most bracing health resort on the East Coast'. Three hundred workmen were employed to lay out roads, build houses and install sewers. Ambitious plans for shops, tearooms, guesthouses and other attractions were drawn up.

The land was divided into 1,500 plots for building and offered for sale. It was hoped that prospective buyers and tourists would come in by special excursion trains and snap up the plots. They were wined and dined and had their fares refunded if they signed up with a deposit, but only a few did, the majority returning home sadly disillusioned. A second platform and passing loop and additional sidings were added to the railway infrastructure. Although a small amount of development did occur around Station Square, with a hotel and vicarage, the hoped-for expansion never happened and by 1913 the consortium became bankrupt and was wound up, leaving a legacy of isolated houses on the clifftop known as 'The Town That Never Was'. So why did it fail? Primarily because there was no safe and quick access to the beach some 600 feet below the buildings, while the village's elevation led to a dense shroud of mist often enveloping the place, which was not conducive to holidays. With the established seaside resorts of Whitby and Scarborough not far away, there was in any event probably not enough trade to sustain a third resort in the area.

Perhaps one of the more successful aspects of Ravenscar station was the Camping Coach, which was a

Another example of hopes dashed are the remains of Ravenscar station. Recovered sections of rail lie cut into convenient lengths following closure of the line in 1965. The former hotel building, which it was anticipated would house visiting tourists, can be seen on the right.

Saplings now grow where trains formerly ran.

popular feature here for many years until 1963. The freight service was withdrawn from Ravenscar on 4 May 1964, just three months before the goods service on the whole line succumbed. Passenger closure came on 6 March 1965. The up platform and the base of the waiting shelter on the down platform survive today but all the buildings have been demolished. Today parts of the unfinished development remain, but the kerbstones of the unfinished streets are eerily quiet with just the strong winds to disturb the all-enveloping vegetation.

14 BOGSIDE RACECOURSE
A day at the races

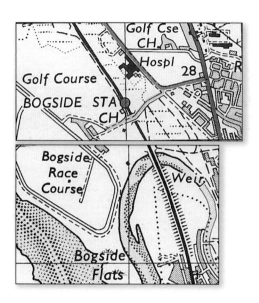

The station opened as plain Bogside on 23 March 1840, although access was restricted until 1 June 1894 when it became fully open to the public. It served the northern part of the town of Irvine, being part of the Glasgow, Paisley, Kilmarnock & Ayr Railway, later subsumed into the Caledonian Railway. The competing Glasgow & South Western Railway had its own branch to Irvine with its own station at Bogside Halt, although this was not so conveniently placed for the racecourse. This branch closed to passengers in 1930. The Caley station was renamed Bogside Race Course on 30 June 1952; however, this was relatively short-lived as, following the closure of the adjacent racecourse, it was once again renamed Bogside on 14 June 1965. The station closed permanently to passengers on 2 January 1967, although trains still pass through on the Ayrshire coast line.

This is Bogside Racecourse station, looking north-west along the ex-G&SWR Glasgow-Ayr-Stranraer main line on 26 September 1961. Closure came in 1967. *Ben Brooksbank*

The nameboard at Bogside Racecourse.

'B1' Class No 61342 halts at Bogside Racecourse signal box with the 'Scottish Rambler No 5' rail tour on 10 April 1966. *George Woods*

The Racecourse located near Irvine on the banks of the River Irvine predated the arrival of the railway, its first meeting having been held on 7 June 1808, although there is evidence of an event known as the Irvine Marymass Races in the area as far back as 1636, claiming to be the oldest surviving race meeting in the world. Initiated by the Earl of Eglinton as his private racecourse, originally Bogside's flat course was an undulating right-handed triangular course of 2 miles in length, and its jumps course was 2½ miles with nine plain fences, two open ditches and one water jump. It was here that the first steeplechase recorded in Scotland took place on 25 April 1839. During its existence it hosted the Scottish Grand National, which is now contested at nearby Ayr, and twice hosted the National Hunt Chase Challenge Cup, which now takes place at the Cheltenham Festival. Its other major race was the Bogside Cup, and among the most notable achievements at the course must be the rides of jockey Alec Russell who rode all six winners in a single day on 19 July 1957. Race-day specials ran from Glasgow's Central station, some running non-stop to Bogside. However, in 1963 the Levy Board opted to cease funding the course, declaring that, 'When Ayr is developed as the main Scottish course the retention of Bogside, only 12 miles away, cannot be economically justified.' The last race meeting was held at Bogside on 10 April 1965, although Point-to-Point meetings took place there until 1994. Some evidence of the former racecourse still remains.

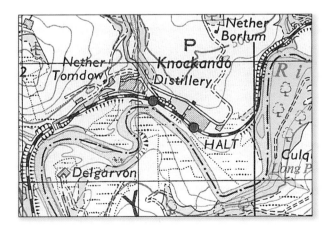

15 KNOCKANDO
Afore ye go

That staple of Highland life, whisky – no 'e' in the Scots spelling – has provided much traffic for the railways of Scotland over the years, in some cases spawning dedicated lines to bring the precious liquor from the distilleries to the branch or main-line station. The most famous of the whisky lines was perhaps the Strathspey route of the Great North of Scotland Railway (GNoS), running from Boat of Garten to Dufftown, which opened in 1863 and served many distilleries en route. Some distilleries even had their own locomotives, known locally as 'pugs', and spurs left this line to serve Dailuaine and Cromdale distilleries. The Dailuaine line was famously worked in its latter years by a 1939 Andrew Barclay-built 0-4-0T locomotive named after the distillery and which is currently on static display at Aberfeldy distillery.

A postcard view of the attractive riverside scenery around Knockando station with the distillery buildings and sidings prominent in the foreground.

To serve the Knockando estate, a 16,000-acre spread of moorland, hill and woodland, a private station was opened in 1869, but it was not until 30 years later in June 1899 that a public station was brought into use, 1¼ miles nearer to the existing station at Blacksboat, at the Knockando distillery siding. This station was originally named Dalbeallie, after a nearby small farm, but this incensed the local villagers who had raised a considerable sum of money, £3,000, to finance the building of a road and bridges to connect Knockando village with the station. It was subsequently renamed Knockando, but not until 1905, when the original private station became Knockando House Halt.

The building of Knockando distillery, which had commenced in 1898, enabled production to begin in May the following year, and this undoubtedly influenced the decision to locate a station here. The name derives from the Scottish Gaelic Cnoc Cheannachd, meaning 'Hill of Commerce'. The village is home to a few other small houses and the larger Knockando House, and is surrounded by woods. In 1904 the distillery was purchased by W. & A. Gilbey, the gin producer from London, becoming part of J&B/Grand Metropolitan in the 1960s and '70s. It is now owned by the multinational firm Diageo. It was the first distillery in Scotland to be built with electric lighting. Cottages for distillery workers were built nearby, as well as a

house for the Customs & Excise Officer. Knockando Distillery is home to a famous selection of casks that went into the J&B Ultima blend in 1994 to celebrate the quincentenary of Scotch whisky. This blend contained 128 different whiskies (116 malt and 12 grain) and one of each of these casks continues to mature in the warehouse.

With only a limited passenger service, generally just three or four daily trains latterly operated by railbuses, passenger traffic was never heavy on this route, whisky being of far more commercial significance. Closure to passengers came not unexpectedly in 1965, although freight continued until 1968. In 1977 the old station was renamed Tamdhu, meaning 'little dark hill', which is also the name of its new owners, another distillery, which has converted the former ticket office and waiting room into a visitor centre. The station contains some railway relics although most relate to the Highland Railway. The GNoS Type 3 signal box has also been restored, being one of only 150 or so survivors of the more than 2,000 that covered Scotland by the time of nationalisation; the remaining mechanical boxes currently in operation are due to become obsolete by 2021. The Knockando box is distinguished by its polychromatic brick chimney and the survival of its original lever frame; fewer than ten boxes by this railway company are known to survive. We'll drink to that!

L. N. E. R. E.3—1,000—8/29 ✠ [M. 9801]

LUGGAGE

From ....

To KNOCKANDO

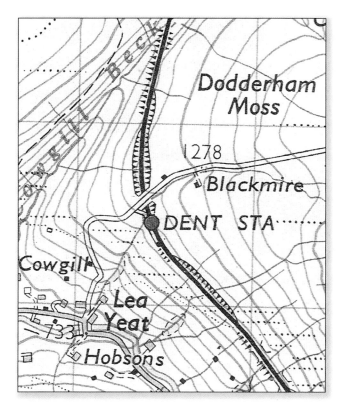

16 DENT
The best of a bad job

In many cases it is fairly obvious where a station should be located in relation to the settlement it is intended to serve, but there are numerous examples where the geography of an area makes a station's actual situation less than ideal. The Settle & Carlisle line is a prime example where the harsh nature of the landscape through which the line passes is combined with the economic imperative of forging a line that would form part of a through trunk route from London to Scotland in the face of competitive routes on either side of the Pennines. As a consequence of

limiting the ruling gradient to 1 in 100 and the need to take maximum advantage of every possible opportunity from an often unfriendly physical landscape, some of its stations were positioned in less than ideal spots, local traffic always being of lesser consideration to the promoters of the line. Kirkby Stephen station, at 300 feet above and 2 miles away from the town, is one example, and another is Dent station, which was perched 600 feet above and 4 miles away from its namesake village.

In fact, Dent and Culgaith were the only two station sites still to be finally settled upon at the time of the opening of the line for goods in August 1875. The original proposals of 1872 for a station to serve Dentdale envisaged a site at Dent Head, but by 1874 the talk was of a site at Arten Gill. An offer by the local landowner, Lord Bective, of a site at Dent Head in 1875 was in the end rejected as being some 7 miles from the village, whereas the site finally selected was a mere 4 miles away! Another issue regarding the chosen location was that of road access, for no matter which site was chosen some hundreds of feet of vertical distance would have to be negotiated by means of very steep roads from the valley floor. The station at Dent was not finally opened until 1877, and was to become one of the least used on the whole line. By the late 1950s and early 1960s fewer than two passengers per day were using the station, but it was still graced with six local services daily.

At an altitude of 1,150 feet, Dent is the highest main-line station remaining on the network in England and proudly displays a board to this effect. There are stone-built passenger waiting rooms on both the northbound and southbound platforms with access to the southbound platform by an unguarded level crossing at the south end of the station for foot passengers; as a consequence of this there is a 30mph permanent speed restriction for non-stop trains through the station. Old wooden snow fences are still in place on the eastern side of the station, drifting being a problem here in the depths of winter. Although closed in 1970 together with the majority of the

The famous snow fences adjoining the line are seen to advantage in this view of Class 47 No 47463 heading south through Dent station on 2 April 1983. *George Woods*

An unidentified Class 47 powers through the isolated Dent station, which in this 1970s view was closed to passengers but still retained its signal box, subsequently demolished in 1981. The highest main-line station in England happily reopened for passenger traffic in 1986 after 16 years of closure.

intermediate stations on the line, apart from Settle and Appleby, a resurgence in fortunes in recent years has seen the reopening of many local stations including Dent in 1986, and annual passenger usage in 2014/15 was a respectable 9,000. Today the station is privately owned and available to hire as holiday accommodation, its former isolation from habitation, once a negative element, being seemingly its main attraction today.

The station was recently offered for sale for £425,000 being described as "handy for the train but a bit of a trek to the shops". This is only the third time it has been on the market since construction in 1877 and with 14 daily rail services stopping here as well as the bonus of seeing steam excursions pass through regularly it will surely prove to be an attractive proposition.

With some snow still lying on the high ground, this is the glorious panorama of Dentdale seen from the southbound 'Thames Clyde Express' in the late 1970s.

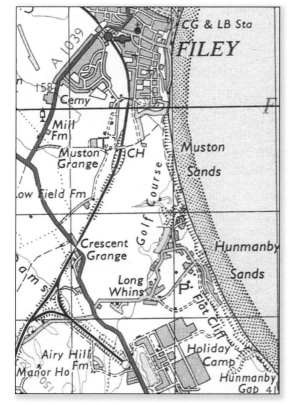

The 09.20 Leeds-Filey service has arrived as the final train of the 1975 season on Saturday 6 September 1975. The Butlins land trains are waiting to take passengers and their luggage under the main road and into the camp. *CH Library*

17 FILEY HOLIDAY CAMP
'Hello campers!'

Holiday camp proprietors such as Butlins, Pontins and Warners tended to choose sites where rail transport was available at not too great a distance from their camps, such as Bognor Regis, Minehead, Barry Island and Skegness. In a few cases dedicated stations and lines were provided to deliver campers to the very gates of the camps themselves. Such stations included Heads of Ayr, Penychain for Pwllheli camp, and Filey Camp station, which was linked to the main line via a short spur from a triangular junction located between Filey and Hunmanby.

Filey Camp station opened in May 1947 and lasted just over 30 years before closure in 1977. The station had no fewer than four platforms, which were lengthy to accommodate the long trains that would bring campers in on summer Saturdays and collect home-going holidaymakers. A signal box was located at the Filey end of the platforms to control train movements. In 1962, for example, there were through trains from Leeds, Manchester, London King's Cross, Newcastle, Penistone and Birmingham. There were never any buildings located on the platforms except for a small ticket collector's hut near the buffer stops. On the large station concourse there was a small single-storey concrete building. Holidaymakers and their luggage were transported from the station to the camp reception by a 'road train' running underneath the main A165 road via a private subway. Apparently one Paul McCartney stayed at the camp in August 1957 with his family and, with his brother, made his first stage appearance in a talent contest.

The declining importance of British holiday resorts as foreign package holidays became more popular in the 1970s, together with the increasing proportion of campers who made their way by private car rather than train, led to a drop in customers for the railway such that the limited-date holiday services became increasingly uneconomic. The final trains ran on Saturday 17 July 1977. Indeed, such was the decline in attendance that Butlins took the unexpected step of announcing closure of the camp in 1983, together with that situated at Clacton. The camp was sold in 1985 to a demolition contractor who reopened it as a holiday centre in 1986 under the name 'Amtree Park', the opening ceremony being performed by Ernie Wise. However, after only a few weeks the scheme failed and the site was sold again to a Birmingham consortium that hoped to turn it into a residential site. The majority of the camp was promptly razed to the ground and the firm went into liquidation. After many years of dereliction it is now prospering as 'The Bay – Filey', a collection of holiday homes with leisure complex, pub and cafes. The platforms of the old station, now of course trackless, and some of the concrete lamp standards still remain in situ although the site is becoming increasingly overgrown as the years go by – a sad testament to the golden years of holiday camp travel.

Butlins, of course, had further railway connections in that Billy Butlin preserved several BR locomotives at his camps and ran miniature-gauge tourist lines within the grounds of the camps including that at Filey, the 2-foot-gauge railway here running from 1953 until closure in 1983.

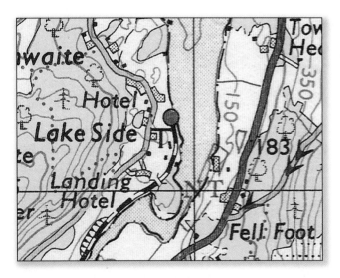

18 LAKESIDE
Lakeside steamers

The Furness Railway (FR) opened a branch line in June 1869 from its Carnforth-Barrow-in-Furness route at Plumpton Junction to the southern end of Lake Windermere. Originally intended to terminate at Newby Bridge, situated where the River Leven enters the lake, it was subsequently decided to extend the line by 1 mile to a new terminus at a spot known as The Landing, which was to be renamed Lakeside. The thinking behind this was to allow the operation of larger vessels on the lake than was possible from Newby Bridge, where the waters of the bottom end of the lake necessitated the use of smaller ships with shallower draughts. To capitalise on the position of Lakeside, the FR purchased shares in the Windermere United Steam Yacht Co (WUSYC) in order to thwart any possible expansionist plans of the Kendal & Windermere Railway, which had opened in 1847 and was by this time part of the London & North Western Railway. In 1872 the WUSYC became fully owned by the FR, which was to take a share in the growing tourist industry of the area. This purchase helped to mitigate the falling off in the mainstay goods traffic, which had been the carriage of coal for the Windermere steamers, iron ore for the Backbarrow Iron Works, and sulphur and saltpetre for the Black Beck and Low Wood gunpowder works. Traffic in the opposite direction was mainly pig iron, gunpowder, pit props, ultramarine 'blue' powder, and wooden bobbins.

At about this time the iron ore industry started to decline and with it the fortunes of the Furness Railway, but at the turn of the 20th century, with a more modern fleet of vessels on the lake, the FR was in an ideal position to encourage and carry train loads of day-trippers and holidaymakers to and from its Lakeside terminus and thence on to its own lake steamers. The golden years of the branch thus began, which were to peak just prior to the First World War when many excursion trains from Lancashire and elsewhere arrived at Lakeside.

The lake steamers owned by the FR included the *Britannia* of 1879, which was the last vessel bought by the FR in 1908 and which was laid up during the First World War and scrapped in 1918 at Lakeside without re-entering service. The *Rothay*, the last of the paddle steamers built for service on the lake, was constructed in 1865 and bought by

The rusting rails and grass-grown tracks tell their own story of dereliction now that the branch line has been closed and trippers will no longer arrive by train at Lakeside to take a journey on the lake steamers.

Resurrection came to part of the line with the opening of the preserved Lakeside & Haverthwaite Railway in 1973. Two of its steam locomotives, an LMS Fairburn tank in steam and Hudswell Clark *Renishaw Ironworks No 6* stabled by the buffer stops, are seen under the roof girders of the terminus. Unfortunately the roof was later removed. The industrial locomotive now resides on the Tanfield Railway.

the FR in 1869, being withdrawn in 1900. The *Swan*, also of 1869 vintage, was bought in 1860 but lasted until 1937. In 1890 the FR commissioned the building of the *Tern*, which was launched the following year and remains the flagship of the Windermere fleet today.

In 1938 the passenger service was suspended for the winter months, then, with the outbreak of hostilities in 1939, the winter service was once more suspended, never to operate again. Even the summertime service ran only until 1941. Newby Bridge station was closed in September 1939 but was occasionally used for the transfer of German prisoners of war to Grizedale Hall POW camp. Summer services were reintroduced in 1946 but by then traffic was declining and BR closed the whole line to passengers on 6 September 1965 and to freight

north of Haverthwaite and the Backbarrow Ironworks sidings. All traffic on the branch ceased two years later.

In the period between closure in 1965 and reopening by a preservation society in 1973, most of Lakeside station, including the tower, was demolished, but not the quayside office of Sealink with its cafeteria above. The overall roof of the station was removed by the British Rail Property Board during the winter of 1978 as being unsafe, so there is little remaining today of the station as it was in its heyday, although steam-hauled trains continue to grace the terminus, running on the 3-mile line of the Lakeside & Haverthwaite Railway. The link between trains and lake steamers, which originally lay behind the construction of Lakeside, is perpetuated today as a reminder of the ambitions of the Furness Railway.

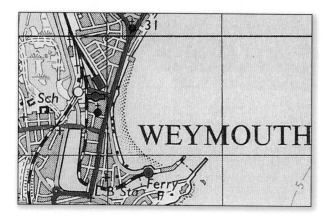

19 MELCOMBE REGIS
Reversal of fortune

Melcombe Regis was a latecomer to the branch line from Weymouth to Portland, not opening until 30 May 1909, some 44 years after the branch had seen its first train. The opening of a station here was facilitated by the replacement of the original timber viaduct over the area of water known as the Backwater, which led to Radipole Lake, by a shorter all-steel construction; the reclaimed land, in the form of an embankment, freed up by this new viaduct was used for the new station. There was no commercial necessity for a station here, but the thinking behind it was twofold. First, it avoided the need for trains to and from Portland to reverse in and out of Weymouth, which they had done previously as the junction of the Portland branch lay to the north of Weymouth facing Dorchester. Weymouth terminus could now be bypassed by depositing passengers at the new platform, where they could walk across to Weymouth station. Second, and perhaps more importantly, it reduced pressure on Weymouth, especially at holiday times, by allowing trains to be diverted to Melcombe Regis, there to unload their holidaymaking hordes. The LSWR had wanted such a station built when the Portland branch had opened, but the

GWR had felt that the facilities at Weymouth were adequate and the promoting railway company, the Weymouth & Portland Railway, did not want the expense of providing an additional station on its line. All branch trains now began and finished their trips to Portland at the new station, which greatly improved punctuality on the line.

After closure of the Portland branch to passengers in 1952 Melcombe Regis continued in this latter role regularly until September 1959. It also played host to certain trains from Abbotsbury until closure of that branch, also in 1952, diverted from Weymouth's station in busy periods.

The station consisted of a single 400-foot timber platform on the down side of the line with a single-storey timber station building faced with corrugated iron. Although the roof extended over the platform to form a narrow canopy, this was found to be completely inadequate in view of the exposed position on the edge of Radipole Lake and the canopy was later replaced with a larger pitched structure, and a cast-iron wind shield was provided opposite the building for additional weather protection. The platform was rebuilt with stone blocks in the late 1930s and was adorned with concrete tank traps during the Second World War.

In the mid-1950s plans were made to rebuild Weymouth station, with Melcombe Regis acting as a relief platform while the work was being undertaken. The station buildings were duly repainted and the platform gas lighting, which had been disconnected upon closure of the Portland branch, was brought back into use in 1956. The last regular use of the station as a relief platform was on 12 September 1959, although there was occasional use after this date.

Melcombe Regis station building was demolished in 1965 and the Backwater bridge remained in situ until it collapsed in a storm in November 1974, being later demolished, the Swannery road bridge being built in virtually the same location. A few vestiges of the platform were still intact in 1999 but these were cleared away during the construction of a retirement and sheltered housing estate in 2000.

Melcombe Regis is seen on 15 May 1964. The girders of the viaduct over the Backwater, now known as Radipole Lake, can be seen in the right foreground; this was demolished in 1974. *Colour-Rail*

Only the platform survives in this view taken in March 1983, looking north. *Nick Catford*

Pannier tank No 3737 is operating a leg of the RCTS 'Greyhound' rail tour on 14 August 1960, which took participants from Melcombe Regis to Easton on the Isle of Portland and return. *Alan Sainty*

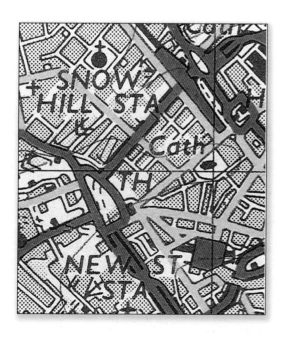

20 BIRMINGHAM SNOW HILL
The biggest unstaffed halt

'The UK's largest unstaffed halt' – such was the sad epitaph for the once great GWR station in the heart of the city of Birmingham. Opened in 1852, as a temporary station, and closed in 1972, with demolition following five years later, its last years were ones of sad decline. The rot started with the decision to electrify the former LNWR main line from London to Birmingham, leaving the ex-GWR route with a much reduced status and with most of its services withdrawn by the late 1960s.

Originally it was never envisaged that Snow Hill would be the GWR's main station in the city, but political machinations between rival railway companies prevented the railway from reaching its originally intended terminus at Curzon Street. Snow Hill station was rebuilt on a much larger scale between 1906 and 1912 to handle increased traffic. The new station building was intended to compete with New Street, which, before the rebuilding of the 1960s into the dreadful place it became, was a much grander building. The rebuilt Snow Hill contained lavish facilities with

The impressive facade of Snow Hill is seen amid the busy street scene of Colmore Row in 1962, just 10 years before complete closure. *Ben Brooksbank*

a large booking hall, an arched glass roof, and splendid waiting rooms lined with oak bars. The main platform area, which was covered by a large glass and steel overall roof, consisted of two large island platforms containing four through platforms and four bays for terminating trains at the northern end. The through platforms were long enough to accommodate two trains simultaneously, with scissors crossings permitting trains to pull in front of or pull out from behind other trains berthed at the same platform, thus effectively creating a 10-platform station.

As late as 1964 Snow Hill still handled 7½ million passengers annually. However, the electrification of the rival route into New Street led BR to concentrate all the city's services on one central hub, thus rendering Snow Hill largely superfluous. In 1966 the decision was taken to end main-line services through Snow Hill once electrification of the WCML was complete, and long-distance services duly ceased to use the station in March 1967, with the tunnel at the south end being closed to all traffic the following year. Local trains from Leamington Spa and Stratford-upon-Avon were then terminated at Moor Street and services to London, the West Country, Stourbridge and Shrewsbury were diverted into New Street, with the branch line to Dudley being closed. The sad remnants left at Snow Hill were a shuttle service of four trains per day using single railcars to Langley Green together with six

daily stopping services to Wolverhampton Low Level; thus almost the entire station became disused, with just one bay platform remaining operational. In March 1972 these last services were withdrawn and the station was finally put out of its misery, being closed entirely together with the lines to Smethwick and Wolverhampton with the exception of a single freight line from Smethwick West to a scrap metal works in Handsworth.

Further ignominy followed with the station being used for several years as a car park. The Colmore Row façade was demolished in 1969, with the bulk of the remainder following in 1977 due to the dangerous state of the building. However, 15 years after closure Snow Hill was reborn, but on a much more modest scale when in 1987 two island platforms were opened for services south to Leamington and Stratford. In 1993 through services to London were reintroduced, but serving Marylebone rather than Paddington. In 1995 services to Worcester and Kidderminster were added. The 'Jewellery Line' to Smethwick followed and a tram link to Wolverhampton also opened as part of the Midland Metro service. So the short-sighted retrenchment of the past has to some extent been undone, but the current starkly functional Snow Hill, situated as it is under a multi-storey car park, can never recapture the grandeur of the former station.

A sabbatarian calm appears to have descended upon an apparently deserted Snow Hill, plentifully supplied with platform barrows. *CH Library*

A much busier scene sees the arrival of an express for Paddington hauled by a 'Western' Class diesel-hydraulic. *CH Library*

The sad sight of a major city station in its death throes. Although unstaffed by the time of this late-1960s view, much of the station's infrastructure is still in situ including the running-in board.

Just one track remains in the sea of devastation, and this was only to last until withdrawal of the shuttle service to Wolverhampton in March 1972.

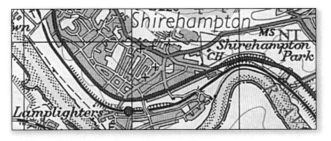

Shirehampton is a station on one of the few lines in the Bristol suburban system to have survived the cuts of the 1960s. In this late-1960s view looking towards Avonmouth the footbridge, signal box and running-in board still survived although the station staff had been withdrawn in 1965. The signal box remained in use until 1970, at which time the track was singled and the down platform abandoned. The station building was later demolished.

21 SHIREHAMPTON
Suburban survivor

One of the few remnants of the once extensive Bristol suburban network is the line from Temple Meads to Avonmouth and Severn Beach. Shirehampton, known as 'Shrampton' in the local Bristol dialect or just plain 'Shire', started life as the headquarters of the Bristol Port Railway & Pier (BPRP) line, which ran from Avonmouth to Hotwells along the bottom of the Avon Gorge. As its status required, the station building was constructed in a style superior to other stations on the route, the original building, which sported an attractive valanced canopy along its length, containing not only a booking office but also a porters' room and an office for the Superintendent of the line. Subsequently the northern platform was lengthened by the GWR and a stationmaster's house built to the west of the station on the up side. The track was doubled in 1903 and the station was remodelled with a new down platform, and a latticed footbridge linking the two platforms. The station building extension was in a different style and had a canopy that did not match the original. A signal box of 20 levers was located at the east end of the down platform.

The line from Hotwells was closed in 1922 to allow construction of The Portway road along the bottom of the gorge. However, train services at Shirehampton continued via the Clifton Extension line from Clifton Down, which was a joint line owned by the GWR and the Midland and which had opened for goods in 1877 but not to passengers, due to concerns about the state of the BPRP track and signalling deficiencies, until 1885. The original three goods sidings were supplemented in 1921 by a fourth, which was extended across an adjacent road into the premises of R. Brodie for the conveyance of materials used in the construction of The Portway. This siding continued in existence until 1985, having served a domestic fuel oil depot for the last five years of its life.

General goods traffic ceased in November 1965 and the station became unstaffed in July 1967, a far cry from the ten staff employed there in the 1930s. The signal box closed in October 1970 when the line was singled and the down platform abandoned. Buildings on the up platform remained in good condition as offices until damaged by fire in the 1990s, after which they were demolished. Under threat of closure in the Beeching Report and from time to time since, the line has seen a resurgence in use in recent years reflecting the increase in timetabled services. The former stationmaster's house remains in residential use. Today a small shelter with a canopy is the only building to be found on the single bi-directional platform, but a respectable 50,000 passengers per annum now use Shirehampton station. There are ambitious plans for Shirehampton to be contained within the Greater Bristol Metro scheme with aspirations for a half-hourly service, with trains alternately terminating at Bath Spa and a rejuvenated Portishead, as well as calls for the reopening of the Henbury Loop line, allowing direct services to Bristol Parkway via Avonmouth. Although long ago swallowed up within Bristol, many inhabitants still view the locality as a village, and one that is fortunate enough to retain a rail link when many other districts of the city have lost theirs.

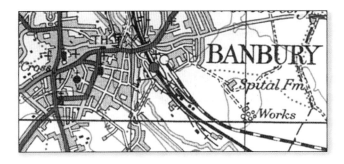

The poor relation at Banbury, this is the exterior of Merton Street station on 24 March 1961, some 10 weeks after closure to passengers. *Ben Brooksbank*

22 BANBURY MERTON STREET
From trunk to branch
– thwarted ambition

Although Merton Street was the first station to serve the market town of Banbury, opening as early as 1850 as the northern terminus of the Buckinghamshire Railway (BkR), it was to be eclipsed by its more powerful neighbour in the shape of the GWR, whose station in the town opened just four months later. The GWR had unsuccessfully opposed the Act of Parliament authorising the construction of the BkR, promoting instead the Birmingham & Oxford Junction Railway scheme, which included a series of loop lines into Buckinghamshire; this scheme was eventually authorised but without the loop lines. It had been the original intention of the BkR to continue lines from Banbury to the north and west further into Oxfordshire. However, with

the expansionist policies of the GWR, whose station at Banbury was located on its London to Birmingham main line, it soon became apparent that Merton Street would in all likelihood remain merely the terminus of a rural branch line linking the town with Buckingham and Bletchley, with connections to Oxford via Verney Junction.

Beginning with a moderate level of prosperity in its early years, the BkR suffered both from the decision to re-route freight through Oxford and Didcot and a depression that affected railway shares in the late 1850s. It was absorbed by the LNWR, which had worked it from the outset, in 1878. With two stations in the town located so close to each other, the LNWR's successor, the LMS, attempted to phase out Merton Street by agreeing with the GWR to combine the two stations into a new joint station to the north of the GWR facility. The outbreak of the Second World War put paid to this idea and it was never subsequently resurrected, although a spur linking the two lines allowed easy transfer of traffic. Although freight from Merton Street held up well, with cattle, milk, and military traffic all being important, passenger traffic declined, with most Banburians preferring to catch trains from Banbury General, the former GWR station that became the main station for the town and which was modernised in 1958. Today it occupies one of the most strategic and important locations in the entire rail network in Britain.

Perhaps anticipating expansion beyond Banbury, Merton Street station was a mean-looking affair that always had a temporary air about it. The wooden main station building was simply built with a low timber island platform covered by a roof supported by steel columns. The timber goods shed initially provided was subsequently rebuilt in brick as goods traffic prospered. There was a locomotive shed, cattle dock and sidings, provided to handle the substantial agricultural traffic; sidings also led to a nearby gasworks and the GWR yard. By the mid-1950s the timber boarding on the station roof had reached a parlous state, and it was removed, leaving only the concourse under cover with the platform open to the elements and with the metal supports of the roof remaining starkly skeletal against the sky, reminiscent perhaps of a greenhouse. Prior to the introduction of lightweight diesel railcars in 1956 the station was spruced up with a fresh coat of paint, but the low unevenly surfaced wooden platforms remained, necessitating the provision of steps to access the railcars.

The experimental railcars, which rather obtusely only operated between Banbury and Buckingham, where passengers had to change to a steam-hauled push-pull service, did not succeed in stemming the line's losses, even though a 400% increase in passengers was reported. Peak-hour services were popular but those off peak ran virtually empty, and even the four-fold increase in passenger usage, when the base figure was so small, could not revive its fortunes. The line between Buckingham and Banbury lost its passenger service from 2 January 1961 with that between Buckingham and Verney Junction lingering on until September 1964, using the diesel units transferred from the closed Banbury section.

Had the BkR been able to expand beyond Banbury in the early days, who knows what might have been its long-term future? After closure to goods in 1966 the main station building at Merton Street and the goods shed were used for a time by British Road Services as a storage depot. The station was subsequently demolished and the site redeveloped for housing.

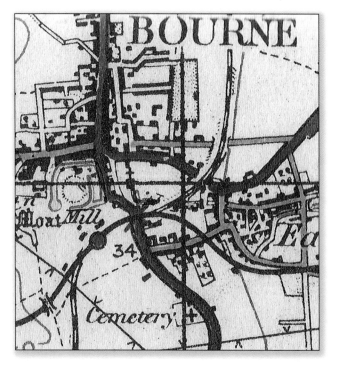

23 BOURNE
Born again

At Bourne we encounter a station adapted from an existing building, as will also be seen later at Staines West, and there were indeed others. Generally, however, these were very much the exception with railway companies preferring to have a station purpose-built from scratch. Between Leicester and Burton-on-Trent the station at Bardon Hill was, in its former life, a coaching inn, and much further afield the station at Cuautla in Mexico was adapted from a former Dominican convent with the former nave becoming a goods warehouse! Closer to home, perhaps the most famous example of station buildings with a former life is here at Bourne in Lincolnshire, a junction of the GN route between Sleaford and Essendine with the Midland & Great Northern Railway (M&GNR) line.

Red Hall, constructed in about 1605, was purchased by the Bourne & Essendine Railway in 1860, becoming the ticket office and stationmaster's house. The line was

The view southwards towards Essendine and Castle Bytham shows the abandoned engine shed in the right background. *Ben Brooksbank*

The station looked intact when photographed in 1961, but it had actually closed to passengers two years before when the M&GNR system was closed wholesale. However, Bourne remained open for goods until April 1965. The ancient Red Hall, dating back to 1605, had been acquired by the Bourne & Essendine Railway back in 1860 and was used as the stationmaster's house. *Ben Brooksbank*

operated by the Great Northern Railway (GNR) and later taken over by that company. Next to arrive was the Bourne & Spalding Railway in 1866, which converted the terminus into a through station. The original down platform remained outside Red Hall after conversion to a through layout, but was no longer used. A single island platform, later reached by an iron lattice footbridge from the disused platform next to Red Hall, was then used by all trains. The footbridge was a characteristic Midland Railway design and was probably provided when the M&GNR arrived, while in 1872 the Great Northern opened a route to Sleaford. The final link was the Saxby to Bourne line, part of the rambling route of the M&GNR, opening in 1894. Thus Bourne became an important crossroads on the railway map of Lincolnshire.

John Thorpe (c1565-1655), one of the foremost architects in Britain during the Elizabethan period, was in all likelihood the designer of Red Hall. Its first tenant was a London grocer by the name of Gilbert Fisher, who had amassed a fortune sufficient to finance such a costly building. The property later passed to the Digby family in the early 17th century and remained in their hands until 1836, when it was leased to various tenants and even used as a private boarding school for young ladies until

sold in 1860 to the railway company. Appreciation for the past was not as strong as it is today and there was an attempt to demolish the hall in 1892 when the railway company required additional space to lay goods sidings. Fortunately a public outcry ensued, forcing the railway to shelve its plans and the building was saved.

Upon closure of the M&GNR system in 1959, which was destined to be Bourne's last remaining rail link, the lines to Sleaford and Essendine having closed in 1930 and 1951 respectively, Red Hall became redundant and was found to be in a poor state of repair. Even at £1 there were no takers when it was offered for sale, and a further attempt was made to demolish it. In 1962 Bourne United Charities came to the rescue, acquired the freehold and over the next decade undertook an extensive programme of restoration. Red Hall reopened in 1972 for public use and as offices for the BUC, and so it remains to this day. The station site was redeveloped in the 1970s as a light industrial estate and the remaining railway buildings were demolished in 2005. In 2014 residential redevelopment was undertaken in the area, but Red Hall still stands proudly defiant, a symbol not just of the Elizabethan period but of the great age of Victorian railway expansion.

24 OTTERHAM
The withered arm – when Hardy set out for Lyonesse

One of Thomas Hardy's short stories, published in *Wessex Tales* in 1888, is entitled 'The Withered Arm', a soubriquet later applied to the LSWR's long meandering rail route through North Cornwall to Wadebridge and Padstow. Hardy's association with North Cornwall derives from his visit to St Juliot near Otterham in March 1870 to undertake church restoration, in the days before he became a novelist and poet and when he was an architectural assistant. Meeting his first wife at the rectory, his attachment to the area was sealed.

His starlit walk that cold March morning began shortly after 4 o'clock in rural Dorset, and was to be the first section in an arduous day's travel of some 15 hours duration to his destination, a remote spot in North Cornwall still untouched by the tentacles of railway development. His journey was to involve Shanks's pony, four changes of train, involving three different railway companies – then still very much a novelty in rural Dorset – and finally a hired trap or 'dog cart' for 16

miles, which Hardy described as 'a dreary yet poetical drive' of 3 hours to his ultimate destination of St Juliot. His future wife, who met him that evening at the rectory, described Hardy's journey in these terms:

'It was a lovely Monday evening in March after a wild winter, we were on the qui-vive for the stranger, who would have a tedious journey, his home being two counties off changing trains many times and waiting at stations – a sort of cross jump-journey, like a chess-knight's move.'

Although there was no railway in the locality when he made his first visit – it did not open until 1892 – after the death of his wife in 1912 Hardy gave vent to his feelings and composed a number of his greatest love poems, many inspired by a return visit made in March 1913, 33 years after his original trip. The route Hardy took on this occasion is not recorded, but by this time he could have taken the LSWR line from Exeter to Otterham to leave him

BR Standard tank No 80041 arrives at Otterham with a service for Okehampton on 15 December 1964. *Roger Joanes*

Shortly before the end the sparse passenger service was reduced to just a single car as seen here as the 14.25 Wadebridge to Halwill Junction service pauses in vain for custom on 1 July 1966. *CH Library, J. Spencer Gilks*

The slate-clad station building at Otterham is seen in the late 1960s some three years after closure. Slate cladding was very necessary here to protect against the strong Atlantic rainstorms that regularly lashed this exposed location.

just 3 miles by road from St Juliot. One particularly pertinent poem, although dated 1870, was not published until after the death of his wife:

> 'When I set out for Lyonesse
> A hundred miles away
> The rime was on the spray
> And starlight lit my lonesomeness
> When I set out for Lyonesse
> A hundred miles away.'

Otterham station was situated in an exposed bleak spot at 850 feet above sea level near the summit of the North Cornwall line and was sheltered from the fury of Atlantic gales by the judicious planting of pine trees. The station building, in typical LSWR rural style, was in local Delabole stone with Portland stone quoins and decorations. Oil lighting remained until the closure of the line in 1966. A terrace of six LSWR houses was built nearby for permanent way men and signalmen. The population of Otterham and the surrounding hamlets was only some 800 in the 1930s. Originally sited to serve as a railhead for Boscastle, passengers tended to prefer using Camelford, which had better road connections. Freight fared better and the location of a wartime airfield in 1942 gave rise to some traffic, but this finished with the closure of the airfield in 1945.

Lavant saw passengers again when the LCGB's 'Hayling Farewell Rail Tour' of 3 November 1963 arrived headed by two Class 'Q' 0-6-0s, Nos 30531 and 30543.

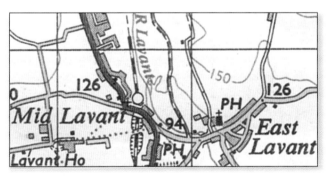

25 LAVANT
The beet goes on

One must empathise with the chagrin that some of the early promoters of the line from Midhurst to Chichester, who had entertained dreams of a through route carrying London to Portsmouth traffic, would undoubtedly have felt had they realised that one of the most lucrative and long-lasting traffics that the railway as eventually built was to carry would be sugar beet, and that Lavant station would play a major role in the transport of this humble vegetable.

The style and scale of Lavant station was in keeping with the grandiose buildings on the rest of the line at Cocking and Singleton, the latter also boasting a refreshment room for racegoers to nearby Goodwood racecourse. Although built of brick to a substantial thickness of 18 inches in places, the second floor of the station building was plastered and strips of wood attached to give the appearance of timber framing in a style that speculative builders would later come to describe as

A later rail tour, of 12 March 1967 headed by the ex-LNER *The Great Marquess,* had Crompton diesel power at its head to traverse the Lavant branch. No D6544 arrives with its train in the loop that had been laid in 1953 when Lavant became the railhead for the sugar beet traffic from the surrounding area.

'Stockbroker Tudor'. Floral designs were etched into the plasterwork, although rain penetration caused some walls to be tile-hung in later years. The platform canopies were supported by decorative columns that were hollow, thereby incorporating roof drainage. The platform level was actually the building's basement and originally comprised a lamp room, a porters' room and a gentlemen's lavatory, and it was these that were subsequently given over to sugar beet administration duties. Timbered entrance porches were also provided and in addition to an internal staircase a wooden external staircase covered with a zinc canopy led from underneath the canopy to the ground floor. An external luggage chute was also provided, enabling luggage to be transferred easily from the station entrance to the platform.

One could only marvel at the scale of accommodation at all the stations on this branch, for it passed through only very modest settlements. The London, Brighton & South Coast Railway (LBSCR) adopted a style of building that was used elsewhere on the system, being particularly favoured during that company's brief period of expansion around 1880, and also to be found on what were latterly known as the 'Cuckoo line' from Hailsham to Eridge and

the 'Bluebell line' from East Grinstead to Haywards Heath and Lewes. Classified as the 'Wealden style' by John Hoare in the publication *Sussex Railway Architecture,* they were to the design of J. L. Myers of Preston, and were certainly among the most ornate station buildings ever provided by the LBSCR.

As previously mentioned, it was hoped that the line through Lavant would form part of a through route from London to Portsmouth. The first plan for such a route had been proposed during the 'Railway Mania' years of the 1840s, and was entitled the Guildford, Chichester, Portsmouth & Fareham Railway. Plans were drawn up by the engineer Joseph Locke and supported by the Duke of Richmond, whose seat was at nearby Goodwood House. However, the scheme was rejected by the House of Lords in 1846 when the more direct route to Portsmouth was approved. A further scheme known as 'Drayson's Line' was the Direct London & Portsmouth & Chichester Railway, which was to run from Redhill direct to Portsmouth with branches to Petersfield and to Chichester branching off

Opposite: Seen after track removal, the crumbling platform presents a sad spectacle.

A diesel shunter heads south from Lavant with a fully loaded train of beet.

near Chilgrove. This also hit the buffers. The final chance for this to become an important through route came in 1865 when the South Eastern Railway (SER) announced its plans for a line from Dorking to Midhurst, following which it would purchase the Chichester & Midhurst Railway, construction of which had started in April that year but had subsequently faltered, and extend that line to Hayling Island, thereby encroaching on LBSCR territory. This prompted the LBSCR to incorporate the Chichester & Midhurst line into its company.

After a relatively short existence, the route closed to passenger traffic in July 1935, but goods continued to be catered for at Lavant for a further 35 years, which must be something of a record for a branch line. Freight services continued to cater for the intermediate stations of Lavant, Singleton and Cocking until the termination of services north of Lavant in 1951. Thereafter Lavant became the railhead for seasonal sugar beet, a traffic that had begun in the 1930s. The sugar beet loading period generally ran from September to January and production increased considerably during the post-war years. With this in mind, a loop was created at Lavant by installing a temporary connection to the branch at the northern end of Lavant goods yard siding on 6 August 1947. Then on 19 November 1951 came the abrupt termination of such through workings when the 9.30am goods from Chichester to Midhurst, consisting of eight wagons hauled by 'C2X' No 32522, ran into the chasm caused by a collapsed culvert to the north of Cocking after a night of storm and torrential rain. Repair of the embankment was deemed uneconomic, so the three remaining railheads had to be served by a goods shuttle from Chichester. However, in view of the annual loss of £19,000 reported for the branch, the two latter stations were closed in August 1953 and the track lifted north of Lavant.

The Lavant-Chichester section was retained primarily for the sugar beet traffic, and at the end of 1953 the former platform loop, which had been removed many years before cessation of the passenger services, was reinstated and a 500-foot-long sugar beet dock constructed by raising and extending the platform, so providing loading facilities for 22 wagons at a time. This sort of investment was obviously felt to be worthwhile and was repeated elsewhere in the South of England, for example at Droxford on the old Meon Valley route, where it helped to keep goods services running until 1962. Outside the season, Lavant continued to be served by a daily general goods service, but this soon became weekly and sometimes less frequently as farmers who had previously used Singleton and Cocking had to incur additional mileage in carting their products to Lavant, this being the subject of many complaints at the time.

From 6 September 1963 further concentration occurred when handling of the West Sussex sugar beet crop in the local area was centralised at Lavant, which catered for production over a 10-mile radius and led to the cessation of beet loading facilities nearby at Barnham, Chichester and Drayton. Although up to 40 wagons and two trains per day now used the Lavant branch, the days of rail-borne beet were numbered as the alternative of road transport continued to grow in popularity. The wagons were marshalled in the still extensive Chichester Goods Yard for onward transmission as block trains via the Mid Sussex line to Norwood and across London to the East Anglian beet refineries. Regular goods services, which latterly consisted of small amounts of coal, ceased on 3 August 1968, when Class 08 shunter No D3662, with one truck and brake van, did the final honours, but sporadic sugar beet trains continued over the increasingly weed-infested track into the autumn of 1969 before finally ceasing altogether in January 1970.

The end of sugar beet workings was not the end of the story for the branch, however, as from January 1972 gravel began to be extracted from a site to the south of the station and, as a condition of extraction, the gravel had to be moved by rail. Gravel traffic was to last until 15 March 1991, a remarkable 55 years after the last regular passenger train had passed over the branch. Today the station building has been converted into dwellings, although the former canopy was dismantled and now does duty at Horsted Keynes on the Bluebell Railway.

Meldon Quarry Halt was a typical product of the SR's Exmouth Junction Concrete Works and is seen here on 19 December 1966 with a school party gracing the small platform on returning from a visit to the quarry. *Roger Joanes*

26 MELDON QUARRY HALT

Railway workers only

Stations solely for the use of railway employees, and sometimes their families, were provided by several companies. Examples were Barassie Workshops, by the Glasgow & South Western Railway, Caerphilly Works, on the Rhymney Railway, Hoo Junction Halt, on the North Kent line, which opened in 1956 to serve a large rail yard, Sugar Loaf Summit on the Central Wales line, built to serve four railway workers' cottages, Durnsford Road Staff Halt in Wimbledon, Battersea Pier Staff Halt, Alderbury, between Dean and Salisbury, and Meldon Quarry Halt on the London & South Western route from Okehampton to Plymouth. As these halts catered for small numbers of people who were not members of the paying public, they were usually simple affairs consisting of just a short platform and minimal or no facilities.

Meldon Quarry opened in 1897 principally to provide railway ballast, but also lump stone for walling and aggregate. The remoteness of the quarry with very limited unmetalled road access made life difficult for the quarrymen and their families who lived in the dozen or so cottages. In the 1920s a halt with two narrow, very short concrete platforms, products of the SR's Exmouth Junction Concrete Works, was installed adjacent to the up and down lines immediately east of Meldon Viaduct. The only adornment was a post-and-rail fence, there being no seat, lighting or nameboard. One up and one down passenger service was generally booked to call when required to take up or set down wives of the company's employees going to or returning from Okehampton.

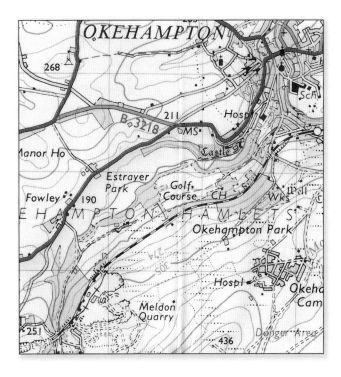

In 1933, for example, the 7.39am service from Launceston was booked to call at the halt on Saturdays with the footnote 'To take up wives of the Company's servants proceeding to Okehampton'; an additional 4 minutes was allowed in the schedule for this. In 1944 a dedicated two-coach train was provided to the Quarry Halt, leaving Okehampton at 6.58am, for quarry and railway workers who lived in the town rather than on site, after which it proceeded to Meldon Junction, to allow the locomotive to run round before returning empty stock to Okehampton. There was a corresponding return from the quarry to Okehampton in the afternoon. In 1947 the footnote in the

59

working timetable reads 'Calls at Quarry signalbox to take up wives of the Company's employees', so perhaps the halt was not in use at this time, although by 1952 the footnote had reverted to a mention of Quarry Halt. By 1958 the service was provided by the 7.00am normal passenger service from Okehampton to Plymouth, but the workmen returned in a coach attached to the 5.10pm stone train from the quarry to Okehampton. The halt was never shown in the public timetable.

Following withdrawal of the passenger service between Okehampton and Bere Alston in 1968, the halt fell into disuse and the platforms were later demolished when modifications to the track layout were implemented and alterations made to the access at the western end of the quarry. Although sold in 1994 to Camas, as part of BR privatisation, stone continued to be shipped out by rail until 2011, when demand declined and the quarry was mothballed by Bardon Aggregates.

The presence of the quarry had ensured the survival of the line from Okehampton, and the Dartmoor Railway (DR) has been running services since 1997. A station on the DR, initially called Meldon Quarry, but changed to Meldon Viaduct in 2015, has been in use since 2000, but not on the site of the original halt. Another of the distinctive aspects of the railway at Meldon Quarry was its signal box, which opened in 1903 and closed in 1970. This had steel mesh screens that could be fitted over the windows to protect the box from flying debris during blasting in the quarry. Another feature was the shed for the resident locomotives that shunted the quarry; these were numbered in the Departmental series and included locomotives of classes 'B4', 'O2', long-term resident 'G6' No DS682, 'USA' tank No DS234, and latterly a diesel shunter.

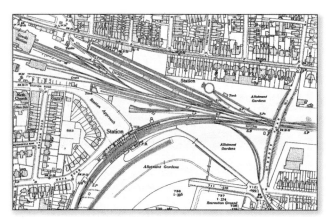

27 WESTON-SUPER-MARE LOCKING ROAD
Day tripper

Excursionists have long been a staple of railway traffic and many stations at holiday destinations catered for them through the expedient of dedicated excursion platforms. Examples include Southport's Chapel Street station, which at its peak had eleven regular platforms and two excursion platforms, although today just six truncated platforms remain and the former Platform 7, which was originally going to be saved and used as an excursion platform for visiting main-line specials, has also been demolished. Bridlington, too, saw excursion platforms added after the First World War to cope with the increasing numbers of day trippers, this market continuing to thrive until the 1960s. By the 1980s rationalisation was overdue as many lines in the station were rarely used except on summer weekends, and the excursion platforms, Nos 7 and 8, were taken out of regular use before signalling changes in 2000 left just three platforms in operation.

In some cases the decision was taken to provide a completely separate excursion station, not just an adjunct of the main station complex. The excursion platforms originally provided at Scarborough were unable to cope with the increasing numbers and, as there was no room to expand the station, the North Eastern Railway obtained powers to build an excursion station, known as Washbeck Excursion station, on the site of an old engine shed half a mile west of the Scarborough terminus. In 1933 it was renamed Londesborough Road, with Scarborough's original station being renamed Scarborough Central.

Weston-super-Mare was another case where a completely separate facility for excursionists was provided. Railways first came to Weston via a single-track branch from the Bristol & Exeter main line in June 1841. The branch was doubled in 1866 when a new station was built, which had an excursion platform added alongside. This early segregation highlighted the class distinction between the regular rail traveller and the 'tripper', the relatively modest fare of 1s 6d return from Bristol attracting an entirely different class of person to the town. Outside the station the railway company ran an 'excursion hall', free to all ticket holders, which dispensed tea at 1½d a cup and even catered for travellers who preferred to make their own brew with ingredients they had brought with them.

In 1884 Weston gained another station when a loop line was constructed enabling through trains between Bristol and Exeter to serve the town. The excursion station was rebuilt in 1907 when the width was doubled and a

A seemingly busy Locking Road station is seen in the distance of this view taken from the Weston loop line. *Colour-Rail*

Hordes of daytrippers no longer throng the platforms of Locking Road, Weston-super-Mare's excursion platform, seen just prior to being swept away for a Tesco supermarket and car park. Dumped 'white goods' seem to be the only traffic here now.

new bay platform added. It was enlarged to four platforms in 1914 and numerous carriage sidings dealt specifically with excursion traffic, and this was now known as Locking Road station. A locomotive turntable was also provided. The excursion station, although rather stark, was located closer to the sea than the main station and in any event weather protection was not of prime importance to a summer-orientated clientele. At its peak a Bank Holiday Monday would see close to 40,000 passengers brought into the town via the excursion platforms. At this time the town's main station attained the grander title of Weston-super-Mare General.

The maintenance of separate stations continued to be an

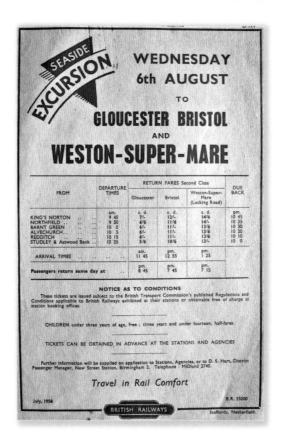

operational necessity until the early 1960s, when excursion traffic declined rapidly. Locking Road closed its doors on its final holiday season on 6 September 1964. After several years being used as a dumping ground for seemingly unwanted 'white goods', the area once occupied by the station and the carriage sidings was replaced with a Tesco store and a large car and coach park. Older citizens of the town no doubt recall those heady days when well-loaded trains, primarily carrying people from the Midlands, occupied all platforms with the excited crowds issuing forth and seeking the delights of a 'kiss-me-quick' British seaside experience.

28 BRENTOR
Putting back the rails
– who will buy?

Although two railways passed through the village of Brentor, only one, the former Plymouth, Devonport & South Western Junction Railway (PDSWJR), decided to serve the village, with a population 105 in 1901, with a railway station. The other, the GWR, feigned indifference and sent its trains sailing through without stopping en route between Tavistock and Launceston; in its wisdom it decided that Mary Tavy, 2 miles to the south, which in a tit-for-tat move the PDSWJR chose to ignore, would be its preferred stopping place.

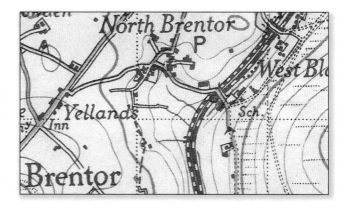

Brentor station was typical of the company's attractive station style. The main building, which was situated on the down platform, incorporated a two-storey station house with single-storey offices, all constructed in local Dartmoor granite with blue-brick facings and dark mortar. The down platform boasted an attractive awning while the up platform contained merely a stone waiting shelter. Right up until closure the station was lit by oil lamps on cast-iron columns, with the station name etched into a blue glass background. Although there was no footbridge, there were steps leading up to the adjacent road overbridge at the end of both platforms.

In spite of the village's small size, the station was quite busy with twenty tickets being issued daily in the late 1920s and early 1930s, not a bad tally for such a small

local population. A small goods yard was located on the down side dealing mainly with coal, minerals and livestock, and a Camping Coach was provided for a few years in the 1930s.

Goods facilities lasted until April 1960, with the signal box closing in June 1961. This was a traditional weather-boarded superstructure upon a masonry base containing a 17-lever Stevens frame. Station staffing ceased in November 1967 after which a few Plymouth-Exeter stopping services continued until the short-sighted closure of the route between Bere Alston and Okehampton in May 1968. For many years the local 4.04pm service from Plymouth Friary terminated here, returning at 5.30pm.

Today the overbridges by the station have been removed, but nearly 50 years after closure the station

The parallel lines of the SR and GWR are very evident here at Brentor, the GWR deigning not to serve this outpost. This view was taken in April 1964 and may be partly replicated again if the diversionary route from Okehampton to Bere Alston is ever reopened as an alternative to the vulnerable coastal route via Dawlish. *Ben Brooksbank*

The LSWR station nestles in the bleak Dartmoor landscape serving the village of North Brentor.

itself is still well cared for and its former role easily recognised as many of its accoutrements have been preserved and enhanced with period pieces such as milk churns, station seats, etc. A couple of years ago the station was put up for sale at just under £600,000, but its prospects were blighted by the possibility that an alternative route to the vulnerable Dawlish seawall line might see trains once again return to the northern slopes of Dartmoor and pass through the old station of Brentor. Reopening the Okehampton-Bere Alston section, though costing many hundreds of millions of pounds, is one of the options currently being examined.

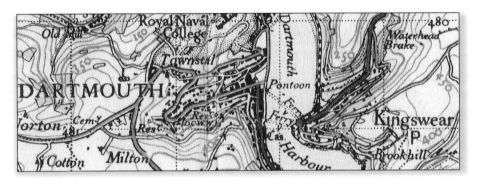

29 KINGSWEAR FOR DARTMOUTH
A bridge too far

Due to the estuary of the River Dart and the difficulty of either constructing a railway bridge or of providing a line down the west bank from Totnes, the intending rail passenger from the town of Dartmouth had first to make a short ferry crossing of the river to reach the terminal station of Kingswear situated on the east bank. Although Dartmouth boasted what passed as a railway station, it only sold tickets and handled parcels, for there were no trains. Kingswear stands on a headland and the railway facilities here all had to be constructed on reclaimed land. The southern end of the platform was covered by an unusual wooden train shed some 100 feet in length.

The original platform was extended in 1929 to 850 feet to accommodate longer trains, of which the 'Torbay Express', which terminated here, was perhaps the most famous.

A wharf, which enabled colliers to unload their cargo direct into waiting trucks at the extensive goods sidings, was rebuilt in 1932 and electrically powered cranes provided. Coal was destined primarily for the gasworks at Hollacombe between Torquay and Paignton. Five parallel carriage sidings were also provided, to stable stock prior to its return workings, and a cattle dock, signal box and turntable completed facilities at the terminus. The turntable had been enlarged twice but was removed in 1966 with the advent of diesels. The wharf closed in May 1964 and goods traffic ceased the following year.

In the dying days of the BR shuttle service from Paignton to Kingswear, a DMU waits to return to the Torbay resort in 1969.

The signal box, which opened in 1894, originally had 45 levers, the frame being replaced in 1960 with one of 30 levers. It closed in October 1968 – the run-down to 'basic railway' status had begun and no signalling was left south of Goodrington. After 1966 the majority of services were provided merely by a local DMU shuttle to nearby Paignton, apart from some through peak season services. The Britannia Royal Naval College at Dartmouth also contributed to passenger revenue over the years as recruits came and went. A run-round loop was retained for engineering purposes at Kingswear.

Following closure by BR at the end of 1972, the line was taken over initially by the Dart Valley Railway and subsequently by the Torbay Steam Railway and it continues to operate it as a commercial steam tourist line today. The station, which has been restored from its rather run-down BR condition, masqueraded as Exeter in the 1981 film *The French Lieutenant's Woman*.

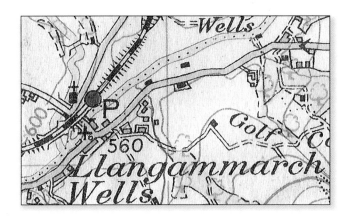

BR Standard Class 5 4-6-0 No 73003 pauses with a Swansea service on a rather wet 3 September 1963 and attracts a little custom. *CH Library*

30 LLANGAMMARCH WELLS
Welsh spa village

The smallest and quietest of the four mid-Wales spas of Builth Wells, Llandrindod Wells and Llanwyrtyd Wells, Llangammarch Wells is a village with a population today of just over 500 people. In the Victorian and Edwardian periods the railway brought in many thousands of visitors to these spas, that at Llangammarch having the apparently magical properties of saline, sulphurous and barium chloride waters. The discovery of the barium spring in the bed of the River Irfon occurred when, in a period of drought, a farmer in search of one of his stray pigs found the animal wallowing in a damp place near the river. Sampling the water himself, he discovered that it had a very different taste from the usual local water

The rather utilitarian original station building is seen at Llangammarch in the 1970s.

supply. Subsequent analysis revealed that it contained, among other minerals, one rarely found in the UK, namely barium, which had a reputation from various European spas as being 'efficacious in the treatment of severe chronic diseases'. The recommended dose was some 1-2 pints daily, *The Lancet* commending the waters as a diuretic and particularly useful in heart and kidney disease.

It is almost certainly true to say that without the railway these spas would not have developed as they did. The arrival of the London & North Western Railway route

linking Swansea in the south with Craven Arms on the Shrewsbury-Hereford line opened up a hitherto isolated area of Wales to visitors and locals alike. The 'season' generally ran from May to mid-September, when accommodation was at a premium. Hotels and boarding houses sprang up to cater for this influx of guests, and at one time Llangammarch could boast three hotels, a golf course, two butchers, two tailors and two grocers, together with a wheelwright, a cobbler, a lending library, a Post Office and a doctor's surgery. Although now sadly in a ruinous state, the Pump Room was situated immediately above the barium spring close to the river and in the grounds of the prestigious Lake Hotel, which continues to offer spa breaks to this day.

In comparison with the hardships endured by stagecoach travellers, the railway provided a swift and relatively comfortable means of transport with easy access from South Wales, the Midlands and London. One hotel advertised 'Two through-trains daily from Euston to Llangammarch', and there were at varying times through services to Manchester, Liverpool, the Midlands, Blackpool and Llandudno.

Today's basic modern station facilities. *Nigel Davies, licensed under the Wikipedia Creative Commons Attribution Share-alike Licence*

Opened in 1867 as plain Llangammarch, the station building provided was somewhat austere, being constructed of glazed red brick without the benefit of a canopy to relieve the stark elevations. A siding ran behind the single platform leading to a small goods yard. In June 1883 the suffix 'Wells' was added to the station name. Closure to freight in September 1964 coincided with a reduction in status to an unstaffed halt. A modern wooden shelter has now replaced the brick station building and attractive floral displays enhance the current scene.

It is a long time since spa water was bottled and sent by rail to all parts of the country, the Llangammarch Wells Mineral Water Company then doing great business. Crates of water were transported to the station, the price of a dozen 5oz bottles of barium water being 4s 6d, carriage paid. The water was not affected by the bottling process and apparently 'travelled well', reaching the customer in perfect condition, unlike many bottled spa waters that tended to lose their potency while on the move.

Like many spas throughout the country Llangammarch experienced a slow decline, its popularity waning as medical knowledge improved, the old cures becoming redundant and somewhat discredited. Not many visitors now come by train, annual passenger usage averaging around 3,000; however, such a remote community is lucky to have retained its rail link of some four trains daily, two on Sundays, in each direction in spite of fears of closure in the post-Beeching years.

31 STAINES WEST
Staines removal

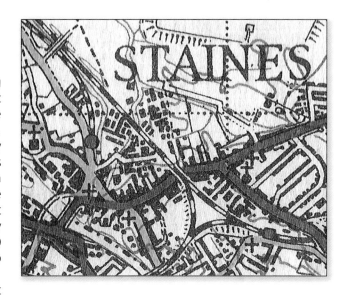

One of Aesop's famous fables concerns a dog lying in a manger full of hay. When an ox tries to eat some of the hay it is bitten by the dog despite the fact that the hay is of no use as food to the dog. Sometimes such an attitude prevailed among rival railway companies such that the company that was perceived as being an interloper was forced to provide its own station when it would have been much more logical to have shared facilities. Staines is a case in point. Lying in that area of no man's land between the Great Western Railway (GWR) and the London & South Western Railway (LSWR) to the south-east of Reading, rivalry between the two companies was intense.

The first station in the town was opened on 22 August 1848 by the Windsor, Staines & South Western Railway, being part of its line from Richmond to Datchet. The line was further extended from Datchet to Windsor on 1 December 1849, by which time the railway had become part of the LSWR. A line from Staines to Wokingham opened in 1856. The GWR was keen to serve Staines from its main line at West Drayton; however, the local company promoting the line had been rebuffed by the LSWR when it indicated its desire to connect with the larger company at the existing Staines station. The LSWR was apparently opposed to this arrangement on the rather questionable grounds that such a connection would be dangerous, that its station had not been built with the facilities that would be required by a terminus, and that consequently it would be unable to handle the additional West Drayton traffic. In truth this was probably just a ploy to keep out the influence of the GWR in its territory, and in this the LSWR was largely successful as the line as eventually built was to standard rather than broad gauge proportions.

The local company ran into financial difficulties and sure enough enlisted the help of the GWR in completing its line. However, the GWR did not wish to alienate the LSWR unduly and only agreed to help the struggling company if it was prepared to countenance its own station in Staines. This was duly opened in November 1885 but, ever mindful of costs, and not wishing to build its own terminus, the company instead decided to convert the Georgian house of a mill owner, one Charles Waring Finch of the adjacent Finch & Rickman's Mustard Mills (later Pound Mill), thereby saving the company £1,150.

The terminus was a fairly plain brick-built villa, modified to undertake its new role as a railway station. It had long platform on the down side of the line with a wide canopy supported by a brick wall, the canopy also covering a concourse at the end of the platform. The upper floor was taken over by the stationmaster and his family, while on the ground floor there was an office, a bicycle room, a booking office and a stationmaster's office. A general waiting room completed the facilities in the main block and there was additionally a single-storey brick extension housing the gents' toilet, porters' room and ladies' waiting room.

A connection to the LSWR route was finally achieved during the Second World War as it was considered to be a potentially useful diversionary route bringing traffic from

An oil tank wagon is parked on the run-round loop at a very overgrown Staines West terminus.

In this exterior view of the architecturally interesting station building, note the former site of the large station sign on the white wall. A couple of bus routes terminated here, as witnessed by the parked vehicles.

the North and Midlands safely round into Feltham Yard or to other points in the south and south-east should the London river crossings be severed by enemy action. Although the suggestion of diverting trains into the SR station was made again, this once more fell on deaf ears and the connecting spur was perversely taken up in 1947.

The WR station became known as Staines West in September 1949. Listed for closure in the Beeching Report, passenger services were withdrawn from the branch in March 1965, although oil freight traffic continued to a Shell Mex and BP private siding established in 1964. The arrival of the M25 motorway in 1981 severed the southern end of the line, so once again a connection was laid in to the SR, to continue to cater for the oil traffic, which lasted until 1991. Fittingly the last special passenger train on 24 January 1981, the 'Farewell to the Staines Branch' rail tour, was unable to run into Staines West by this time and ran into Staines SR station. Thus the original intentions of the promoters had at last been achieved. Staines West station was converted into office accommodation and still stands today.

The never-to-be-opened station of Lullingstone in the process of being demolished in March 1955. *Sid Nash*

32 LULLINGSTONE
Built but never opened

Having gone to the expense of building a station, one might have expected the railway company to have actually opened it to traffic. However, this was not to be the case with Lullingstone, situated on the line from Swanley through Eynesford to Sevenoaks in Kent. The electrification of the route in 1935 had resulted in significant increases in passenger traffic at the nearby stations of St Mary Cray and Chelsfield where considerable house-building programmes had provided a significant number of additional dwellings. Capitalising on the electrification, in what was called the 'sparks effect', the SR was alive to the possibilities of generating additional revenue from planned housing developments near its tracks. The Kemp Town Brewery, which had purchased 5,000 acres of land at Lullingstone with a view to building a large housing estate, signed an agreement with the SR in April 1937 by which the railway company agreed to construct a station at Lullingstone to serve this development. The brewery donated the land for the station site and £5,000 towards the anticipated construction costs of nearly £14,000, half being payable upon signature of the agreement, and the balance upon opening of the station.

The platforms and footbridge were to the SR's standard concrete design, while the building itself was of brick. With the station virtually complete, the summer rail timetable for 1939 declared that the opening date would be advised by special announcement. With the advent of the Second World War only weeks away, the planned opening was postponed, as indeed was the start of the housing development.

By the war's end the situation had changed radically, and in 1947 the Greater London Plan had rescheduled the Lullingstone area as 'green belt' with draconian restrictions upon speculative house-building. In 1948 all hope of generating any traffic for the unopened station had evaporated and there was talk of demolition, which began with the station canopies being recovered for use at Canterbury East. It was not until 1954 that the process of abrogating the agreement with the brewery and returning the land to it had been settled. The costs of demolishing the station were estimated at £5,000, although there was expected to be some £1,400 worth of recoverable materials. In the event vandalism and theft forced the railway to demolish the buildings in 1955 and take up the platform edging.

This was not the first time that a development scheme for Lullingstone had come to nothing, for back in 1935 Lullingstone Park had been selected as a possible airport to help overcome the problems being experienced by Croydon, then London's main airport but situated in the London 'fog belt' and as a consequence suffering many diversions. Commissioned by the SR to look at suitable alternatives, Sir Alan Cobham, the aviation pioneer, had come up with Lullingstone. Plans were drawn up for a station here with a spur leading into an airport terminal station. Some preparatory work on the airport was undertaken with the ground being levelled, and during the war a decoy airfield with dummy planes was fabricated here to fool the Luftwaffe intent on bombing nearby Biggin Hill airfield. However, this scheme too came to nothing, probably to the relief of the inhabitants of the surrounding areas.

Thus a railway station at Lullingstone was to be doubly thwarted, and today the only evidence of the grand plans are a solitary iron gate on the station approach road and the fact that the conductor rails are located away from the site of the former platforms at this spot.

The isolated rural position of Chalder is very evident in this view of a Selsey-bound Ford railcar halted at the platform prior to loading the milk churns onto the baggage truck sandwiched between the two railcars. Weeds have colonised the platform and the seat appears to be missing its cross-member. Passengers both on the train and on the platform appear to be in short supply.

33 CHALDER
Big name – small halt

The rather grandly named Hundred of Manhood & Selsey Tramway, to give the line its full title, was a short-lived rural line connecting the cathedral city of Chichester with the coastal village of Selsey. Opened in 1897, it expired less than 40 years later when the final trains ran in 1935. Although only 7½ miles in length, it boasted no fewer than eleven stations and halts, one of which, Chalder, is featured here.

Chalder was typical of the many hundreds of generally rather insubstantial light railway stations dotted across the country, which, as the economies of operation worsened, became ever more ramshackle in appearance. Colonel Holman F. Stephens was appointed Engineer in 1897, and the line was later taken over by that renowned collector of semi-moribund railways and became part of his empire. Chalder was located where the line crossed a private farm road leading to the eponymous Chalder Farm, the railway company paying the local landowner the sum of £2 per annum for permission to locate a station here. While it might not appear to be located in a very propitious spot to attract local traffic, it was more conveniently sited for the northern part of Sidlesham village, the largest intermediate population on the whole line. The station was close to Sidlesham Common, just a quarter of a mile from the local 13th-century parish church, a third of a mile from the main road and more, importantly perhaps,

The remains of the former Chalder station platform are seen in the 1960s.

the local pub! The station at Sidlesham itself was located to the south of the village near Pagham Harbour.

The gravel-topped platform at Chalder was of concrete construction with Staffordshire blue-brick platform coping stones with a length of some 38 yards. Cast-iron ventilators were provided at either end of the platform. The building provided, being 20 feet by 9ft 9in, was of corrugated-iron and timber construction; it was divided into two compartments, each with its own window, lined with matchboarding and containing fitted cupboards and seating. The door consisted of four square glazed panels above three wooden panels. The colour scheme, as with the other stations on the line, was white with woodwork picked out in black. It had been the intention to provide a rear door to the building, but this was never constructed. A canopy was provided, and a bench and nameboard with timber lattice fencing completed the ensemble. In addition to passengers, milk was an important commodity handled here.

Local goods sidings were provided at three locations in the vicinity. The first was to the north of the station at Hoe Farm, which also had a private halt, to the south of the

station at Church Farm Lane, and at Chalder itself, running behind the platform. The siding at Chalder was used by the landlord of the local Anchor Inn, one Dredge by name, who also acted as the local coal merchant for some years. In 1933, for example, the rental income for use of the coal siding at Chalder was £5, then being operated by Charlton. Sacks of hay were also despatched, one former employee recalling that sacks marked 'Chalder Farm' reached him in the Middle East while serving in the First World War, to provide fodder for Army horses.

Unsurprisingly no staff were provided at Chalder, although a Lad/Porter was provided to cover the Hunston-Sidlesham section, which included Chalder, and to cater for parcels deliveries. Chalder was unlit during the hours of darkness. A Foreman/Platelayer patrolled the section southwards to Selsey each morning, while a similar duty was undertaken by another platelayer northwards to Chichester. Today little remains here to show that a railway ever existed other than the concrete platform, which was cleared of undergrowth a few years ago, revealing the foundations of the station building.

Adlestrop station and goods yard are seen looking in the down direction. *CH Library, Real Photos*

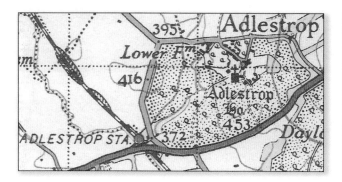

34 ADLESTROP
Remembering Adlestrop

The preserved station sign and a copy of Edward Thomas's famous poem can be found in the bus shelter at Adlestrop, seen here in 2007.
Graham Horn, licensed under the Creative Commons Attribution Share-alike 2.0 Generic Licence

Edward Thomas's famous poem of the same name recalls the unexpected halting of what he describes as an 'express' at this Gloucestershire wayside station in the summer of 1914. He was travelling from London to Ledbury to meet with the American poet Robert Frost. There is some doubt as to the nature of this 'express', as Thomas's own notebooks record that the stop was made at 12.45pm, which corresponds exactly to the scheduled stop of a stopping train and not the unscheduled stop of an express. Be that as it may, the stop, however occasioned, has given immortality to this one village station out of the many thousands that once peppered the countryside. Jane Austen was another literary visitor to the area, visiting Adlestrop House, formerly the Rectory, several times; she is thought to have drawn inspiration from this and the village for her novel *Mansfield Park*.

Originally opened as Addlestrop & Stow Road in 1853 on the banks of the River Evenlode, the suffix was dispensed with in March 1862 and the second 'D' was dropped in July 1883. A signal box, goods shed and substantial station house complemented the usual station features; the box was operational from 1906 and

contained 25 levers, although it was usually only opened when shunting the yard was required. Although the goods shed contained a 1-ton crane, a mobile crane was usually brought in by rail to unload the quantities of timber that were handled here. The main station building on the up platform was timber-built and originally designed by Brunel, the construction being completed by John Fowler. On the down side a wooden waiting shelter was provided, behind which was the station house constructed in alternating courses of red and grey bricks.

In the early years of the 20th century some 6,000 tickets were issued annually, but thirty years later this had dropped to just over 2,000, illustrating the downward trend in rail usage over the years. The 1930s train service of four trains each way daily, with two on Sundays, had reduced to just two down and three up services by the late 1950s. Goods facilities were withdrawn in August 1963, with the signal box closing in April 1964. The station site was cleared after closure to passengers in January 1966, although one relic, a station seat, has been preserved and is to be found, with a plaque recording the poem, adorning the local bus shelter, which also contains a station running-in board.

Thomas never saw his poem in print, being killed in France in 1917. Today trains on the Cotswold Line still pass through though non-stop, 'unwontedly' or by design, as before.

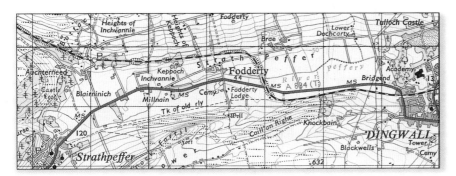

35 STRATHPEFFER
McNimby

Where stations were less than ideally situated for the local populace, there were often calls for a more convenient site to be found. This was often not possible due to the nature of the local geography – for example, Shaftesbury, sited on a hilltop, had to make do with Semley down in the valley some miles away – or opposition from a local landowner. Where a railway company saw an advantage in better serving a town, it was sometimes prepared to overcome the constraints of the local topography or aristocratic objections and somehow find a way to answer the residents' calls. Such was the case with Strathpeffer.

When the Dingwall & Skye Railway was opened in 1870 it had been intended to serve Strathpeffer, being the largest community en route, but opposition from Sir William Mackenzie, whose land the line was to cross, caused the route to turn sharply northwards, climbing at a steep gradient to a local summit at the Raven's Rock and thence continuing west to meet the originally intended route. Not only did such a deviation increase the cost of construction, but it also made working the line more difficult and of course also meant that the people of Strathpeffer were denied a conveniently located station.

What they did get was a station some 2 miles from the town at the top of a steep hill. Ironically Sir William Mackenzie died before the opening of the line and his heirs were much more railway orientated, although by then it was too late to alter the route. Blessed with a number of chalybeate mineral water springs, as well as the strongest sulphur springs in the country, the town developed spa facilities attracting large numbers of visitors, who found the inconvenient location of the station very trying. The Highland Railway was approached to build a line to the town itself and, since the demise of the previous objector, this was done

2P 0-4-4T No 15199 is at rest in the terminus at Strathpeffer on 12 June 1936. *Colour-Rail*

The beautifully restored station building at Strathpeffer, seen in 2011, now does duty as a tourist information centre and retail outlet. *RuthAS, licensed under the Wikipedia Creative Commons Attribution Share-alike Licence*

with the opening of a branch line from Fodderty Junction in June 1885 heading west to the outskirts of Strathpeffer along the route originally intended to serve the town. The earlier Strathpeffer station remained open but was renamed Achterneed. Thus a connection with Dingwall was made and through trains operated between the two towns. However, a change of train at Fodderty was required if one wished to head towards Skye, a situation that would not have obtained had the original route been allowed.

No expense was spared with the new station, which comprised a single-storey timber-clad building incorporating a booking office, waiting rooms, toilets, parcels office and a railway telegraph office. A continuous glazed gabled canopy ran the full length of the platform elevation supported on twelve cast-iron columns with decorative cast-iron brackets. In addition there was a run-round loop to the south of the platform line and a goods yard with three sidings running behind the passenger platform. A bow-fronted gable, embellished with intricate bargeboards, enhanced the rather plain frontage, which faced onto a wide and sweeping approach. In short, it was a station suitable for an up-and-coming spa resort.

In 1911 the Highland Railway built its own hotel in the town and began running a Tuesdays-only train in summer called the 'Strathpeffer Spa Express', which lasted until 1915. *The Scotsman* newspaper was moved to designate the town 'The Harrogate of the North'. In 1908/09 there was even a through sleeping car service from London, a carriage being detached at Dingwall for the spa. After the end of the First World War the town never resumed its former importance as a tourist centre and no further 'exotic' trains were operated. The 1930s saw rapidly declining usage, but it was not until March 1946 that the passenger service was withdrawn. Goods continued for a while, but this too succumbed in 1951. In 1965 the station at Achterneed also closed, meaning a journey to Dingwall to catch the nearest train, or to Garve, 8 miles further along the line. After standing empty for several years the former railway station was restored in 1979 and currently houses the Highland Museum of Childhood, a gift and Fairtrade shop, a book shop and a cafe; there are even plans to reconnect the town with the main line.

The scant remains of the short-lived Salcey Forest station, seen on 29th April 1966. *John Evans*

36 SALCEY FOREST AND STOKE BRUERN
Errors of judgement

Sometimes railway companies just got it plain wrong when siting their stations. Such was the case when on 1 December 1892 the Stratford-upon-Avon, Towcester & Midland Junction Railway (STMJR) opened a station to serve Salcey Forest on its line from Towcester to Ravenstone Wood Junction, the latter situated on the Midland's Northampton to Bedford line, which had opened for freight in 1891. This was a former medieval hunting forest situated in the south of Northamptonshire close to the Buckinghamshire border. The station was in an isolated spot to the north of the forest and was not located near any settlement. One can only surmise that the railway company anticipated leisure traffic developing in the area of the forest. Another theory is that it was provided at the request of the Duke of Grafton, who lived at nearby Salcey Lawn. However, it remains a mystery as to why, if a station was required at all, it was not sited either at Forest Road, Piddington, or adjacent to the main Northampton to Newport Pagnell road (B526).

At the outset, passenger services consisted of four stopping trains daily, operated by hiring in a Midland Railway locomotive and three coaches, but patronage was so dismal that it was reported that just one person alighted from the first service at Salcey Forest, and none joined, while at the neighbouring station of Stoke Bruern (it was never spelled correctly after the local village with a final 'e'), seven joined and one alighted. Apparently the service attracted no more than twenty passengers a week and the railway company incurred a loss of £40.

To make matters worse, substantial station facilities had been provided at both Salcey Forest and Stoke Bruern stations in anticipation of traffic that never materialised. The imposing brick station buildings were later occupied by railway employees until closure of the line. The short approach road to Salcey Forest station led from the original (pre-turnpike) Old London road that ran through the village of Piddington. When the new turnpike road was built, taking in Horton and Hackleton, the original Old London road was reduced to its present bridleway status. A more substantial access was never justified in view of the disappointing levels of usage. Realising its error, the railway company promptly set about withdrawing services from Salcey Forest, giving it,

Better preserved is the neighbouring Stoke Bruern station, now a private house and seen here on 5 April 1966. *John Evans*

together with Stoke Bruern, the dubious distinction of having had the shortest passenger service ever provided at a British railway station. Both stations closed to passengers on 31 March 1893, just four months after opening, and passenger services were never to be restored. Inhabitants of the surrounding areas found Roade station, sited on the LNWR London-Rugby main line, much more useful than either of the STMJR stations.

The STMJR duly went into receivership in 1898, and in 1908, together with the other associated impoverished railway companies, the East & West Junction Railway and the Evesham & Redditch Railway, it was combined into the Stratford-upon-Avon & Midland Junction Railway, which itself could never be classed as a successful venture. Closure to freight at Salcey Forest came in 1908; the signal box was removed in 1912 followed in 1915 by the single loop goods siding controlled by a ground frame. Nearby Stoke Bruern continued to handle goods traffic until 1952.

The occasional passenger special still passed through the two ghost stations, such as a St Pancras-Stratford-upon-Avon excursion of 18 April 1927 and a race

excursion from Newmarket to Stratford for Control Board staff on 30 March 1930. Through freight continued to use the line from Towcester to Ravenstone Wood Junction regularly, especially from Wales to North East England, that is until June 1958 when the line closed. Once the bridge over the London main line had been removed at Roade in 1960 the two stubs of the route were used for storing redundant wagons and coaches for a couple of years. Stock was often brought in by powerful 9F locomotives forging a way through the waving grasses that progressively covered the rusting tracks. By 1964 all tracks had been lifted.

While Stoke Bruern station building is now an attractive dwelling, the only traces of Salcey Forest are the remains of the platform, which can be seen largely intact in the undergrowth, the buildings having been demolished in the 1950s. The trackbed is now a path running between fields forming part of the Midshires Way long-distance footpath – a sad epitaph for a station that I'm sure the railway company would have preferred to forget it had ever provided.

Class 52 No D1060 *Western Dominion* passes Stoke Gifford yards with the 09.15 service from Swansea to Paddington on 8 August 1971 as the new platforms of Bristol Parkway are taking shape. *CH Library*

37 BRISTOL PARKWAY
The 'Parkway' concept

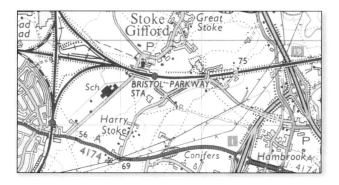

There are now in excess of 30 new or renamed 'Parkway' stations on the national network, including Alfreton, formerly known as Alfreton & Mansfield Parkway, Bodmin Parkway, Didcot Parkway, Luton Airport Parkway, Oxford Parkway, Port Talbot Parkway, Southampton Airport Parkway, Tiverton Parkway, Warwick Parkway and the progenitor of them all, Bristol Parkway. The definition of a 'parkway' railway station is one that primarily serves a 'park and ride' interchange rather than being located in a town. The suffix at Bristol's new station originally referred to the M32 motorway, known as the Bristol Parkway, which was located near the new railway station and had been built through parkland, hence its name. Thus the station was not in fact named after its construction as a 'park and ride' facility, but the name has stuck to other new stations built to serve such facilities.

Bristol Parkway is located in the northern suburbs of the Bristol conurbation and was opened in 1972 as the first in a new generation of such stations. Situated on the Badminton cut-off route, which opened in 1903, the station was built on the site of the Stoke Gifford marshalling yard, which closed on 4 October 1971, having become surplus to requirements with the cessation of wagonload freight. The original structures, built by Stone & Co of Bristol, were pretty basic, being just two island platforms connected by an open metal footbridge, with a wood and brick building containing the booking facilities and waiting rooms. Platform 1 on the north side of the line was for trains towards London and Birmingham and

Platform 2 served trains to South Wales and Bristol Temple Meads. The station opened with only a 600-space car park. Platform canopies were added in 1973 together with a cover for the footbridge. Further minor improvements were implemented over the next thirty years, including a new booking office and small extensions.

Bristol Parkway is now the third most heavily used station in the West of England after Bristol Temple Meads and Bath Spa, and in the period 2002-12 the number of passengers starting or ending a journey at Bristol Parkway grew by one million per year to 2.25 million, with a further 740,000 passengers changing trains there, giving an annual footfall of just under 3 million passengers. Currently there are three platforms, to which a fourth will be added when the line is electrified. Road access is excellent, situated as it is close to three motorways, the M4, M5 and M32, as well as the Bristol Ring Road.

Due to the rapid growth in passenger numbers, work started in 2000 on a completely new station building, which opened on 1 July 2001, and featured lifts and greatly enhanced facilities. This ultra-modern sweeping metal construction contains a booking office, waiting

These two shots recall the fairly primitive initial station, showing the somewhat sparse facilities provided upon opening of this 'Parkway' concept station, with little protection for the intending passenger, an uncovered footbridge and a very small station building. Notice also the early car park and relatively few cars. Today there is parking for more than 1,100 cars.

Quite an improvement over the initial basic facilities, this is the revamped Bristol Parkway station seen in 2009.
Matt Buck, licensed under the Creative Commons Share-alike Licence

rooms, payphones, cash machines, shops and toilets, and is a far cry from the basic station of 45 years ago. A dedicated bus interchange was built in 2003, and in 2006 construction started on a third new platform face on the north side of Platform 1 in order to ease congestion for trains towards Birmingham and London; the new platform, numbered 4, was opened on 9 May 2007. With the impending electrification of the line from London to Cardiff a further platform face, to be numbered Platform 1, will be provided to the south side of the station. Bristol Parkway and the 'parkway' concept must count as one of the great railway success stories of the past forty years.

38 BRECON
Four into one will go!

In the days before the railway Grouping of 1922/23, several of the larger Welsh towns were notable for the number of distinct railway companies that served them. Cardiff and Merthyr both had no fewer than six, while Newport and Swansea both had four – five in the case of Swansea if the Mumbles tram is included. In all cases this multiplicity of provision arose from the lucrative traffic to be had in coal and heavy industry.

Surprisingly, in the heart of mountainous country, almost devoid of industry, and 50 miles from the coast, the small county town of Brecon was served by four different railways, each arriving from different points of the compass, whose inter-company rivalry could match that of much more important towns. The rapid run-down of services in the early 1960s led to complete passenger closure of all four routes by the end of 1962, leaving Brecon isolated and one of the first significant towns in the principality to be completely denuded of passenger

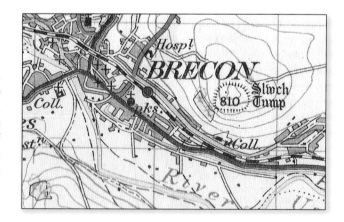

services. This decline also graphically illustrated how, in the absence of the artificial stimulus that railway competition gave to the promotion of lines in the Victorian era, such lavish route provision could not hope to withstand the onslaught of the rise of motor transport.

Back in time, the first to arrive had been the Brecon & Merthyr Railway (B&M) in 1863, coming in from Newport to the south-east. 1864 saw lines arrive from Hereford to

79

At the eastern end of the station Ivatt 2-6-0 No 46520 is ready to depart from the bay platform with a Mid Wales line service in 1957. © *www.railphotoprints.co.uk*

What a difference five years make – not just in the weather but in the survival prospects for the railway at Brecon. A snowy scene sees pannier tank No 9616 arrive on the penultimate day of rail services with the 8.03am service from Newport on 28 December 1962. The attractive station building provided here is seen to advantage in this view.

Hugh Ballantyne, © *www.railphotoprints.co.uk*

the north-east and the Mid Wales route coming in from the north-west. The Neath & Brecon route, coming up from the south-west, completed the map, being the last to arrive in June 1867. The B&M, the Hereford, Hay & Brecon Railway and the Mid Wales line used the B&M station at Watton, while the N&B had a temporary station at Mount Street, to which the Mid Wales line services moved after a time because of congestion at Watton.

It was decided to consolidate the stations into a new joint facility at Free Street, which opened in 1871, although the N&B did not terminate here until 1874 when its Mount Street station closed to passenger traffic. However, such was the continuing rivalry that the tender for the contract to construct the station specified that a separate booking office, of identical dimensions, should be provided for each of the four companies! The B&M actually built the station, with the other companies paying rent, although it took more than three years to agree terms.

Brecon station was an imposing building with intricate architectural details and sporting an attractive canopy. It had two through platforms, the outer face of that on the south side being generally used by Neath trains. On the

north side platform there was a terminal bay and a small turntable. Surprisingly for such a large station, no footbridge or subway connection between the platforms was ever provided, an unsupervised board crossing sufficing, and the island platform never had any form of shelter. A 27-lever signal box was originally provided, but replaced by one with 44 levers in 1931. Some thirty-five staff were employed here during the 1930s. Like other junction stations, such as Halwill in Devon, there were specific times of day when the railway came alive with arriving terminating services and departing trains being concentrated into a relatively short space of time.

The end came swiftly with the very limited services on the N&B route, latterly just one train a day with two on Saturdays, being withdrawn in October 1962. The remaining three routes went at the end of December, leaving Brecon isolated from the rail passenger network, although regular freight continued on the B&M route for a further eight months, complete closure coming in May 1964. Following demolition of the attractive building a different type of station stands on the Free Street site today – one occupied by the local fire brigade.

39 DOVER MARINE
Continental departures

As its name suggests, Dover Marine was built specifically to service the cross-Channel ferry services operating from the port. Erected on infilled land to the side of the Admiralty Pier, upon its opening in January 1915 it was initially called Dover Admiralty Pier, but from 1918 until 1979 it was known as Dover Marine. A final name change saw it become Dover Western Docks. Although completed in January 1915, it was unable to be used by the public until 1919 due to the First World War, when Admiralty Pier and the new terminus were taken over solely for military use, becoming the principal ambulance railway station. It has been estimated that more than 1¼ million wounded men passed through the port during the conflict. During the early years of the war the station was still in an unfinished state, and the large customs examination shed in the station was used to process demobbed troops after the war finished.

The station had four platform faces with a steel and glass trainshed some 800 feet in length and 170 feet wide. Beneath this trainshed there were two 60-foot-wide concrete island platforms, each 693 feet in length, capable of handling large crowds and their luggage. On each platform there were three large blocks of brick buildings, each 100 feet in length and 25 feet in width. These performed a variety of purposes, including waiting rooms, tea rooms, dining and refreshment facilities, post and parcel sheds and railway staff rooms. At the end of each platform nearest the Admiralty Pier provision was made for a Post Office, and at the end of the other

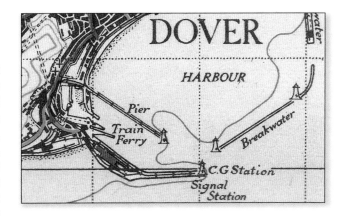

platform there was a large Customs Examination and Clearance Shed. Somewhat unusually for a UK station, signs were bilingual, although these were replaced in later days with signs in English only.

Although the trainshed was virtually complete by the outbreak of the conflict, construction of the impressive stone façade at the north end had not yet been started. This bold architectural statement was to comprise an ashlar frontage with rusticated dressings. The central section had a large central round-headed opening for two tracks with a rusticated surround and an enriched keystone above carrying the inscription 'S E & C R'. There were flanking full-height narrow arches within which were high circular windows above pedestrian entrances. The flanking lower bays had rusticated round-headed arches and end quoins, each for a single track. The sides and rear of the building were of red brick with ashlar dressings. The south-east elevation had pilasters at regular intervals and some black brick dressings. Pedestrian access

The impressive facade of Dover Marine is seen in May 1990, just four years before closure. This view is looking south-east towards the buffer stops, and behind to the left is Hawkesbury Street Junction and Dover Priory, while to the right is the line from Archcliffe Junction and Folkestone. The line crossing in the foreground leads to Admiralty Pier.
Ben Brooksbank

A 4-CEP electric multiple unit is seen within the confines of the station waiting to depart for London. Note the unusually large station signs provided for continental travellers.

The bustle of a continental departure port is well captured in this view of the 'Golden Arrow' premier service taken in the early 1960s.
CH Library

was through a detached entrance block opposite the famous Lord Warden Hotel. A wide stairway led up to a 455-foot-long enclosed glazed footbridge, which was suspended above the double tracks of the former Admiralty Pier. The footbridge was divided down the middle by cast-iron railings to separate people bound for the pier and passengers for the station.

The line was electrified from Faversham in June 1959 as part of the Kent Coast scheme, and in order to accommodate 12-car multiple unit trains the two island platforms at the Marine station were extended by 114 feet with 24-foot ramps. The extensions comprised prefabricated concrete components manufactured at the Southern Region's Exmouth Junction Concrete Works.

The most famous train to grace the station was the 'Golden Arrow', introduced in 1929, which ran until September 1972. Its other famous train was the 'Night Ferry', which had been introduced in 1936 and saw its carriages being shunted on to ferries enabling passengers to board a train in London and wake up in Paris. This service was withdrawn in 1980 and, with the prospect of the Channel Tunnel finally becoming a reality

in 1994, closure of the station loomed. This duly took place on 25 September 1994, although unadvertised passenger trains continued to Faversham until November of that year. After closure the station remained in operational use for train berthing and cleaning purposes until all rail movements finally came to an end on 5 July 1995 with the closure of the signal box.

Demolition and track-lifting commenced at the beginning of 1996 as the Dover Harbour Board hoped to demolish everything to build a new cruise terminal. However, the trainshed and the entrance building on Lord Warden Square had been given a Grade II listing by English Heritage in 1989, so the only demolition that could be undertaken related to the platform extensions of 1959. Dover's £10 million Cruise Terminal, now known as 'Cruise Terminal 1', was opened in June 1996, and involved infilling the trackbed up to platform level to create car parking. All the buildings within the trainshed were retained as was the covered footbridge to the pedestrian entrance, a lasting testament to the great days of coordinated train and cross-Channel ferry services.

Unit No 151002 calls at Sinfin Central on 3 September 1986, where railway staff seem to outnumber the passengers.

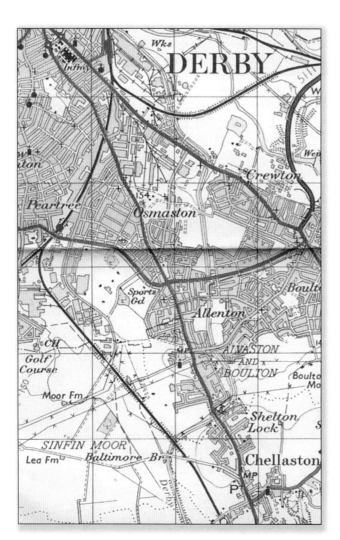

40 SINFIN CENTRAL
Decongestant

The Derby to Ashby-de-la-Zouch line was never particularly successful and closed to passengers in 1930. Were it not for the acute peak-period traffic congestion that Derby experienced during the 1970s, it might have stayed that way. However, with County Council funding an interesting experiment was undertaken to alleviate problems that the considerable north-south flow of commuters, from Belper and Duffield in the north to Peartree and Sinfin in the south, was creating for city centre road traffic. Used for freight at the time as far as Sinfin, the track and signalling were upgraded to take passenger services and the former station at Peartree & Normanton was reopened, with modest new halts provided at Sinfin Central and Sinfin North. The Sinfin area also served several industrial premises, including that of Rolls-Royce.

On 4 October 1976 a service commenced with two trains each way daily, the City Council aiming to emulate Birmingham's new Cross City line. The service was integrated with that covering the Derwent Valley route to Matlock. However, for a variety of reasons the trains became very poorly patronised and by 1992 just a single early-morning service survived. Both Sinfin stations were naturally unstaffed and consisted of little more than a couple of waiting shelters on platforms that could accommodate three-car DMUs. Although both halts were advertised in the public timetable, Sinfin Central could only be accessed by the public via a 360-yard footpath from a nearby road. Employees of Rolls-Royce could use a gate, controlled by security staff, leading from the platform directly into the Rolls-Royce site. Sinfin North was accessible only from two adjacent factories, as there was no public right of way.

The limited DMU service lasted until 17 May 1993, when the Derwent Valley line was turned over to 'Sprinter' units, which unfortunately were incompatible with the track circuits in use on the Sinfin line. After this time the service was famously, or should that be infamously, turned over to a taxi service, which of course attracted the attention of the press:

> 'There is a train service where passengers recline in leather seats, chat with the driver and get dropped off at their destination's door. It is not a futuristic vision of Britain's rail service, but the story of the taxi ride that masquerades as the 6.48 morning train from Derby to Sinfin, an industrial suburb of the city. The downside is that the service is only one way. Returning in the evening they have to walk and take the bus – or a normal taxi at £3.20.'

Thus ran a story in *The Independent* in 1998.

The reasons behind the failure of the line involved the city's declining industrial base, which meant that the factories and workshops served by the new stations were either reducing the numbers of staff employed or were closing down. There was also inflexibility in working hours, which did not always allow workers to fit in their shifts with the times of trains, an example being a service leaving 10 minutes before workers clocked off at Rolls-Royce in the evening. The line to Sinfin survives as a freight route serving Rolls-Royce, and there is occasional talk of reopening the line and extending it to Chellaston, which had been proposed as part of the initial reopening to Sinfin, and even on to East Midlands Airport, but such plans seem unlikely to come to fruition at the present time.

In more recent years Peartree station had its service enhanced, but this also proved to be not particularly successful and is now served by only a few trains daily. The overgrown platforms at Sinfin testify to the failure of a bold experiment, and meanwhile Derby's traffic problems continue to grow…

41 SWANSEA VICTORIA
A thrust to the heart
– we are not amused

Anumber of stations in the UK had the suffix 'Victoria', including examples at Manchester, Sheffield, Nottingham, Norwich and, of course, the London terminus of that name. One of the lesser known was Swansea Victoria, the terminus owned by a succession of railway companies following its opening in 1867, but perhaps most famously by the LNWR and its successor the LMS. It formed the terminus of the Central Wales line from Craven Arms and Shrewsbury and brought a competitor right into the heart of Great Western Railway territory in Swansea.

Two platforms with a middle road were provided at Victoria for arrivals and departures, topped with a glazed overall roof that was badly damaged during an air raid in the Second World War. The missing glazing was never replaced, admitting the weather to part of the platforms and concourse, although some of the arrival platform roof remained partially covered by the undamaged section of roof, which also afforded a degree of protection to the parcels and administrative offices. A series of rather makeshift huts adorned the departure platform providing some of the usual station facilities, and the whole place had a run-down air during its final years.

A GWR connecting line from that company's High Street station and North Docks complex ran around the

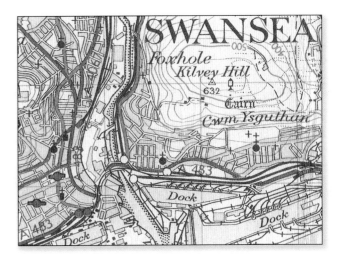

south side of Victoria station to the South Docks connecting with the Swansea Harbour Trust lines. A six-road engine shed at nearby Paxton Street was provided to service the locomotives, but this was closed in 1959. A goods shed and yard completed the railway infrastructure. For the last four years of its life a 20mph speed restriction was imposed on the line from Swansea Victoria to Pontardulais as a prelude to abandonment, and there were recurring problems with sand being blown across the tracks in the area of Swansea Bay station, necessitating the operation of special ballast-cleaning trains.

Cited in the Beeching Report for closure, the Central Wales line itself survived, but the section from Swansea Victoria to Pontardulais closed in 1964, trains being diverted to run via Llanelli to Swansea High Street station,

'Black 5s' were common motive power on the Central Wales line, and this is a view of the arrival of No 45298 on 29 June 1962 with the 12.00pm through train from Shrewsbury, a trying journey of no less than 4¼ hours and twenty-eight stops! *Ben Brooksbank*

Another member of the class, No 45283, leaves with the 10.25am departure to Shrewsbury while 0-6-0PT No 4650 shunts the yard on 10 June 1960. *Hugh Ballantyne, © www.railphotoprints.co.uk*

from where they still operate today over what is now called the Heart of Wales line. The section of line closed in 1964 was expensive to operate and was well covered by bus services. There were five services daily from Swansea Victoria in the final timetable in 1963/64, with four short workings, three to Pontardulais and one to Llandebie.

Goods traffic, via the GWR connecting line, continued to Victoria station until October 1965. There was a difficult start for trains leaving Victoria with a 1 in 45 incline on a sharp curve to be negotiated. A leisure centre and small park now cover the site of the demolished station.

42 THE DYKE
Beauty spot

Stations serving local beauty spots are not uncommon on both main lines and branch lines, such as Forge Valley station on the Pickering-Seamer line and Falls of Cruachan station on the Oban line, but a complete branch line devoted to reaching such a place is something of a rarity. The Brighton & Dyke Railway Co, noting the increasing popularity of the Devil's Dyke, a large 100-metre-deep valley on the South Downs to the north-west of Brighton, decided in its wisdom to construct a 3½-mile-long single-track branch in 1887 to bring tourists to the attraction. It was also hoped that residential development might occur near the summit, but this never took off and a hotel was the only building to be erected. The LBSCR was the company that operated the branch.

Local folklore explains the valley as the work of the Devil, who was digging a trench to allow the sea to flood the many churches of the Sussex Weald. His labours disturbed an old woman who, according to different versions, either lit a candle, or angered a rooster causing it to crow, making the Devil believe that the morning was fast approaching, and causing him to flee, leaving his trench unfinished. The same legend has it that the last

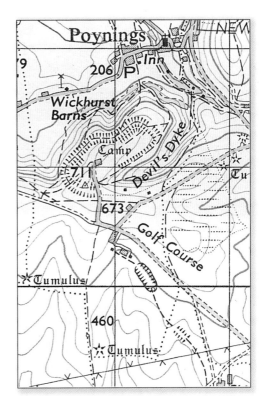

A postcard view showing the rudimentary Dyke railway terminus.

DEVIL'S DYKE NEAR BRIGHTON. — VIEW OF THE RAILWAY STATION SHOWING TRAIN READY TO START FOR BRIGHTON. THE QUAINT REFRESHMENT ROOM ON THE LEFT IS KEPT BY AN OLD RAILWAY GUARD.

Posted in 1934, this postcard view shows the deep valley known as the Devil's Dyke.

The Devil's Dyke near Brighton.

883
Copyright

shovelful of earth that he threw over his shoulder fell into the sea and formed the Isle of Wight. A more prosaic explanation lies in the erosive power of large amounts of water from thawing snow running off the Downs during the last Ice Age when the frozen chalk prevented any further absorption of this water, the valley being deepened by the 'sludging' of the saturated chalk.

In late-Victorian times the Dyke became a tourist attraction, complete with a fairground, two bandstands, an observatory, a cable car, a funicular steep-grade railway and a camera obscura. So popular was it that on Whit Monday 1893 some 30,000 people visited the site.

The railway was necessarily built with some stiff gradients, up to 1 in 40, rising 400 feet on sinuous track. Even then it stopped 200 feet short of the summit in an isolated and exposed position near Dyke Farm, leaving visitors with a further half-mile climb. A small corrugated-iron building served as the railway terminus and a disused coach body did duty as a summer tearoom, apparently operated by a retired railway guard. There was a Saxby & Farmer signal box provided at the terminus, containing a 15-lever rocker frame, and one member of staff doubled as booking clerk, porter, signalman and shunter. Freight was negligible, although there was a small goods yard that dealt with some coal and cattle food inwards and the occasional load of hay going out. In 1917 the service was withdrawn as a wartime economy measure, not recommencing until 1920.

However, with increased competition from motor buses, which could take trippers right to the summit, the railway closed in 1938. A small portion of the brick-faced platform still lies in the undergrowth near the farm and traces can be found of many of the former attractions, including the remains of the concrete pylon supports once used by the cable car system.

Remains of the platform at The Dyke are seen in August 1982. *Nick Catford*

This view of the former platforms that served the colliery dates from November 1982 and shows the typical basic SR platform composed of standard concrete components from the SR's own works at Exmouth Junction. *Nick Catford*

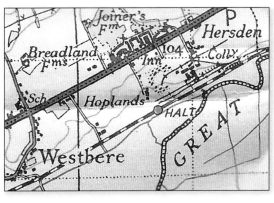

43 CHISLET COLLIERY HALT
Black gold

In coal-mining areas railway halts were sometimes provided to cater for colliers who would often arrive by special 'workmen's' trains'. For fairly obvious reasons, as coal dust and the best moquette did not make the ideal travelling companions, these trains were often made up of the tattiest carriage stock the railway companies could muster. In South Wales, for example, halts were provided at Ammanford Colliery, Bedwellty Pits, Cefn Coed Colliery and Cwmaman Colliery. The Kent coalfield too had an example in the shape of Chislet Colliery Halt, opened by the South Eastern Railway in 1921, located on its route from Ashford to Ramsgate near Sturry.

The presence of coal in Kent had been confirmed by test borings undertaken in connection with the original Channel Tunnel scheme put forward in the 1870s, and although many of the subsequent collieries were relative failures, four main sites emerged – Snowdown, Tilmanstone, Betteshanger and Chislet – which between them produced some million tons of coal annually. Chislet was fortunate in being located near a railway line, as was Snowdown, and in 1911 the Anglo-Westphalian Coal Syndicates Ltd was set up and leased land near Chislet. German industrialists were involved in this project in the beginning, but the advent of the First World War ensured that these influences were speedily removed, the company changing its name to North Kent Coalfield Ltd and subsequently to Chislet Colliery Ltd.

Sinking resumed in 1915, but due to difficult conditions progress was slow and the situation was not helped by a series of strikes in the 1920s. In 1929, when the company was in serious financial difficulties, a leading mining engineer, Forster Brown, reorganised operations with the result that output increased and the company's fortunes revived. Many Chislet miners were Welsh and until the mid-1920s the majority lived in the Ramsgate area, travelling to work by train, initially to Grove Ferry station but after 1921 to the newly opened colliery halt. In 1924 the Chislet Colliery Housing Society was formed, building a small colliery village of 300 houses at Chislet, the village being later renamed Hersden.

Following coal nationalisation in 1947 the colliery was extensively modernised. However, much of the market for its product, top-grade steam and coking coal, was the steam-powered railway, but the declining numbers of steam locomotives together with the UK's gradual conversion to natural gas decreased the need for coking coal; this spelled the end for production, and the colliery closed on 25 July 1969. More than 1,500 men who had worked at Chislet were transferred to the other three Kent pits, the last of which, Snowdown, remained open until 1987. Chislet Colliery was later demolished and a small industrial estate now occupies part of the site.

Facilities at Chislet Colliery Halt were fairly basic. It originally had wooden platforms with a wooden shelter, but these were later replaced with concrete components, typical products of the SR's Exmouth Junction Concrete Works. In the last full year of train services, 1970, a regular electric service from London or Ashford to Ramsgate and Margate continued to call up to 20 times each weekday. Closure of the halt took place on 4 October 1971, its primary function gone.

44 BEXHILL WEST
The poor relation

Where a latecomer to the railway scene arrived in a town already served by an established company, it was invariably the case that, in spite of grandiose buildings or pretensions of improved service, rail travellers tended to prefer the route to which they had become accustomed. Probably the Great Central route was the prime example of this, but there were smaller cases as evidenced by the 4½-mile branch line of the South Eastern Railway (SER), which branched off its route from London to Hastings at Crowhurst Junction in an attempt to give the citizens of Bexhill an alternative to the London, Brighton & South Coast Railway (LBSCR) route when it came to rail travel.

The LBSCR had arrived in the town way back in 1846, although the first railway station was only a small country halt as the settlement at that time was not very large. It was to be the 7th Earl De La Warr who transformed the rural village of Bexhill into an exclusive seaside resort in the last years of the 19th century. A new station was opened in 1891 to serve the growing resort, but it was not until 1902 that the current station opened, the same year that a competitor in the shape of Bexhill West also opened its doors. Although built by the nominally independent Crowhurst, Sidley & Bexhill Railway Co, the line had the backing of the SER, which absorbed the company in 1905. The hope was that as this line could offer a shorter route to the capital, 62 miles as against the 71¾ miles of the LBSCR, passengers would be attracted to use the new service.

An additional incentive was the provision of a lavish station reflecting the SER's ambitions for the line. It was constructed from yellow and red brick with a Bath stone dressing. The slate-covered roof was crowned with a clock tower. The main building comprised a large and airy booking hall, ticket and parcels offices, a waiting room and ladies' toilet, as well as the stationmaster's and inspector's offices. At right angles to the building stood a smaller block that contained a refreshment room, gents' toilet, porters' and lamp rooms. Two 700-foot-long, 30-foot-wide island

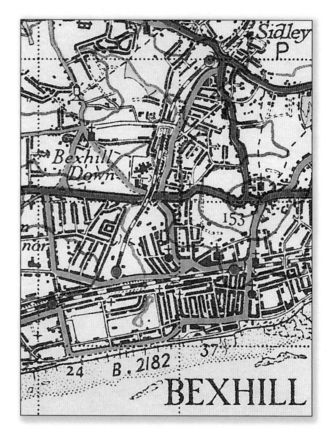

platforms were provided, Nos 1 and 2 being covered by a glass canopy extending to a distance of 400 feet, which also covered the concourse between the tracks and building.

Such provision would not have disgraced a major station in a large town; however, two factors mitigated against the dreams of the promoters being realised. One was the position of the station, which was in a valley on the west side of the growing town, but unfortunately this was the side that had not yet been developed. The second factor was the inbuilt inertia that had to be overcome, for rail passengers had grown used to the LBSCR's services, operating from a more centrally located station, over the past half-century, and it would prove to be very difficult to dislodge the traditional patterns of travel.

Closing at the start of 1917, due to wartime economy measures, passenger services did not restart until 1919.

BEXHILL STATION-DEPARTURE PLATFORM.
SOUTH EASTERN & CHATHAM RAILWAY.

An Edwardian postcard view of the platforms at Bexhill West.

Renamed plain Bexhill, with the main station becoming Bexhill Central – which reinforced the more favourable position of the LBSCR station – a further renaming in 1929 to Bexhill West drove home the point more forcefully. Even with coaches being dropped off at Crowhurst from main-line trains for onward transmission down the branch to Bexhill, thus avoiding the need to change trains, passenger traffic never lived up to expectations. The construction of a link between the two lines in Bexhill, discussed in the 1930s, came to nothing, as did proposals to electrify the branch. The two coaches of the DMU service introduced in 1958 seemed rather lost at the vast platforms of the forlorn-looking terminus, Platform 3 being rarely used and Platform 4 never having had any track laid. Inclusion in the Beeching Report sealed the fate of the branch, which met its end in June 1964.

The ornate exterior of Bexhill's other station, built of yellow and red brick with Bath stone dressing crowned by a clock tower, is seen after closure in the late 1960s. A fine array of cars of the period can be seen parked outside.

The SLS 'West Wales' rail tour of 16 May 1964 is captured at the terminus of Newcastle Emlyn. A three-car Swindon Cross Country DMU set was used on this leg of the tour, which traversed the Aberaeron branch, while pannier tanks Nos 1655 and 1665 were motive power for visits to other destinations visited that day. *David Pearson*

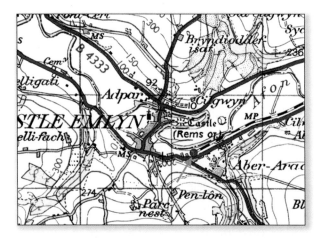

45 NEWCASTLE EMLYN
Thus far and no further

It was never intended that the small town of Newcastle Emlyn, with a population of just 1,138 in 2011 and straddling the border of Ceredigion and Carmarthenshire, should have had a terminus station. Originally conceived as a broad gauge line from Carmarthen to Cardigan, the Carmarthen & Cardigan Railway (C&CR) was formed in 1854, with construction beginning in 1857. Initially the line was planned to halt temporarily at Newcastle Emlyn, a distance of 26¾ miles, the intention being to later extend the line by a further 12 miles to Cardigan, where the company planned to build a deep-water port. The extension to Cardigan was authorised by an Act of Parliament in July 1863, but was never in fact built.

In 1860 the line was opened from Carmarthen as far as Cynwyl Elfed, with a further extension to Pencader and Llandysul opening four years later. 1869 the C&CR had formed a new company for extending the line to Newcastle Emlyn and eventually on to Cardigan, but it failed to get sufficient local support and an approach to the LNWR to buy the line and build the extension also failed. Conversion to standard gauge followed in 1872, but the company was by that time bankrupt due to the high cost of construction, especially Pencader Tunnel, together with the purchase of two tank engines, which had exhausted the company's coffers. The GWR stepped in to buy the line and, although the necessary land for the extension had all been purchased by 1885, the company, which had always been reluctant to build the line, ensured that work progressed as slowly as possible – it took over ten years to reach Newcastle Emlyn.

Only the platform remains while a solitary box van, a loading gauge and rusting tracks testify to the fact that Newcastle Emlyn is just about open for goods in this 1970 view. It would be another three years before total closure came.

The extension finally opened on 1 July 1895, some 38 years after the C&CR had originally been formed. The impetus for reaching Cardigan had by now disappeared, largely due to opposition to the intrusion of the line into an area of natural beauty that was becoming increasingly popular with tourists. In any event, a branch line from Whitland to Cardigan had opened in 1886, rendering a second route to the town somewhat superfluous. Thus it was that a bus service, initially provided by the GWR, operated from Newcastle Emlyn to Cardigan, and Newcastle Emlyn was destined to remain the terminus of the line.

The station was furnished with a single platform on the down side with a long single-storey brick building at the west end boasting a wide canopy that ran the full length of the building. All the station facilities, including booking office, station offices, waiting rooms and toilets, were contained within this one building. There was a large goods yard containing a goods shed and sidings laid out on both sides of the platform together with a run-round loop adjacent to the platform line. A cattle dock and a large grain warehouse were provided together with a two-storey warehouse, the latter being the only remaining railway artefact on the site today, which has been redeveloped as a garage. A 17-lever signal box, corrugated-iron engine shed and turntable completed the infrastructure; the shed closed in 1952 and was demolished 12 years later.

Passenger services ceased in 1952, but goods services, mainly serving the adjacent Co-op Creamery, lasted until September 1973. Although attempts to preserve a standard-gauge line to Newcastle Emlyn were not successful, a restoration project eventually got under way in 1981 when a group of enthusiasts bought part of the trackbed at Henllan. After several false starts the railway is currently operating services over a short section of track.

The remains of Acrow Halt looking towards Bartlow in September 1969, with the factory behind the halt on the left. *Nick Catford*

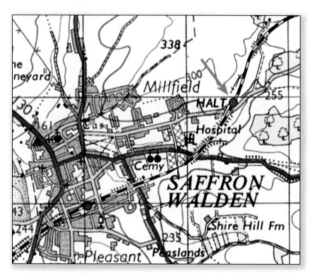

46 ACROW
Company halt!

Private companies occasionally sponsored their own dedicated railway stopping places, such as Ampress Works Halt on the Lymington branch, which served the Wellworthy Engineering Co from 1956 until closure in 1989, when the engineering works ceased production. The station here never appeared in any timetable. Similar facilities were provided at Daimler Halt in Coventry, Salvation Army Halt in St Albans, serving a printing works rather than the religious organisation, the Singer Works Platform on Clydeside, and Acrow Halt on the Audley End-Saffron Walden-Bartlow branch.

Acrow (Engineering) Ltd produced the famous Acrow props used by the building industry, the firm being named after the founder's solicitor, Mr A. Crow. It also produced formwork for the D-Day Mulberry Harbours, and for its own halt, constructed in concrete, donated to BR, and opened on 1 April 1957.

The company's Coronation Works had been served by a steeply inclined siding from about 1957. This left the line via a trailing connection at the east end of the platform and after a short distance split into three sidings accessed via a ground frame released by a key on the single-line token. The new, though rather austere and functional, halt consisted of a concrete platform with an open concrete waiting shelter in the centre. At the rear of the shelter a concrete path led up to the factory. There was no lighting provided at first, but subsequently two electric lights were added over two yellow nameboards that displayed the company 'Acrow' logo. Power to these lights was achieved through the simple expedient of an overhead cable strung from the factory. With a view to economy, the lights were only switched on when services were due to call during the longer periods of darkness in the winter months. Some of the concrete edging was also painted yellow, as that was the company livery.

Quite how much use was made of the halt by Acrow staff is not clear. Its opening was attended by the Mayor of nearby Saffron Walden, and the crew of the first train to call, hauled by 'N7' Class No 69651, were presented with a bottle of champagne. Unlike Ampress Halt, Acrow was shown in the timetable, although the limited service only called at convenient times for the clocking on and clocking off of the workforce.

The introduction of diesel railbuses in July 1958 failed to avert closure of the branch line, which came in September 1964, and track-lifting was largely complete by 1968. Today the remains of the halt lie mouldering amongst undergrowth and fly-tipped rubbish, the platform and graffiti-daubed waiting shelter being still extant, although a planning application was submitted in 2014 to redevelop the whole 45-acre Acrow site. Thus ended a short-lived but interesting experiment that the company obviously felt to be a worthwhile investment. Other company halts have also fallen by the wayside either as a result of factory or line closures.

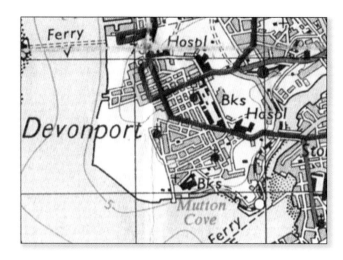

47 DEVONPORT KINGS ROAD
About face

This impressive station, formerly known as Devonport & Stonehouse, announced the arrival of the LSWR in the city of Plymouth with trains originally arriving from the east somewhat inconveniently via GWR tracks from Lydford and Marsh Mills. The Devonport area was considered more important than Plymouth at the time owing to the vast traffic from the nearby naval dockyard.

No 34104 *Bere Alston* leaves the station under clear signals with the 2.25pm Plymouth to Waterloo service on 29 August 1961. *CH Library, R. C. Riley*

A sad conclusion for this once important station as demolition proceeds in 1970 with part of the main building roof having already been removed.

The station served as a terminus between 1876 and 1890 when the route from the west arrived courtesy of the Plymouth, Devonport & South Western Junction line from Lydford and Bere Alston. It was then a case of 'about face', as the up and down lines were consequently reversed with London trains arriving from the west. There were four tracks through the station, although the middle two roads were sidings ending at stop blocks. The platforms were spacious, intended to accommodate large numbers of naval personnel and their kit, and a refreshment room was provided that was no doubt a welcome facility for the matelots. In 1928, for example, some 63,000 tickets were issued and more than 100,000 collected, many of them from naval personnel.

The main entrance was on the north side and graceful end gable walls in stone with glazing gave the impression of grandeur and an almost ecclesiastical feel to the trainshed. A tall tower graced the main building, which was embellished with steep gables and decorative chimneys, situated on the original departure platform. Conflicting evidence suggests either that the station was originally designed as a through station, to cater for the eventual arrival of the PDSWJR line, or that the west wall of the former terminus was subsequently pierced to allow for the extension.

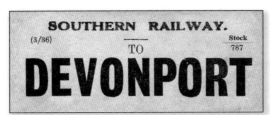

SOUTHERN RAILWAY.

(3/36)　　　　　Stock

TO　　　　787

DEVONPORT

The fine overall roof was badly damaged by enemy action in 1941, the Plymouth dockyards being a prime target for the Luftwaffe. Demolition of the roof together with the remains of the gable at the west end left the station looking rather gaunt, with the platforms being subsequently covered by canopies. The suffix Kings Road was added in 1949 to differentiate the station from the GWR's Albert Road station in Devonport. An engine shed, which closed in 1909, was provided by the LSWR together with a turntable. In addition to local services there were a number of Waterloo trains, together with the very useful Plymouth-Brighton through service, which included a portion for Portsmouth, thus connecting the two important naval centres.

The fall from grace was fairly rapid. The refreshment room closed in 1962, the signal box controlling the area closing in 1963, and closure of the station followed in September 1964 when the few remaining services were diverted over the WR route to St Budeaux; however, the goods yard remained in operation until 1971. The station was subsequently demolished and City College Plymouth built on the site, although the decorative railings atop the approach road wall in the delightfully named Paradise Road still remain as a reminder of former glories.

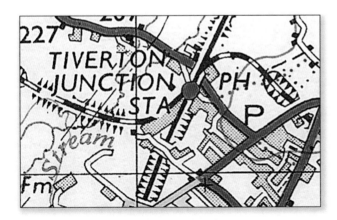

48 TIVERTON JUNCTION
A brace of branches

There are some junction stations that assume a greater importance owing to the fact that they served more than one branch line, for example Kemble in Gloucestershire, where one could change for both the Tetbury and Cirencester branches, Yatton in Somerset, where no fewer than three branches led off to Clevedon, Blagdon and Witham, Titley Junction in Herefordshire,

serving the Presteign and Eardisley branches, and Tiverton Junction, which had branch lines to Tiverton and Hemyock.

Opened in 1844 as Tiverton Road, the station was renamed Tiverton Junction in 1848 when the branch opened to the market town of Tiverton, 5 miles away. Later in 1876 the Culm Valley branch ran into the junction from Hemyock. The 1930s saw the track through Tiverton Junction quadrupled, resulting in the demolition of the old station.

Although it retained its junction name until closure to passengers in 1986, when it was replaced by the new Tiverton Parkway station situated 2 miles to the north on the site of the closed Sampford Peverell Halt, conveniently sited next to the M5 motorway and North Devon Link Road, the station had ceased to be a passenger junction some years before. The first casualty was the Hemyock line, which closed to passengers in September 1963 followed by withdrawal of the remaining shuttle service to Tiverton in October 1964. Freight continued to Tiverton until June 1967 and to the creamery at Hemyock until October 1975.

Tiverton Junction station consisted of four platforms connected by a footbridge, which also led to the station forecourt; the outermost platform faces were used by the respective branch-line trains. A locomotive shed was provided, but this closed in 1964, and a large signal box with a 120-lever frame was sited on the up platform. This closed in March 1986, after which time access to the

Tiverton Junction is seen looking towards London in the late 1960s with old signage, semaphore signalling and the branch to Hemyock still in situ, seen curving away in the centre right of this view.

The large platform-mounted signal box witnesses the departure of an HST en route to London via Newbury.

loops was controlled from Exeter. Cattle was an important commodity carried to the adjacent slaughterhouse, and numerous cattle docks were provided. A 'butter platform' also existed to handle dairy products from the adjacent dairy. Esso oil tanks were served by two sidings until 1983, the facility having been established here by the Air Ministry during the Second World War.

Once the branch lines had closed, passenger services were minimal for the last 20 years or so of the station's existence, with just a couple of trains daily in each direction. Part of the former Hemyock line was used for a time as a siding for the loading of tiles made at nearby Burlescombe, but this traffic ceased in March 1990. The buildings were not demolished until 1991, some five years after closure, and today just the platforms are evident, the site being known as Tiverton Loops, where engineers' sidings and loop lines remain.

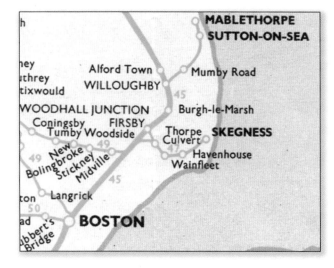

49 FIRSBY
Out of all proportion

Looking at the small settlement of Firsby on an OS map one might think that a wayside halt on the nearby railway line might be all that would be justified. However, Firsby, a classic junction station in the middle of nowhere, owes its origin and size to its location on the East Lincolnshire line, running from Grimsby to Louth and Boston, and its proximity to the popular seaside resort of Skegness. There was also a branch line leading westwards to the small market town of Spilsby. Firsby's importance was emphasised by the graceful brick-built station building complete with a canopy roof that was provided here, such provision only being justified by its strategic location and the resulting presence of thousands of holidaymakers en route to 'Skeggy' on summer weekends.

On 7 February 1970, in the last year of operation, there are trains to Boston on the left and Skegness on the right at Firsby. Note the unusual double set of level crossing gates provided at this location. *CH Library*

An attractive floral display and the decaying overall roof are evident at Firsby as trains to Skegness and to Grimsby provide connecting services. This image was taken on 9 July 1969. *CH Library, J. A. M. Vaughan*

The station was adorned with an elegant three-arched porticoed entrance, and three platform faces, each 220 yards in length, were provided, the bay platform generally accommodating the connecting shuttle to and from Skegness. The stationmaster's house abutted the platform at the north end of the site and a door marked 'Residence' opened directly onto the platform, making 'living on the job' somewhat of an unavoidable necessity. The station had an independently run refreshment room as well as no fewer than three waiting rooms – General, Ladies and Gentlemen – crew rooms, staff canteen facilities and the usual conveniences and parcels offices. An attractive cast-iron and glass canopy covered much of the platform area and appeared most out of place in the wilds of rural Lincolnshire. A signal box adjacent to the level crossing at the south end completed the picture. Even the crossing gate configuration was unusual, consisting of two sets of four gates crossing a double and a single line of track.

Originally, before the triangular junction to the south of the station was constructed, all trains from the south had to reverse at Firsby to gain the Skegness line, but once the south curve was added they could proceed directly to the seaside town. The triangle was also used for turning locomotives following the removal of the turntables and turning triangle at Skegness.

The Spilsby branch was closed to passengers back in 1939 as a wartime economy measure and never reopened, although freight continued until 1958. Goods traffic ceased at Firsby in December 1964 and, after a long campaign following the initial TUCC enquiry held in 1964, the East Lincolnshire line lost its passenger service in October 1970 together with the route from Lincoln. Firsby station was subsequently demolished, leaving just the house at the south end of the former station standing forlornly today amid a sea of desolation. As one contemplates the scene today, trains can still be seen in the distance as they take the spur line to and from Skegness.

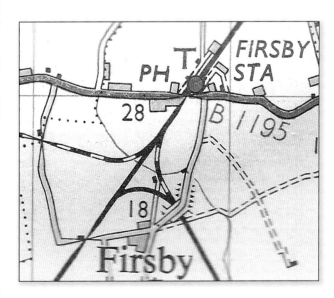

Table 47 — FIRSBY and SKEGNESS

MONDAYS TO FRIDAYS

Miles from Firsby	Station		am			am (TC from Grimsby Town Table 45)	am		am (dep 7 57 am) (TC from Retford Table 63)	am		am	am (TC from Derby (Friargate) Table 52 dep 8 20 am)	am	am		am (TC from Manchester (Piccadilly) Table 63 dep 9 10 am)
45	London (King's C.)	dep	1 15	..	..	4 0	..	..	5 55	..	..	8 20	..	..	..	..	..
45	Peterborough (Nth)	,,	3 5	..	..	6 54	..	..	8 48	..	..	9 56	..	..	..	..	..
44	Doncaster	,,	..	..	..	3T17	..	..	7J21	..	..	7J21	..	..	9T14	..	..
63	Sheffield (Victoria)	,,	..	..	..	3T 8	..	..	6V22	..	..	6V22	..	..	7T37	..	1018
49	Lincoln (Central)	,,	..	..	..	..	..	..	8 41	..	..	9B10	..	..	..	..	12p4
45	Boston	,,	4 5	..	..	7 53	..	..	9 38	..	..	1051	1059	..	..	..	..
45	Grimsby Town	,,	..	..	..	7 30	..	..	8 51	..	..	..	..	..	1137	..	..
			am			am	am		am	am		am	pm				pm
—	Firsby	dep	6 44	..	..	8 22	..	..	10 5	..	..	1119	..	..	1252	..	..
2¼	Thorpe Culvert	,,	6 48	..	..	8 26	..	..	10 9	..	..	1123	..	..	1259	..	..
4¼	Wainfleet	,,	6 53	..	..	8 31	..	..	1014	..	..	1128	..	..	..	..	..
6	Havenhouse	,,	6 57	..	..	8 35	..	..	..	..	..	1132	..	..	..	..	..
9¼	Skegness	arr	7 3	..	..	8 41	..	..	1023	..	..	1138	1144	..	1 8	..	1 17

MONDAYS TO FRIDAYS — continued

Station		pm (TC from Grantham dep 12 35 pm Table 50)	am			am		pm		pm	pm		pm (TC from Lincoln)		pm
45 London (King's C.)	dep	11C 0	..	..	..	..	1 20	..	2 20	..	..	4 5	..	6 50	..
45 Peterborough (Nth)	,,	12p46	..	..	..	..	2 49	..	3 48	..	..	5 30	..	8 15	..
44 Doncaster	,,	10N56	..	..	11L 0	..	..	1T51	..	..	3L 7	..	6H21	..	..
63 Sheffield (Victoria)	,,	9T52	..	..	10L18	..	..	1T 8	..	..	3L45	..	5L47	..	..
49 Lincoln (Central)	,,	..	..	..	2p 5	..	..	..	..	..	6 25	..	7B30	..	..
45 Boston	,,	1p40	..	..	..	..	3 33	..	4 32	..	6 25	..	8 0	..
45 Grimsby Town	,,	1 2	..	..	..	..	..	3 49	..	5 7	6 4	..	8 0	..
		pm	pm			pm		pm		pm	pm		pm		pm
Firsby	dep	2 4	..	..	3 16	..	4 0	..	4 58	6 4	..	7 4	..	9 37	..
Thorpe Culvert	,,	2 8	..	..	3 20	..	4 4	..	5 2	..	..	7 8	..	9 41	..
Wainfleet	,,	2 13	..	..	3 25	..	4 9	..	5 7	6 11	..	7 13	..	9 46	..
Havenhouse	,,	2 17	..	..	..	..	..	..	5 11	..	..	7 17	..	9 50	..
Skegness	arr	2 23	..	..	3 34	..	4 18	..	5 17	6 20	..	7 23	..	9 56	..

SATURDAYS ONLY

Station		am	am (TC from Grimsby Town)	am	am (TC from Lincoln)	am	am (dep 6 25 am)	am	am (TC from Radford Tables 55 and 62)	am (TC from Derby (Friargate) dep 7 10 am Table 52)	am (Runs 20th July to 31st August TC from Nottingham (Victoria) dep 8 12 am Table 52)	am	am (Runs 3rd to 24th August TC from Leeds dep 7 3 am Table 2)	am (TC from Peterborough)	am	am (Not after 31st August TC and MB from King's Cross Conveys also passengers for Butlin's Holiday Camp Second Class only)
45 London (King's C.)	dep	1 15	..	4 0	..	..	..	..	..	5 55	..	8 10
45 Peterborough (Nth)	,,	3 5	..	6 54	..	..	..	..	..	8 45	9 20	9 33
44 Doncaster	,,	..	..	3T17	5L55	..	..	..	9 25	..	..	..
63 Sheffield (Victoria)	,,	..	..	3T 8	6L22	7D 5	..	..	..	..	8 6	1022
49 Lincoln (Central)	,,	..	..	..	8 1	8D39	..	..	9 43	..	7L 5	..
45 Boston	,,	4 5	7 53	..	..	..	..	..	..	..	9 13	9G10
45 Grimsby Town	,,	..	7 30	..	..	..	..	..	..	..	..	1013
		am	am		am		am			am	am	am	am	am		am
Firsby	dep	6 44	8 22	..	..	..	..	..	..	..	..	6N25
Thorpe Culvert	,,	6 48	8 26	..	..	..	..	..	..	..	..	..
Wainfleet	,,	6 53	8 31	9 4	..	..	..	..	..	8 6	..	..
Havenhouse	,,	6 57	8 35	..	..	..	..	..	..	..	9G10	..
Skegness	arr	7 3	8 41	9 14	9 27	9 48	..	10 0	1020	1026	1048	11 1

B Via Boston
C Except on 2nd and 5th August passengers can dep King's Cross 11 20 am by Pullman Car train to Peterborough. Supplementary charges
D Applies until 27th July and on 31st August and 7th September
G Except 3rd, 10th, 17th and 24th August. Via Boston

H Via Grantham
h Via Doncaster
J Via Retford and Lincoln
L Via Lincoln
N Change also at Hitchin. Applies 13th July to 31st August inclusive
n Lincoln (St. Marks)

MB Miniature Buffet Car
p pm
T Via Grimsby
TC Through Carriages
V Via Lincoln. Except on 2nd and 5th August passengers can dep Sheffield 7 20 am by Pullman Car train to Retford. Supplementary charges

For continuation of Saturday and Sunday Trains, see page 340

The attractive stone building at Clifford is slowly swallowed by vegetation although the GWR paint scheme on the door survives years after its last repaint.

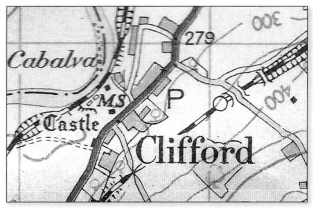

50 CLIFFORD
A place of no importance

In spite of its soubriquet, the 'Golden Valley' route as it was known, running from Pontrilas on the Abergavenny-Hereford line to Hay-on-Wye, on the Hereford-Brecon line, gave a far from golden return for its investors. One of the most vociferous critics of the railway was one Mr Archer Clive of Whitfield, a sceptic who observed at the outset of the scheme: 'Of the many unpromising schemes which are afloat, I think this the most silly. There can be no passenger traffic and but very little goods, and the capital, if any should be invested, will probably be sunk unprofitably.' His son, Mr Meysey Clive, also did not mince his words, when giving evidence to a later parliamentary committee, saying that the line '… leads from a place of no importance to a place of no importance and appears to be practically useless and involves a wasteful expenditure of money.'

This scheme, although dating from the 1870s, was typical of some of the earlier plans thrown up by the 'Railway Mania' of the 1840s when schemes were promoted more through enthusiasm rather than sound economic judgement. Local landed gentry wishing to ensure that their part of the country was not omitted from the burgeoning railway map were optimistic backers of such projects, and this was true in the case of the Golden Valley route. A total expenditure of some £335,000 for construction realised a paltry £9,000 when the impecunious concern, following closure in 1898 through lack of funds, was sold to the GWR for a song in 1899 – a financial disaster for many of the local backers.

The line never returned an operating profit nor the promised dividends to the shareholders before it was sold to the GWR, and although it provided a useful service to the inhabitants of the area this was really a luxury that could never have been economically justified. The GWR managed to make a small profit until the outbreak of the Second World War and, following withdrawal of

A striking survivor at Clifford was this water tank, its provision at such a lowly wayside station being explained by the fact that there was an engine shed located here until 1897.

passenger services in 1941, the line continued as freight only for the duration. Following nationalisation the last goods train to Hay ran in 1949 and to Dorstone in 1953. The surviving rump from Pontrilas serving an Ordnance Depot hung on until 1969.

Clifford was typical of the stations on the line, serving a small rural population that even in 1901 numbered only 730 souls and which sixty years later was reduced to just 586. Sandwiched between the Golden Valley route and the Hereford-Brecon route, a station was never provided on the latter and passengers had to journey to Hay-on-Wye to make connections for this line. Clifford station was constructed of stone and surprisingly boasted a water tank, the presence of which may be explained by the fact that there was an engine shed located here until 1897. The GWR initially provided a staff of two men to look after the station. A small goods siding and cattle dock were also

provided, the siding being been converted into a loop in 1888 to enable trains to pass, but this later reverted to siding status. The GWR initially provided three trains each way daily, but this was reduced to two and then to a solitary passenger working, reflecting the basic problem that there was just not enough traffic to warrant a passenger service. Track was recovered in 1949 following closure of the route between Dorstone and Hay.

Although Clifford's medieval castle was perpetuated in the name of one of the GWR's 'Castle' Class locomotives, No 5046 *Clifford Castle*, today the forlorn remains of the village's station building and water tank are poignant reminders of dashed hopes and unfulfilled dreams reflecting the underlying drastic changes in social history and economic circumstances experienced by such rural communities.

Wherwell station seen in a period postcard view. *Wikipedia*

Wherwell Station.

51 WHERWELL
Keeping the beggars out

The corollary of invasive lines by one railway company into another's territory was the provision of a 'blocking line' built to discourage such invasions. Such a line was that built by the LSWR from Hurstbourne, on its main line from Basingstoke to the West, over a distance of 7½ miles to Fullerton on the line from Andover to Romsey and Southampton. This went by the grandiose name of the 'Northern & Southern Junction Railway'. The perceived threat came from the Didcot, Newbury & Southampton (DN&S) company, which although it was originally authorised to run only from Didcot to Micheldever, where it was expected to make a connection with the LSWR route to Southampton, together with a connection at Whitchurch with the West of England main line, decided to attempt an independent route all the way south to Southampton. This would have allowed access to the lucrative market on the coast using its own metals, and it was in at attempt to forestall this that the LSWR built the aforementioned blocking line, which, by means of a connection at Whitchurch, would enable DN&S trains to reach the South Coast port without the need for further southwards independent construction.

Although appearing eminently sensible to the LSWR, the DN&S thought otherwise and, although it received no financial backing from the GWR as far as is known, undoubtedly the bitter rivalry between that company and the LSWR was behind the reluctance on the part of the DN&S to take up the LSWR's offer. In the event, it tried to pursue its own way to Southampton, which in fact only got as far as Winchester, where the money ran out; in the end the DN&S was forced to utilise the LSWR route from Shawford Junction southwards.

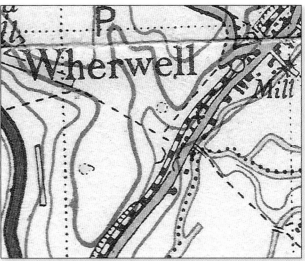

Two stations were provided on the Hurstbourne-Fullerton line, at Longparish and Wherwell, neither of which could hope to sustain a viable passenger service run purely as a local operation without the benefit of through traffic. Double track was provided upon opening in 1885 and there was an attempt to save face by stating that the new line would 'expedite the journey time from London and Bournemouth', although this would have required a west-facing curve at Redbridge, necessary to avoid reversal at the junction with the Southampton-Bournemouth line. Although authorisation was given for this curve in 1906, it was never constructed.

Queen Victoria apparently preferred her trains from Windsor to run this way while she was en route to Osborne on the Isle of Wight in order to avoid the tunnels north of Winchester, or so rumour had it. Faced with the prospect of remaining a rural backwater the line to Fullerton was singled in 1913 and closed to passengers in July 1931, due mainly to the usual story of bus competition proving more attractive for passengers wishing to go to Andover, the train service being infrequent and involving a change of trains. Before closure to passengers the line was used in the making of a silent film version of the play *The Ghost Train*.

Goods continued from Fullerton to Longparish, primarily to service the ammunition dumps in Harewood Forest, until May 1956, following closure of the Air Ministry depot there the previous year. Although Wherwell remained theoretically open for freight, by the end it contributed little if anything in the way of traffic and just one siding was in situ in the last years. Thereafter the line was used to store withdrawn freight wagons and life-expired electric units, and for the testing of the new Hampshire DMUs until track was removed from the majority of the remaining line in 1960.

Wherwell station was provided with a full range of facilities upon opening, which remained underused for much of its latter existence, although hay and game birds,

shot in Harewood Forest, were important traffics in years gone by. Attractive curved station canopies were provided for both platforms, which were situated on a 40-chain-radius curve with reverse curves of the same radius at each end. This would have precluded any fast through running although, as things turned out, this requirement never materialised.

The station had an attractive railed porch on its road entrance elevation above which there was a dormer window increasing illumination to the booking hall below. A signal box containing 15 levers was provided, although this closed in July 1913 with the singling of the line. Following total closure, the site was sold to the local Rural District Council for development, and although bungalows were built on either side, the station building survived, as it does today, in residential use. The motorist entering Wherwell from Andover still has to negotiate a hairpin bend before crossing the old line as the railway was constructed here on a shelf of the steep-sided valley of the River Test.

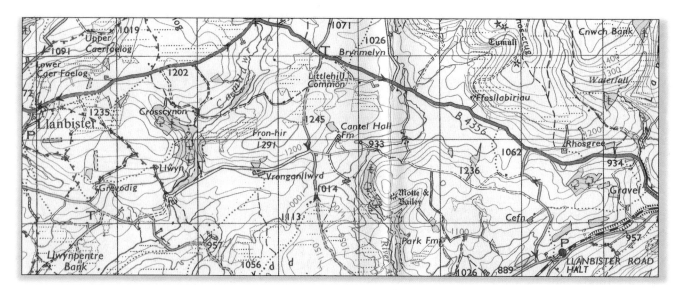

52 LLANBISTER ROAD
Stretching a point

This station is one of many throughout the country that carries the suffix 'Road', a sure sign that the intending traveller is likely to have a considerable journey after alighting from the train in order to reach the settlement that gives its name to the station. The Great Western were particularly fond of this device and other instances that come to mind include Bodmin Road, almost 4 miles from Bodmin, but at least there was a connecting rail service, Gwinear Road, 2 miles from its namesake village, Grampound Road, 2½ miles from its village, and Mitcheldean Road, also some distance from Mitcheldean itself.

Five and half hilly miles separate the small settlement of Llanbister, population 382 at the 2011 census, from its namesake railway halt on the Central Wales line. The village's main claim to fame is that it was the birthplace of

the Victorian actress Eleanor Bufton, who spent the majority of her career in London playing Shakespeare, burlesque, and a variety of comedy and drama roles. Railways were to play a part in her career, which was temporarily halted after she was injured in a railway accident at South Kensington station on 2 August 1871 when she was thrown to the floor following a collision. Sustaining injuries to her knee and forehead, she was unconscious for a time and was subsequently awarded £1,600 in compensation. Although she suffered memory loss, she was able to resume acting again after a couple of years.

Even in Victorian times, when people were prepared to travel some distance to catch a train, it is doubtful whether the railway company attracted much business to its halt from the villagers. It would not be unsurprising to

BR Standard Class 5 No 73003 comes to a halt with a Swansea-Shrewsbury service on 3 September 1963 as the signalman waits to hand over the token.
CH Library, Andrew Muckley

Although the station house is still occupied in private ownership, today's passenger only has the comfort of a basic waiting shelter at Llanbister Road.
David Medcalf, licensed under the Wikipedia Creative Commons Attribution Share-alike Licence

learn that few made their way over the intervening miles in the 19th century to avail themselves of the service, and this is even truer today when only some 1,200 passengers per year used the station in 2014/15.

In the wilds of central Wales where there was, and to a large extent still is, not much in the way of habitation, the London & North Western Railway adopted the expedient of naming its station after the nearest settlement of any size, and this just happened to be Llanbister.

The station house was sold off for residential use some years ago and the passing loop and signal box closed. Today just one platform and a small waiting shelter serve the public, who have the choice of four trains daily to Llanelli and five to Shrewsbury, with two services in each direction on Sundays.

Taken from the Madgwick Collection, this is a view of Shoreham Airport station, where you could also alight for Bungalow Town. The train seen passing through is the 12.00pm Brighton-Plymouth service on 11 May 1938. Air services were operated to Jersey, Birmingham and Liverpool, the two mainland routes being run by Railway Air Services on behalf of the SR and GWR. *Royal Pavilion & Museums, Brighton & Hove*

53 BUNGALOW TOWN/ SHOREHAM AIRPORT
Split personality

It is unusual for a station to have two incarnations, but such was the case with this small halt located to the west of Shoreham-by-Sea. The reasons for its first life can be traced back to 1898 when a pioneering American film director by the name of William Dickson built a studio on an area of shingle spit to the south of the town and began film-making. Other film companies followed, including the Sunny South Film Co and the Progress Film Co. So successful were these ventures that the need arose for local accommodation for the film crews, technicians and indeed the actors. The LBSCR also decided to relocate its carriage works from the cramped Brighton site to Lancing, a short distance along the coast from Shoreham, beginning construction in 1911 and opening for business in January 1912. The disposal of redundant railway carriages, a bargain at £10 each plus £3 for carriage along the adjacent River Adur using lighters drawn by horses when the tide allowed, coincided with this requirement for accommodation.

Although Progress Films had promised to make Bungalow Town 'the Los Angeles of British productions', a series of setbacks in 1922 put paid to that ambition and the company suffered, as did all British companies then, from the cut-throat competition of US studios. A fire broke out that, although it spared the main studio, destroyed 'Studio Rest', which was a 20-bedroom railway carriage bungalow used by the repertory company whose members included, at one time, Sybil Thorndike.

Although the days of the nascent film business were numbered, the need for accommodation continued and a rather ramshackle development grew up on Shoreham beach that came to be known by the soubriquet 'Bungalow Town'. Attracting 'arty types' and those without the means to purchase the more traditional forms of dwelling, the transport needs of this burgeoning 'shanty town' were met by the LBSCR when in 1910 it opened a small halt to serve the local populace. The halt was of wooden construction with small waiting shelters and was located where New Salts Farm Road met the airport perimeter. Bungalow Town continued to develop, becoming more of a holiday-home community, although the lack of electricity and the necessity for purchasing water, at twopence per bucket, were inconvenient aspects of living here. The train service eventually ceased on 1 January 1933 with the coming of electrification to the line from Brighton to Worthing.

However, only 18 months passed before the station reopened in July 1935 in its new guise as Shoreham Airport, the nameboard including the subtext 'Alight here for Bungalow Town', making it, by a small margin, the first airport station in the country, predating the original Gatwick Airport station, which opened in September of that year. The airport at Shoreham was originally developed in 1911, making it the oldest licensed airport in the UK still in operation. It was used by the Royal Flying Corps, the precursor of the RAF, during the First World War for cross-Channel sorties. Subsequently developed to

Since it closed in 1940, images of the station are rare. This is a view of the Art Deco-style Grade II-listed airport terminal dating from the 1930s.
Les Chatfield, licensed under the Wikipedia Creative Commons Attribution 2.0 Generic Licence

provide civilian services between the wars, including the construction of a fine Art Deco terminal building, now Grade II listed, destinations included Jersey, Birmingham and Liverpool, the latter two routes being operated by Railway Air Services Ltd on behalf of the SR and GWR.

The halt finally closed in 1940 at the same time as most of the bungalows were demolished, due to the threat of invasion, the occupants being given just 24 hours' notice. The airfield was then made secure for its role in the forthcoming Battle of Britain, when it was home to Lysanders, Spitfires, Hurricanes and Defiants, and it became an air-sea rescue base using Supermarine Walrus aircraft. A tarmac runway was not laid until 1981 and it is currently used by privately owned light aeroplanes, flying schools, and for light aircraft and helicopter maintenance and sales. The airfield unfortunately hit the headlines in 2015 when a Hawker Hunter taking part in the local airshow crashed nearby.

Of the small railway halt that once served it there is now no trace, and Bungalow Town has also passed into distant memory, Shoreham Beach now being the name of the community that still occupies the beach area and where one of the older properties still reveals its earlier railway carriage origins.

On 26 March 1966 grimy No 34012 *Launceston* slows on the curving approach to Dorchester; it will then set back into the up platform seen on the right. *Mark B. Warburton courtesy Mrs Margaret Warburton*

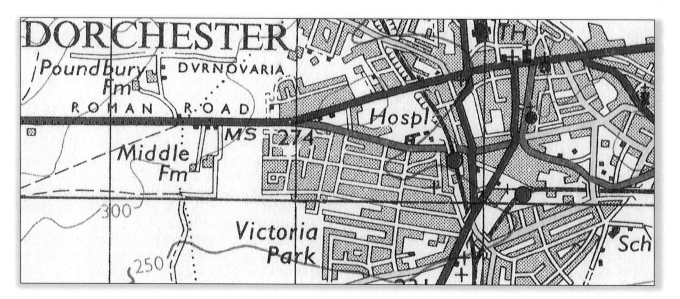

54 DORCHESTER SOUTH
A change of direction

The operationally inconvenient layout of the old Dorchester South station stems from the original plan to extend the line westwards to Exeter. A number of schemes were put forward in the years of the 'Railway Mania' during the mid-1840s, including the Exeter, Dorchester, Weymouth Junction Coast Railway, and the alternative South Western & South Devon Coast Junction Railway. In 1851 the Dorchester & Exeter Coast Extension Railway's proposal also foundered, as did several attempts by the GWR, such as the Devon & Dorset Railway from Maiden Newton to Exeter, to build a line from its Wilts, Somerset & Weymouth route across to Exeter. The opening of the LSWR route from Salisbury through Yeovil to Exeter in 1860 effectively ended the hopes of a coastal route from Dorset to the Devon county town, and Dorchester was stuck with a station facing in the wrong direction.

The new up platform is in use here, accessed by a temporary walkway from the former facility seen in the background in this view taken on 12 August 1986. The old up platform and buildings would subsequently be demolished.
CH Library, J. Critchley

The station at Dorchester had opened on 1 June 1847 when the Southampton & Dorchester Railway reached the town. It was built as an east-facing terminus with the intent of continuing the line westwards. However, these plans came to naught and instead another line was built southwards towards Weymouth, opening in 1857, which joined with the GWR's line from Dorchester West, continuing as a joint line to Weymouth.

Dorchester South station, which had an overall roof until about 1938, remained a terminus with just one platform for both up and down trains. Services from Bournemouth had to enter the station, then reverse out to continue towards Weymouth. The procedure for trains from Weymouth was equally convoluted in that they had to pass the station, reverse into it, then proceed eastwards again towards Southampton. This time-consuming process caused delays and was far from ideal operationally, particularly in the days before more flexible diesel or electric power.

Following an accident in 1877 a curved platform was provided for southbound trains the following year, so removing the operational complexity at least for trains bound for Weymouth; eastbound trains were still required to reverse into the original platform until June 1970, when a new platform was built on the curve to serve Southampton trains.

A cantilevered signal box was located at the eastern end of the down platform, with its lever frame unusually positioned at right angles to the main line, until this was replaced in February 1959. There was also a motive power depot and turntable, although this also closed in 1959. The buildings on the trackless original platform remained in use until 1989, linked to the new platforms by a raised walkway. As part of the modernisation work preparatory to electrification in 1988 a new booking hall was built on the curved platform, replacing the building on the original platform, which was then demolished.

The station was renamed Dorchester South in 1949 to distinguish it from the former GWR station on the route from Westbury, which gained the suffix West. One of the penalties of having a station with tightly curving platforms is the train guard's lack of visibility of passengers boarding and alighting from trains. To alleviate this problem CCTV monitor podiums have been installed on the London-bound platform to afford guards better oversight of the platform.

Above: The basic concrete halt at Lympstone Commando is seen in May 2006 with its rather threatening notice to passengers intending to alight here.
Wikipedia Public Domain Kicior99

Left: First Great Western DMU No 142001 picks up a solitary passenger at the Commando station on 13 December 2010.
Geof Shepherd, licensed under the Wikipedia Creative Commons Attribution Share-alike Licence

55 LYMPSTONE COMMANDO
Alight at your peril

Stations that at one time had a large military clientele could be found at several places on the network, for example at Liss and Bordon in Hampshire, where connections could be made with the Longmoor Military Railway, at Milford & Brocton, where connection was made with the Cannock Chase Military Railway, and at Codford near Warminster, where the Codford Camp Railway connected with the GWR main line.

However, a private station solely for the use by the military, in this case Lympstone Commando on the Exeter-Exmouth branch serving the Royal Marines' Commando Training Centre, is something more unusual. Opening on 3 May 1976, the platform of cast concrete sections was second-hand, coming from the redundant second platform at Weston Milton Halt when the loop line from Weston-super-Mare to Worle Junction was singled in 1972. A basic waiting shelter is provided at this request stop.

Apart from the arrival and departure of individual commandos in training at the camp, of which there may be up to 1,000 housed in the barracks at any one time, special troop trains used to be run to bring in and take out troops in bulk. The short platform, which is all that is needed to cater for the short service trains that regularly ply the branch, meant that the troop trains, which were often lengthy, had to pull up several times to discharge their passengers. The absence of run-round facilities also meant that such trains had to operate with locomotives at both ends. Their operation today would be more difficult in view of the much more intensive branch service. In addition to specials there is a useful traffic in evening and weekend journeys made by the staff and trainees when off duty. In 2013/14 some 56,000 passengers were recorded at this station. On average, 1,300 recruits, 2,000 potential recruits and 400 potential officers attend training courses and acquaint courses at CTCRM every year. In addition, the Training Wings run upwards of 320 courses a year for a further 2,000 students. On average it takes 32 weeks of intensive training to turn out an RM Commando.

The halt is a rare example of a passenger station on the national network that is not open to the general public, being exclusively for the use of the military and visitors to the training centre. The Ministry of Defence has accepted that it is the property of Network Rail and as such there is no prohibition for ordinary members of the public to alight at the station; indeed, there is public access to it via a footpath. However, exit from the station is through a locked gate and signs on the platform indicate that 'Persons who alight here must only have business with the Camp'.

Some confusion was caused for passengers wishing to travel to Lympstone who alighted at the Commando station, and this has been partially solved by the renaming of Lympstone station as Lympstone Village. On 28 May 2010 a section of the Exe Estuary Trail opened between Lympstone Village and Exton a quarter of a mile to the north. At Lympstone Commando station this trail runs between the platform and the entrance to the camp, both of which are locked and guarded. In these times of heightened security, anyone taking photographs from the platform should be aware that this might attract interest from the security staff at CTCRM Lympstone, particularly if photographs of the camp are taken. To avoid any such concerns, individuals wishing to take photographs of trains, etc, should contact the CTCRM Guard Room and inform them of their intentions beforehand. Anyone trying to buy a ticket to the station online is greeted with the message 'MOD only'. As the station gates are normally locked, access to the trail is denied to the rail passenger, though of course not to the walker.

56 MONKTON COMBE
Fame at the flicks

Enjoying a quiet existence as a passenger station for only some seven years before handling only freight for a further 25 years, Monkton Combe may well have passed into history with nothing to differentiate it from hundreds of other closed minor rural stations. However, the arrival of a film crew in 1952 changed all that for ever as it was to become the station for the fictional village of Titfield in the classic Ealing comedy *The Titfield Thunderbolt*.

Originally opened in 1910 with the extension of the Hallatrow-Camerton line through to Limpley Stoke on the GWR line from Bath to Westbury, Monkton Combe's limited passenger service was suspended just five years later as a wartime economy measure, and did not restart until 1923, only to finish completely in 1925. The station was operated by one man who was responsible for the level crossing gates, handling tickets, parcels and goods, but still with plenty of time spare to maintain the gardens.

The wooden station building sported a small canopy, although corrugated metal cladding was later overlaid onto the original wooden panelling. A loop line and one siding were provided, the station being constructed on the site of an old canal that had formerly carried away the coal from the Somerset coalfield. No signal box was provided but two ground frames, of five and two levers respectively, controlled the points and crossing gate locking mechanism. Distant signals were fixed from 1932 onwards. Goods services continued to run through with

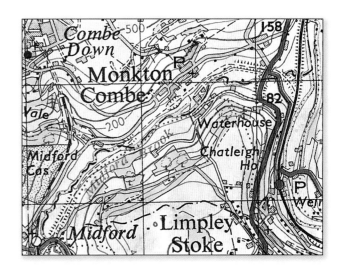

coal from collieries back up the line towards Camerton, flock for mattress filling from the nearby mill in Monkton Combe, and special trains carrying the luggage of the boys at the prestigious boarding school in the village. In the last full year of operation, 1950, just one goods service per day arrived at the station, continuing to Camerton Colliery only once every two weeks; latterly this was reduced to just once a month as the colliery wound down production and finally closed. The line officially closed in February 1951.

That might have been the end of the matter had it not been for a film studio wishing to find a location to film the railway scenes for its forthcoming comedy the following year. The moribund line between Camerton and Limpley Stoke proved to be the ideal location, and indeed had

A 1947 view of the halt
with some coal trucks
positioned on the loop
line.
CH Library, Real Photos

This is the view looking west at the slowly decaying Monkton Combe station on 9 January 1955, a couple of years
after the film-makers had moved in, the *Titfield Thunderbolt* motion picture having been released in 1953. Note that
the level crossing gates are still in situ. *Rail Photoprints, Hugh Ballantyne*

featured in previous films such as *The Ghost Train* and *Kate Plus Ten* in the 1930s. For *The Titfield Thunderbolt* the station canopy was extended and the surroundings generally spruced up to represent the village of Titfield, which was due to lose its railway service. As is well known, the plot revolved around the efforts of a group of locals to run the train service themselves, and many scenes feature Monkton

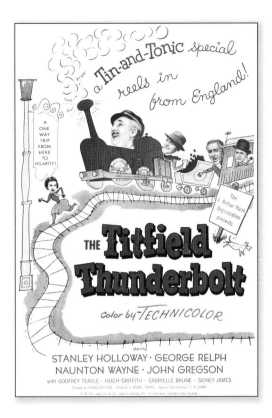

Combe in its new incarnation. An ex GWR 0-4-2 tank locomotive and a coach recently retired from the Kelvedon & Tollesbury branch line in Essex completed the ensemble.

Although the station was demolished in 1958 and tennis courts for the public school were built on the site, it has undoubtedly secured its place in railway folklore.

57 PARK HALL HALT
Visiting time

In addition to railway lines built solely to serve hospitals and mental institutions, such as the Whittingham Hospital Railway in Lancashire and the Hellingly Mental Asylum Railway in Sussex, a number of stations were opened on main and branch lines to serve such facilities. There was, for example, Knowle, a small halt on the line from Fareham to Eastleigh, which opened in 1907 to serve the Hampshire County Lunatic Asylum, later Knowle Hospital. This station went through a variety of name changes from Knowle Asylum Halt, to Knowle Platform and finally plain Knowle Halt. Although it closed in August 1963, it reopened the following day due to trade union objections, finally closing in April 1964. Another was Rosslynlee Hospital Halt on the route from Edinburgh to Galashiels via Peebles, which opened as late as 1958 only to close four years later.

Park Hall Halt was on the route from Gobowen to Oswestry, which had opened in 1848 and was in a similar category. During the Great War a barracks and military hospital with more than 800 beds had been developed, and in 1921 it was transformed into the Shropshire Orthopaedic Hospital. To serve this the halt was opened by the GWR on 5 July 1926.

By their very nature such halts were generally pretty basic affairs, and Park Hall was no exception. It was located on the east side of the line south of an overbridge that carried a minor road over the line, and was quite close to the A483 Oswestry-Gobowen road. The hospital was a short distance away on the north side of the minor

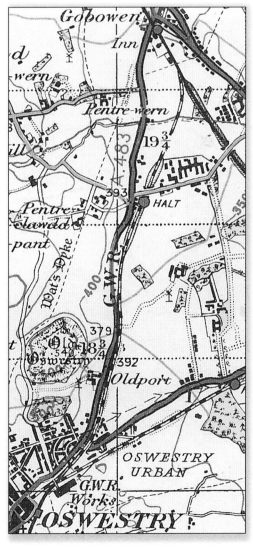

A Class 101 DMU shuttle from Oswestry to Gobowen pauses at the halt in the 1960s.
RCTS Archive

road just to the east of the halt. A very short platform, faced with sleepers, and a simple waiting shelter with a corrugated-iron roof sufficed. The large nameboard, out of all proportion to the size of the halt, stated rather baldly 'Park Hall Halt for Hospital'. A solitary oil lamp completed the infrastructure. Some 22 services daily stopped here, being mainly the shuttle that ran frequently between the main line at Gobowen and Oswestry. These autotrains were supplemented by some through workings between Ruabon and Wrexham.

The basic platform and corrugated-iron shelter are seen in the 1970s during the period when freight traffic from Blodwell Quarry still passed through. This traffic ceased in 1986, but there are plans by the Cambrian Railways project to reopen the route from Oswestry to the main line at Gobowen, which will once again see passenger trains serve this halt.

In view of the increase in hospital activity during the Second World War, some improvements were made to the halt to cater for the increased number of passengers visiting the hospital and for troops at the military camp situated to the south-east. These included an extension to the platform, so that it passed underneath the bridge, which received a new span. The nameboard was moved to the other side of the bridge so that it was sited on the platform extension. A new building was even provided to the north of the original waiting shelter, which was transformed into a 'Gents', consisting of a corrugated-iron shed with a pitched roof together with a flat timber canopy. After the war the military camp was taken over first by Canadian troops, then by the Royal Artillery, and finally did duty as a training centre for Infantry junior leaders. Closure of the camp came at the end of 1975.

Although not mentioned for closure in the Beeching Report, the closure of the former Cambrian route from Whitchurch to Oswestry effectively left the latter town with just the shuttle service to Gobowen. Closure duly came in November 1966 and Park Hall Halt was closed completely, the line to Oswestry continuing for goods until December 1971, after which its only traffic was the Blodwell Quarry trains, which lasted until 1988, when the line was mothballed. The final passenger train to call at the halt was a rail tour of May 1976.

Today, with its buildings long demolished, the overgrown platform and rusting tracks are still in situ awaiting a possible resurrection of the service linking Oswestry with Gobowen. The hospital, which was renamed the Robert Jones and Agnes Hunt Orthopaedic Hospital in 1933, still operates today as an NHS Foundation Trust hospital.

58 RAMSEY
Never the twain shall meet

With a population of some 5,000 inhabitants, the small Cambridgeshire town of Ramsey seems an unlikely candidate to have two railway stations. This, however, was not the original intention. A proposal was made in 1859 for a branch line from Somersham, located on the Great Northern & Great Eastern Joint line from March to St Ives, through Ramsey to join the Great Northern Railway (GNR) Huntingdon-Peterborough main line at Holme, a distance of some 13 miles. The proposal progressed well through Parliament and the scheme was placed on the list of unopposed Bills. However, owing to a shortfall in available funds to the tune of £3,400 – some £387,000 at today's prices – the line was abandoned in 1860.

The first line to reach Ramsey was the branch from Holme in 1863, promoted by the Ramsey Railway but worked by the GNR, although the Great Eastern Railway (GER) maintained a majority interest in the line. The GER was concerned that this branch was the first sally in a long-term bid by the GNR to reach Ely, which was well inside GER territory. Consequently in 1875 the Ramsey Railway was vested in the GER. To act as a further insurance policy, the GER lent its support to a locally promoted independent company, the Ramsey & Somersham Railway, which was authorised to run to Ramsey from a junction with the St Ives-March line at Somersham. With the situation seemingly tied up to its advantage, the GER passed the original Ramsey branch back to GNR control on a lease. The Somersham branch was not completed until September 1889, due in no small part to the lack of enthusiasm for the project on the part of the GER.

Thus Ramsey found itself with two stations, the more recent one being named Ramsey High Street, but with no immediate prospect of them ever being linked, even

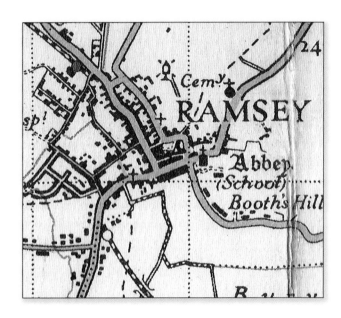

though the distance separating them was only about a mile. In 1923 both branches came under the control of the London & North Eastern Railway (LNER), and one might have thought that in the interests of economy the two stations, then named North and East, might have been joined. However, given that the LNER felt that two separate lines to such a small town was hardly justified, particularly as neither branch was very well patronised by passengers, it came as no surprise that the more recent branch to Somersham closed to regular passengers as early as September 1930 and to freight as far as the intermediate station at Warboys in 1956, closing completely to freight in 1964. It did, however, see the occasional seaside excursion train to East Coast resorts such as Clacton in the early 1950s. Its rival, the original line to Ramsey North, closed to passengers in October 1947, although freight traffic continued here until 1973. Had the two branches been joined and operated as a

Ramsey East plays host to the RCTS 'Fenman' special of 24 July 1955 headed by 'J17' Class No 65562.
Rail Photoprints, Hugh Ballantyne

Following closure to passengers in 1947, freight remained the only traffic at Ramsey North until July 1973. The buildings were demolished in 1974 and Ramsey Auction Rooms now occupies the site.

through route, perhaps the passenger service might have lasted a little longer.

Both termini were single-platform affairs, although the style of building differed in that Ramsey North was a rather unimpressive wooden construction while Ramsey East had an 'H'-shaped brick building. This was adorned with a pitched tiled roof on each of the two end pavilions, which were decorated with bargeboards and finials. The central section had a sloping roof that projected over the platform in the form of a canopy with a deep fretted valance. Both termini have now been demolished, although the goods shed at Ramsey North remains.

The line from Ramsey North might well have played an instrumental part in a wartime spy drama had things turned out rather differently. On 31 January 1941 a German spy, Josef Jakobs, parachuted into a field near Ramsey with the task of making his way to London to report back on the capital's weather patterns. A train from the local station, which by that time would have meant only Ramsey North, would probably have been his obvious route. However, he had broken his ankle when he landed and the following day, wishing to attract attention, he fired his pistol into the air, which brought two farmers running, who reported the intruder to the Home Guard. He was apprehended still wearing his flying suit and carrying £500 in British currency, forged identity papers, a

Ramsey North station is seen in June 1973.
Geoffrey Skelsey, licensed under the Wikipedia Creative Commons Attribution Share-alike Licence

radio transmitter, and, although this may be a later embellishment to the tale, a German sausage! All other German spies condemned to death in the UK during the Second World War were executed by hanging at either Wandsworth or Pentonville prisons in London, but Jakobs achieved notoriety by being the last person to be executed at the Tower of London. Sitting on a chair, due to his ankle injury, he faced a firing squad on 15 August 1941.

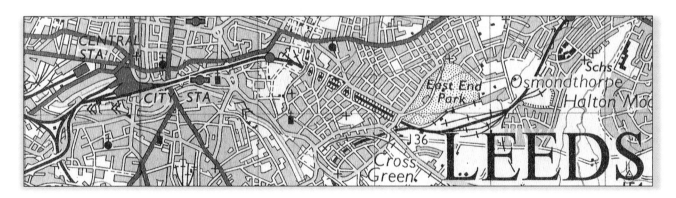

59 LEEDS CENTRAL
Realising the assets –
Leeds decentralised

The fate of Leeds Central was typical of many inner-city stations where concentration of services upon one site made operational and economic sense in the period of great rationalisation during the 1960s. At the peak of railway development in the Yorkshire city in the 19th century, Leeds played host to six different railway companies that worked into five different main stations. The Leeds & Selby Railway worked into Marsh Lane, the North Midland into Hunslet Lane, the Leeds & Bradford into Wellington station, and the Manchester & Leeds into

Central, with Leeds New station opening in 1869 to be run jointly by the LNWR and NER. By 1923 Leeds was down to just three main stations, Wellington, New and Central, and in 1938 the adjacent New and Wellington stations were combined into 'City'.

British Railways had always intended to close Central and divert trains into City, but reconstruction of City proceeded very slowly and it was not until 30 April 1967 that Central was able to shut its doors. Various trackwork alterations were required to cater for services coming into

The impressive overall roof of the terminus at Leeds Central is seen on 3 July 1965. *Rail Photoprints, Chris Davies*

the city from all points of the compass. Leeds City is now the second busiest station in the UK outside London, handling some 110,000 passengers daily.

By the end, Central station, which some have described as being undistinguished architecturally, was beginning to show its age and was the subject of many complaints from passengers and businesses alike. It had seven rather cramped platforms with two bays, housed underneath a twin-span roof and catering for some 4,500 passengers daily. Some prestigious services could be boarded here, however, including 'The Yorkshire Pullman', 'The Harrogate Sunday Pullman', 'The West Riding' and 'The White Rose' expresses. With the provision of extra capacity at City station these numbers were catered for and easily absorbed.

One would have thought that the release of a lucrative city centre site would have given rise to a rapid redevelopment of the site of Central station; however, this was a long time coming. Royal Mail initially built a sorting office on part of the site, but offices and restaurants have now been built, leaving just part of the approach viaduct and a wagon hoist, which connected the upper and lower goods yards, as the only tangible reminders of the former station. Some might have called the closure 'asset-stripping', but concentration of train services in one location has obvious benefits to the travelling public, making interchange that much easier. Similar contraction and concentration was practised in other cities such as Birmingham, with the closure of Snow Hill (which in the end turned out to be somewhat premature), Edinburgh, with the closure of Princes Street, Sheffield, which lost Victoria, and Manchester, which saw its own Central closed.

A view taken of the exterior of the station during the visit of a railtour from Waterloo on the 23 November 1952.
© www.railphotoprints.co.uk – Hugh Ballantyne

60 BISLEY CAMP
Going out with a bang

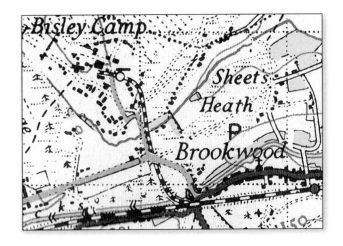

The National Rifle Association (NRA), which was designed to encourage rifle shooting proficiency amongst the rifle and artillery voluntary corps formed following a war scare with France in the 1850s, was for many years located on part of Wimbledon Common. Forced to vacate this site in 1888, the LSWR was keen to keep the NRA's new headquarters within its own operating area and, by offering to help with construction costs and by making cheap fares available, it managed to ensure that a site at Bisley near its main line at Brookwood was chosen, after the NRA had enjoyed a brief sojourn at Churn, south of Didcot. Even though trains would generally run for only one month during the year, when the NRA's annual meeting was held in July, it was still considered a worthwhile investment and the 1¼-mile branch line opened in 1890.

Services were later introduced at other times of the year, including a Saturday afternoon service that ran throughout the April-October shooting season from 1900 to 1914. The operation of the occasional special and troop train was supplemented by irregular goods services and trains for shooting competitions held at Bisley as part of the Olympic Games in both 1908 and 1948. The LSWR agreed to provide the locomotive and carriages to work the services in return for 50% of the gross receipts, but as the line was only used for these limited periods, and in times of national crisis during wartime, it is perhaps not surprising that it was never a great money-spinner.

The participants had transferred to an ex-LSWR Turnchapel push-pull set at Brookwood propelled by M7 tank 30027.
© www.railphotoprints.co.uk, Hugh Ballantyne

However, at the start of the First World War some 150,000 troops underwent training at Bisley in just four months, many coming by train. Track extensions were built totalling 3 miles from Bisley Camp to serve other camps built at Pirbright, Deepcut and Blackdown. There were also three narrow-gauge tramways, one carrying competitors to a distant firing range, another carrying targets to shooting butts, and one to carry targets on a short stretch of track.

There were originally two stations at Bisley Camp, but in 1891 a new centrally located station was decided upon, which consisted of one long brick-faced platform with a passing loop. The unassuming timber station building comprised a waiting room, booking hall and office. Crossing gates were positioned at the end of the platform to accommodate one of the camp's internal roads, and three sidings and an unloading dock were also provided. The platform was subsequently extended and a canopy added at right-angles to the station building. Economies during the 1930s saw some rationalisation of the track layout, which thereafter required subsequent push-pull operation of trains, generally with a two-coach set. Trains left from a branch platform at Brookwood.

London and South Western Ry.

787

FROM WATERLOO TO

BISLEY CAMP

The military camp extension lines did not last long following the end of hostilities, and the track was lifted in 1928. However, about a mile was relaid during the Second World War, but again this did not long survive the outbreak of peace.

With expenses and maintenance costs exceeding receipts after the First World War, no further payments were made to the NRA until the 1930s. With deteriorating track and the ever-increasing cost of maintaining the service the possibility of replacing trains with buses was investigated, but was not pursued and the track was upgraded. After proving an asset again during the Second World War, the branch became an increasing financial liability, and 1952 saw the last rail-served NRA annual meeting and the 'Bisley Bullet', as the train had been affectionately dubbed, operated for the final time on 19 July of that year. The platform and station still exist at Bisley as the headquarters of the Lloyds Bank Rifle Club, and a Mark 1 sleeping car has been positioned on a length of track as dormitory accommodation by the platform, a fitting reminder of this unusual operation.

Chard Town, acting in a goods-only capacity, is seen in July 1961. *CH Library, R. C. Riley*

61 CHARD TOWN
Relegated to goods

Changing circumstances often cause a change in the importance or function of a railway station. Such was the case with the declining fortunes of the LSWR station in Chard, known as Chard Town. Opened in May 1863, it linked the Somerset town with the LSWR West of England main line at Chard Junction, initially Chard Road, and enjoyed a monopoly of traffic from Chard for some three years until the arrival of the GWR route from Yeovil, which came into the town from the north in 1866.

Although known locally as the 'tin station' due to its corrugated-iron cladding, quite a contrast to the substantial brick-built goods shed, the building at Chard Town survived in passenger use until December 1916, when it closed as a wartime economy measure and passengers had to travel on to Chard Joint, not nearly so conveniently located for the town centre. A goods yard, goods shed, signal box and engine shed were all provided initially, and an extra siding to serve the local firm of Hockeys was added in 1905. A 5-ton crane, located in the yard, was supplemented by a mobile crane in later years. The service from the Junction was extended to the GWR

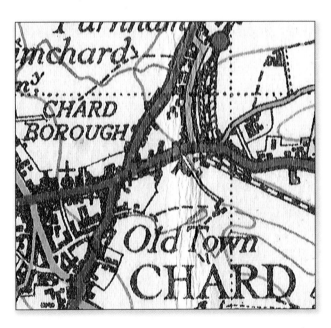

Chard Joint station in 1867, although the necessity for trains to back into and out of the LSWR terminus to continue southwards or northwards remained an operational problem until a platform was built on the connecting curve in 1871. Tickets still had to be purchased from the original terminus building before passengers proceeded to this new platform. At the time of the closure

Firemen damp down after the blaze at the old station at Chard Town. *Martin Boddy*

of Chard Town and the new platform the signal box was replaced by a two-lever ground frame to work the connection between the station area and the link line. All the points in the station area were converted to hand operation and all the signals removed. Use of the engine shed ceased the building being demolished in 1929.

Following diversion of the passenger service via the connecting spur to the GWR station, the LSWR terminus was used solely for goods and became known as Chard Goods. As coal was one of the principal traffics handled, staithes were located on the former passenger platform to cater for this. A private siding was added to serve the firm

of Brecknell, Willis & Co, which were specialists in railway electrification, particularly pantographs and contact shoes, and they continue to be located in the town to this day.

Following the closure of the route between Chard Junction and Yeovil for passengers in 1962, the yard at Chard Town was closed in April 1964, with all sidings taken out of use in July. Goods continued to pass by from Chard Joint to the Junction until total closure came in April 1966. The 'tin station' building was subsequently damaged by fire and today the whole site of the former LSWR presence in the town is covered by a Tesco supermarket.

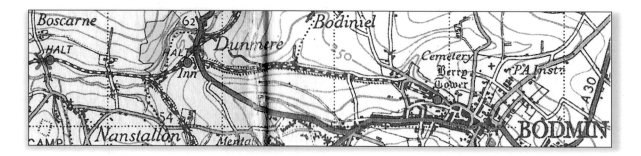

62 BOSCARNE EXCHANGE PLATFORM
Here today – gone tomorrow

An intriguing entry in the book *Passengers No More* reads 'Boscarne Exchange Platform – Opened 15.6.64 – Closed 18.4.66 – Reopened 2.5.66 by order of MOT – Closed permanently 30.1.67 with line.'

This highly unusual sequence of events for such a short-lived facility makes the history of this platform unique. Following the failure of diesel railbuses to avert the closure of the Tetbury and Cirencester branches in April

The short-lived Boscarne Exchange platform. It would appear from this view taken in 1969, after closure to passengers, that a second-hand signboard has been reused from Bodmin Road station to serve this interchange point.

1964, four AC Cars units were released for use in the West of England, two being maintained at St Blazey shed and two at Yeovil Town shed. For two and a half years the Cornish pair were to provide a service in the Bodmin and Wadebridge area.

In anticipation of their arrival, a new exchange platform was constructed at Boscarne Junction where the lines from Bodmin Road via Bodmin General (WR) and from Bodmin North (SR) converged en route to Wadebridge and Padstow. In May 1964, at a cost of £2,000, a simple wooden platform of one coach length with no shelter was built on the Bodmin General line with a nameboard, reclaimed as it turned out from Bodmin Road, which announced 'Boscarne Junction Change for Dunmere and Bodmin North', although in fact in the printed timetable it was always known as Boscarne Exchange Platform. A gravel path, illuminated by three oil lamps, led from the halt the few yards to the Bodmin North line where passengers had to access the air-operated central sliding door of the connecting railbus via retractable steps from a platform of sleepers located at rail level, no raised platform ever being constructed here. There was no road access to the sleeper-built platform, no tickets were issued and no staff were ever provided; the halt thus possessed all the characteristics of the classic interchange point.

The aim of this move was to reduce costs by concentrating the two independent Bodmin-Wadebridge services on the ex-GWR line from General station, and dispensing with the need for duplicate running from Boscarne Junction to Wadebridge inherent in having a separate service from Bodmin North to Wadebridge. Prior to the establishment of the platform it had been rumoured that the WR wished to reduce operational costs in the area by closing the Bodmin North section altogether and concentrating all trains on the Bodmin General route. Diesel railbus services, which began with the introduction of the summer timetable on 15 June 1964, consisted of four trains each way per day on the 2-mile branch from Bodmin North to Boscarne Exchange Platform, connecting with the Bodmin Road-Wadebridge/Padstow services. The WR service from Bodmin Road, which had hitherto not generally called at the intermediate stations of Nanstallon and Grogley, which had been traditionally served by the SR services from Bodmin North, now made additional stops at these points.

Simultaneously with these developments, however, BR entered into negotiations with the unions regarding closure not just of the link to Bodmin North but of the whole line. This was all the more surprising to locals given the investment represented by the recent introduction of diesel units, the provision of a new station, albeit an

The ground-level platform at Boscarne serving the branch to Bodmin North is seen on 10 October 1964 with railbus No W79978 ready to receive passengers via its folding steps. *Roger Joanes*

the railbus shuttle service was withdrawn – temporarily as it turned out – and Boscarne Exchange Platform closed.

Bodmin North continued to be served – just – but only in the down direction, by diverting trains from Bodmin Road to reverse at Boscarne Junction and run into Bodmin North. Although North station was nearer the town centre, the economics of operating into two stations in a relatively small town must have been doubtful. At North station the railbuses reversed and retraced their steps to Boscarne Junction and on to Wadebridge, thereby doubling the journey time from Bodmin General to Wadebridge, for example, from 17 to 34 minutes. This doubtless adversely affected the attractiveness of the service to through passengers who did not wish to enjoy the delights of a detour via Bodmin North.

No trains were provided for passengers from Bodmin North who wished to travel up country, unless they wished to avail themselves of the morning departure for Padstow, change at Nanstallon, the first halt after passing the closed Boscarne Exchange Platform, hang about there for some 47 minutes, then retrace their tracks to Boscarne, branching off to Bodmin Road via Bodmin General, taking in all a leisurely 71 minutes for the journey from Bodmin North to Bodmin Road! No doubt they made their way to General station to access the service to Bodmin Road, which could be reached in a much more reasonable 7 minutes.

Words were not minced at BR's Plymouth HQ when it was stated that, 'The trouble with these seaside branch lines is that they only take money in the summer. Take out June, July and August and the rest of the year is a dead loss.' Following many objections from local travellers to this level of service, the Ministry of Transport stepped in and took the most unusual action of ordering BR to reopen Boscarne Exchange Platform forthwith, which it did from 2 May 1966. The railbus returned and continued to ply up and down to Bodmin North from Boscarne until closure of the whole line to passengers could be implemented nine months later in January 1967. Thus the short life of Boscarne Exchange came to an abrupt end after just 2½ years.

unstaffed halt, and the general rationalisation indicating that perhaps their line was safe at least in the short term in spite of inclusion in the Beeching Report. As a prelude to closure, Bodmin North became unstaffed on 3 January 1966 and attained 'Halt' status on 18 April, a somewhat unusual situation for a terminus. Rationalisation only went so far, however; the signal box remained manned to handle the arrival and departure of a handful of passenger services daily, goods traffic having ceased in 1965, until closure of the line the following January. On 18 April 1966

The station at Macduff perched on the hillside overlooking Banff Bay features on this early-20th-century postcard.

63 MACDUFF
Lay on, Macduff!

The North Aberdeenshire coastal resorts of Banff and Macduff lie on opposite banks of the River Devoran and are separated by little more than a bridge. One might have expected that just one station would have been sufficient to serve this community, which in the 1860s had a combined population of just 11,000. However, two independent lines were laid, one to Banff and the other to Macduff, and they were never linked. The Banff, Portsoy & Strathisla Railway, later known as the Banffshire Railway and opened in August 1859, connected Banff with the Great North of Scotland Railway (GNoSR) main line initially at Grange but subsequently at Tillynaught, when the coastal route to Elgin opened. The railway was merged with the GNoSR in August 1867 and was to provide a quicker link than the subsequent Macduff

A close-up view of the station at Macduff.
CH Library David Lawrence

branch to the Aberdeen-Inverness main line. Instead of extending the line over the river to its neighbour, Macduff was served from 1860 by the Banff, Macduff & Turriff Railway, later also absorbed by the GNoSR, running from Turriff, on a branch line that had opened in 1857 from Inveramsay on the Elgin-Aberdeen line.

Initially the station was located high up at a spot known as Gellymill, due to the steeply sloping nature of the land on the south side of the Hill of Doun, some three-quarters of a mile from Macduff town and a quarter of a mile from the river bridge and nowhere near its important fishing harbour. A tramway to connect the station and harbour was mooted, but the 1 in 30 incline proved too much of a deterrent and the scheme was dropped. This terminus was rather optimistically known as Banff & Macduff.

In 1872 the line was extended around the hill closer to the town to a station known as Macduff, whilst the original station closed on 1 July of that year and was demolished. Such was the altitude of the Macduff branch that it was not feasible to bridge the River Devoran and thus connect to Banff, leaving the two towns separated by a circuitous rail journey of 75 miles! A station was, however, opened at Banff Bridge conveniently sited near the bridge over the river that divided the two towns. In spite of financial incentives offered by the railway company, traders in Banff preferred to use Banff's own station rather than transport their goods across the river bridge and up the steep hill to Macduff station.

Thus the GNoSR found itself the owner of two routes to the two towns. Although the distance from Macduff to Aberdeen via Inveramsay was some 15 miles shorter than that from Banff via Tillynaught, traffic did not develop as hoped and generally three or four trains each way daily, providing connections to and from Aberdeen at Inveramsay, constituted the basic passenger service. Passenger closure came as early as October 1951 with freight north of Turriff ceasing ten years later. The Tillynaught to Banff branch closed to passengers on 6 July 1964 and completely on 6 May 1968, the coastal route to Elgin having closed to passengers in May 1963.

The second line to open thus proved to be the first line to yield to rationalisation, with Macduff closing to passengers a good dozen years before Banff, so in Shakespearian terms I guess Macduff was the first to cry, 'Hold, enough!':

'Lay on, Macduff; and damned be him that first cries "Hold, enough!"' (*Macbeth*)

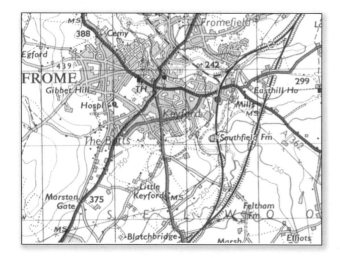

64 FROME
Cut off in its prime

Cut-off lines constructed to shorten mileage and therefore journey times usually had the effect of changing the status of station stops on the original route. Such was the case with the GWR's development of its new route to the West of England, which began in 1900 with the doubling of the Berks & Hants extension from Hungerford to Patney & Chirton and the construction of a new route between Patney & Chirton through Stert to Westbury. The other gap in the line was between Castle Cary and Taunton, which was filled in 1906. This brought Taunton 20 miles nearer to London than via the 'Great Way Round' through Bristol. By-passes around Westbury and Frome were opened in 1933. These developments led to the reduction in status of Devizes, formerly on the original route from Hungerford to Westbury, and of Frome, whose station now sat on a loop line. None of the through expresses called at Frome nor Castle Cary, which is today a railhead for that part of Somerset and sees a regular London-West of England service. Frome has enjoyed the occasional through train

A service from Bristol via Radstock arrives at Frome on 18 April 1959. *Roger Joanes*

from time to time, and in 2016 there was one through service to London in the morning with a return in the evening, together with a London-Taunton and return service that called at Frome in both directions, but the majority of services are locals between Weymouth, Bath and Bristol. South West Trains also operates some services from Waterloo to Yeovil Pen Mill via Frome.

Frome station has a wooden overall roof, one of many that used to grace the GWR network such as Ashburton, Thame, Exeter St Thomas and Cheddar, and remarkably it has survived to the present day protected by Grade II listed status. The roof was designed by J. R. Hannaford in 1850 for the opening of the route from Westbury, and is one of the oldest such structures; it is 120 feet by 48 feet (36.5 by 14.6 metres), supported by twelve composite trusses with a span

of 49 feet (15 metres), and is the only example remaining in railway use in the West of England. The line was extended to Yeovil in 1856 and to Weymouth the following year. A small locomotive shed, a sub-shed of nearby Westbury, was located to the west of the station until closure in 1963.

Although both platforms remain, one is now unused since singling of the loop in August 1970. Upon the opening of the avoiding line a new signal box, one of four in the vicinity and known as South Box, was located at the end of the down platform. It closed when the loop was singled and was later demolished. A branch line from Frome ran via Radstock to Bristol, but this closed to passengers in 1959 although stone traffic is still heavy from nearby quarries. An extension to the up platform was completed in 1893, the bay catering for the Radstock service.

Although one track has been removed, Frome station still sports its now redundant footbridge and signal box, not to mention the brown and cream running-in board.

A modern view of the splendidly restored station boasting one of the oldest through trainsheds still in operation in the UK.

65 MERTON PARK
When trams took over

Trams are making a comeback, and in the case of Tramlink route No 1 through Merton Park from Elmers End to Wimbledon they are utilising the trackbed of a former railway. A little bit of history is in order here, as the railway developments in this area are somewhat involved. Although the line from Wimbledon to Mitcham Junction and West Croydon opened in 1855, no station was provided at Merton Park. It was not until October 1868 that a station was opened on the route at Lower Merton, jointly promoted by the LBSCR and LSWR, from Streatham through Tooting to Wimbledon, continuing on through Lower Merton and Merton Abbey forming a loop back to Tooting. Almost as an afterthought, on 1 November 1870 a single platform was opened on the West Croydon route to complement the two platforms provided on the Tooting route, the station having changed its name to Merton Park in September 1887.

The line from Merton Park to Tooting closed for almost six years from 1 January 1917 as an economy measure, and although it reopened in August 1923 it did not prosper and closed to passengers in 1929, leaving the West Croydon line platform as the only operational one. Freight continued on the Tooting line although the junction was severed at the Tooting end and one track lifted, leaving just one long siding from Merton Park until freight traffic ceased in 1975. The line from Wimbledon through to West Croydon was electrified in July 1930. The route was particularly busy in peak hours; in 1969, for example, more than 150,000 tickets were sold.

Facilities were only provided for the original Lower Merton station, where a brick-built station house incorporating a booking office was located on the up platform. A small canopy was provided at the front of the building with another at the rear over the entrance. A

This view of Merton Park, photographed from a passing train, shows the former platforms and the line leading to Merton Abbey.

An exterior view of the old BR station at Merton Park taken on 30 March 1976. *CH Library, J. Scrace*

The old order changeth: Merton Park tram stop is seen in November 2008. *Nick Catford*

small brick waiting shelter was located on the down platform, passengers having to cross the tracks to reach it as no footbridge was provided. No buildings were provided on the Croydon platform. Upon closure of the Merton Abbey line to freight, a temporary wooden walkway was provided across the former trackbed, but this was later replaced with a more permanent fenced earthen walkway. The main booking office continued to be used but before closure of the Croydon line in 1997 it had become disused, vandalised and partly burnt out. The building was later restored, however, as a house, and

further housing has been built on the former Tooting trackbed. To the north of the station a signal box controlling a level crossing was in use until CCTV cameras were installed in 1982.

The last train ran on 31 May 1997 and the line closed on 2 June for most of it to be reused in the Tramlink network in May 2000. The tram stop occupies part of the site of the former railway station with services running every 12 minutes throughout most of the day, a far cry from the basic half-hourly service offered by British Rail 50 years ago.

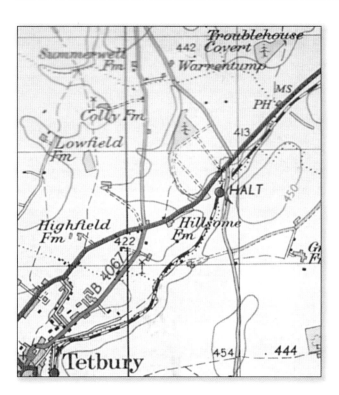

66 TROUBLE HOUSE HALT
Going to a lot of trouble

A Tetbury-bound AC Cars railbus pauses at Trouble House halt. *CH Library, Andrew Muckley*

In an effort to reduce operating costs and increase passenger traffic, consideration was sometimes given to the provision of a new station, or more often than not merely a very basic halt, on a branch line that otherwise might have been a possible candidate for closure. To improve the profitability of the two ex-GWR branches connecting Cirencester and Tetbury with the main Swindon-Gloucester line at Kemble, the Western Region of BR adopted a two-pronged attack. The replacement of steam by diesel railbuses occurred from February 1959 with an improved service, and immediately passenger numbers rose. The second development was the opening of new halts on the two branches. On the Cirencester branch there was no intermediate station until Chesterton Lane Halt opened on 2 February 1959, with Park Leaze Halt following on 4 January 1960.

Similar new provision occurred on the Tetbury branch, which did already have three intermediate stops at Jackaments Bridge Halt, open from 1939 until 1948 primarily for RAF Kemble construction workers, Rodmarton Platform, which had opened in 1904, and Culkerton, which was open from the beginning but had closed in 1956. Culkerton was subsequently reopened in February 1959 with the advent of the railbuses and additionally two new halts were provided at Church's Hill and

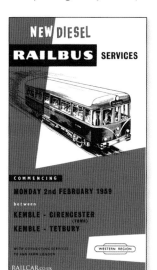

Trouble House. As might be expected, the halts were very simple affairs, being just long enough to accommodate the single-car diesel railbus. A low sleeper-built platform and a small noticeboard with timetable comprised the facilities, the railbuses having retractable steps to allow passengers to alight and board. Folklore has it that the landlord of the nearby public house supplied a beer crate to enable passengers to board, although the condition of any such passengers is not specified!

The primary purpose of locating a halt at this spot was to serve this drinking establishment, known as the Trouble House Inn. Apparently it was so named to reflect various problems, possibly legendary, that beset a series of landlords in the 18th and 19th centuries. Built in about 1754 it was known as 'troublesome' at that time due to its poor quality and habit of flooding. Two landlords reportedly suffered bad luck, one losing a number of wives who died young and another who experienced financial problems when many of his male regulars were forcibly abducted by HM press gangs to fight in the American Revolution. The pub was then embroiled in the agricultural riots of 1830 as local farm labourers vented their displeasure at the introduction of mechanical haymaking and threshing machines. One unlucky farmer transporting a new piece of machinery hidden in a laden hay wagon was spotted in Tetbury and chased by an angry mob who eventually surrounded the wagon outside the Trouble House and set it on fire. Another owner apparently embarked on a refurbishment that bankrupted him, so he hanged himself from a beam in the pub. The half-reconstructed building was taken over by another innkeeper who also fell on hard times and drowned himself in a nearby pond. The pub was then purchased by a wealthy businessman who renamed it The Trouble House in honour of its possibly apocryphal history. Sightings of a ghostly 'Lady in Blue' complete the tall tales.

Trouble House Halt was in fact one of the few stations in the country built specifically to serve, and be named after, a pub; Berney Arms station in Norfolk performs much the same function. But the railbuses and the halts were all too little too late, being unable to save either the Tetbury or the Cirencester branches, and they duly closed to passengers in 1964, the last trains running on the evening of 5 April. Even the closure was troublesome and not without incident, for when the last passenger train from Tetbury arrived at Trouble House Halt a coffin, made by the landlord of the pub and his brother, covered with inscriptions and filled with empty whisky bottles, was loaded onto the train by several bowler-hatted mourners. On arrival at Kemble the coffin, addressed to Doctor Beeching as the architect of the closure, was transferred to a London train. As a final gesture, the last passenger train to Tetbury found its approach to Trouble House Halt blocked by bonfires of burning hay bales placed across the tracks. The halt would go on to be immortalised by Flanders and Swann in their song 'The Slow Train'.

Table 107	KEMBLE and TETBURY										
	WEEK DAYS ONLY—(Second class only)										
Miles		am	am S	am E	am S	am	pm	pm	pm	pm	pm
	105 London (Pad.) .. dep	5 30	8 0	9 5	9 5	11 45	..	1 45	2S 0	4 55	7 0
—	Kemble .... dep	8 35	1030	1130	1150	1 45	2 42	3 45	5 0	7 3	8 55
3	Rodmarton Platform.. ..	8 43	1038	1138	1158	1 53	2 50	3 53	5 8	7 11	9 3
3½	Church's Hill Halt........	8 46	1041	1141	12 1	1 56	2 53	3 56	5 11	7 14	9 7
4½	Culkerton Halt.. .. .	8 49	1044	1144	12 4	1 59	2 56	3 59	5 14	7 17	9 10
5½	Trouble House Halt.......	8 53	1048	1148	12 8	2 3	3 0	4 3	5 18	7 21	9 15
7½	Tetbury .. .. .. arr	8 59	1054	1154	1214	2 9	3 6	4 9	5 24	7 27	9 21
Miles		am	am	am S	pm		pm	pm	pm	pm	pm
	Tetbury .. .. .. dep	7 40	9 17	11 0	1220	..	2 15	3 11	4 25	5 58	7 35
1½	Trouble House Halt.. ..	7 45	9 22	11 5	1225	..	2 20	3 16	4 30	6 3	7 40
2½	Culkerton Halt..	7 50	9 27	1110	1230	..	2 25	3 21	4 35	6 8	7 45
3½	Church's Hill Halt.. ..	7 53	9 30	1113	1233	..	2 28	3 24	4 38	6 11	7 48
4½	Rodmarton Platform.. ..	7 55	9 32	1115	1235	..	2 30	3 26	4 40	6 13	7 50
7½	Kemble .... arr	8 4	9 41	1124	1244	..	2 39	3 35	4 49	6 22	7 59
98½	105 London (Pad.) .. arr	9 55	12 5	..	2 47	..	..	6 0	6 35	9 1	1043

E Except Saturdays   S Saturdays only

67 CALLANDER
Trossachs springboard

The attractive Perthshire town of Callander might have remained merely the terminus of a short branch line from Dunblane had it not been viewed as a useful 'jumping-off point' by a railway company with a vision of connecting Oban on the far west coast with the rest of the Scottish railway network. The Dunblane, Doune & Callander Railway (DDCR) did not succeed in opening its modest 10-mile line until 1858, some 12 years after the plan was first mooted. Callander was the western extremity of relatively lowland terrain, for beyond lay the rugged Highlands, very challenging country for railway builders. The promoters of a line to Oban, some 71 difficult miles to the west of Callander, decided in 1864 that the market town would make a good starting point for their line to penetrate the Highlands, and it would become known as the Callander & Oban Railway (C&O).

In view of the vast sum of money that the construction of the route was expected to entail, the only way that

finance could be raised was to involve some well-established railways in the scheme. The Scottish Central Railway (SCR) was prepared to put up some £200,000 and the authorised capital was £600,000 with loans of £200,000. The DDCR was duly absorbed by the SCR on 31 July 1865, which itself amalgamated with the Caledonian Railway the following day. The original Callander terminus station closed on 1 June 1870 and became a goods yard when a new replacement through station was opened together with the first section of the C&O between Callander and Glenoglehead. This new station underwent subsequent expansion in 1882, the enlarged layout being later controlled from two signal boxes, the East box containing 45 levers, and the West box with 27 levers. It had five platforms comprising two bays at the south end, one at the north end, and two through roads. The line from the station to Callander & Oban Junction, three-quarters of a mile to the west, was doubled in 1903.

It was to take until 1880 before the whole route was opened, but the monopoly of the C&O's route to the west coast was broken in 1894 by the opening of the West Highland line from Fort William, which crossed the C&O at Crianlarich, a connecting spur between the two routes being constructed in 1897. The population of Oban realised that there was now a potentially quicker route to Glasgow,

An undated view of Fairburn 2-6-4T No 42199 pausing at Callander. *CH Library*

Looking towards the north on 3 April 1961, the DMU forms one of the popular 'Six Lochs Landcruise' specials, the passengers detraining to enjoy the spectacular scenery. Note the tall signal cabin in the background. *CH Library, S. Rickard*

it being 17 miles shorter via the West Highland line of the North British Railway (NBR) than over the C&O via Callander. This duplication remained until formal closure of the C&O route between Dunblane and Crianlarich on 5 November 1965, although a landslide in Glen Ogle had precipitated closure when it blocked the line on 27 September. From that date all Oban services were diverted to run via the former NBR route from Glasgow to Crianlarich and thence over C&O metals to the coast.

Track to the west of Callander was lifted in early 1967 and to the east of the station in 1968, the attractive station building being demolished in the spring of 1973. The site is now a car and coach park, although the impressive cast ironwork on the road bridge to the east of the station was refurbished before infilling in 2012. The site of the original terminal station is now occupied by housing.

Callander had a brief period of fame in the 1960s when the BBC TV series *Dr Finlay's Casebook* featured the town and its setting as a backdrop, with the railway station also featuring occasionally. Today one can stay at the Arden House B&B in the town, once the fictional home of Doctors Cameron and Finlay and their housekeeper Janet.

Chedworth station basks in the summer sun untroubled by trains or passengers.
Mark Warburton, courtesy of Mrs Margaret Warburton

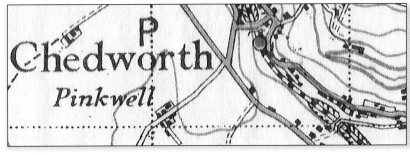

68 CHEDWORTH
Just one train a day

If you lived in the Gloucestershire village of Chedworth, famous for its Roman villa, from 1958 to 1961 you would not have been spoilt for choice as regards train services, there being just one train daily in each direction on weekdays only. Leaving at 10.20am, you could be in Cheltenham half an hour later and have some 3 hours available for shopping or any other business before being forced to catch the only return train available at 1.56pm. In the opposite direction the only southbound train of the day would take you to Marlborough, Swindon, Andover or Southampton. With such a level of service it is hardly surprising that passenger numbers at Chedworth were pretty negligible. This was a far cry from the heady days of 1915 when Chedworth enjoyed five departures in each direction as well as the benefit of some Sunday trains. Even in the 1930s some 2,500 passengers and 6,000 parcels were handled each year.

The Midland & South Western Junction Railway (MSWJR) line northwards from Cirencester to the junction with the GWR at Andoversford had opened to passengers in August 1891, but initially no station was provided at Chedworth, which was situated near the 637-foot summit of the line. After complaints from locals, who faced a considerable walk to the nearest station at Foss Cross, a station was provided in the village in October 1892. It was a rudimentary affair comprising a small single platform some 150 feet in length, at the south end of which stood a small office with an awning that was placed hard against an old carriage body planted on the platform. Access was via a zigzag path down the embankment opposite the platform and a board crossing, which was not ideally situated as the line was on a curve. Although parcels were handled at the station, which had a staff of two, no goods facilities were provided, the company maintaining that there was insufficient space to provide siding accommodation.

Upon doubling of the line in June 1902, a new station was provided with a new wooden station building and lamp house, a small signal box by Duttons with 14 levers, four of which were spare, and a shelter on the former original platform that appears to have been adapted from the original building with the doors removed. Crossovers were put in, which allowed a loop clearance of some 650 feet. Although the company managed to find space for a very small siding adjacent to the signal box, goods facilities were never introduced here and the siding was subsequently removed. Following singling of the line in 1928 the new platform and building became the only one to be used, and the signal box, which was not staffed by a signalman but by the stationmaster, had fallen out of use by the following year. The box was subsequently advertised for sale by the Stores Department at Swindon and was used as an extension to a bungalow, surviving until demolished in 1970.

The station became unstaffed in February 1954 and slumbered on, disturbed by very few train movements, until closure on 11 September 1961 together with the rest of the MSWJR line from Andover to Andoversford. The economics of this route, like so many others that crossed the grain of the country, could not survive on local traffic alone, and it really only came into its own as a through route, particularly useful in times of war. The cutting by the station was infilled and all trace of the railway hereabouts has been lost, local memories of the line in action living on only in the minds of inhabitants aged 60 or more.

69 RUGBY CENTRAL
Rugby's rump

Opened by the Manchester, Sheffield & Lincolnshire Railway, the line was to be rebranded as the grandiose Great Central, which planned a route through the heart of England linked to France via a Channel Tunnel. The last main line built in England was opened to the Marylebone terminus in 1899 but never fulfilled its early promise. Rugby Central, which was situated approximately half way along the London Extension, was a stopping point for London-Manchester expresses and was also a changeover point for local services south to Woodford or Aylesbury and north to Leicester or Nottingham. Its fortunes were to suffer a slow decline, accelerated by the withdrawal of the expresses in 1960s, leaving only semi-fast and local services until just the rump of a shuttle service from Nottingham Arkwright Street remained at the very end of its life.

Always a more modest affair than the LNWR's main-line station on the route to Euston, it did attract a loyal clientele but had to work hard to compete with the more established routes serving the towns through which the GCR also passed. In spite of its suffix, the station was situated on the eastern outskirts of the town and consisted of the standard GCR island platform with access via a glazed stairway from the street-level building, which contained the booking office and parcels office. The building was finished in Gothic style in red brick with white Mansfield stone, and a glazed walkway provided a separate exit from the station in addition to that via the main building. There was also a goods lift to facilitate movement of goods from the platform to road level.

The stationmaster's house was not built from new but was adapted from a dwelling, Laurel Cottage, already existing on Hillmorton Road, which crossed the railway by means of an overbridge. Canopies were provided along part of the 600-foot platform, protecting the usual station facilities that included three waiting rooms and toilet facilities. 'Parachute' water columns were provided at each end of the platform, although difficulties in obtaining a good water supply meant that the original intention to provide a locomotive shed here was changed to Woodford Halse. Extensive goods facilities were provided, but freight services finished in June 1965 when through freight services were transferred away from the line as a prelude to closure as a through route in September the following year.

One part of the overall closure plan could not be implemented as it was felt necessary to continue to provide services, operated by DMUs, between Rugby and Nottingham, initially to Victoria but latterly to a reopened Arkwright Street when Victoria was demolished and redeveloped as a shopping centre. Rugby station became unstaffed and this last service rump continued until May 1969 when it was also discontinued; a few days later the embankment north of Rugby was severed by works for the M6 motorway, the station being demolished the following year, although the platforms are still extant. As John Betjeman said in his poem 'Great Central Railway, Sheffield Victoria to Banbury':

'And quite where Rugby Central is
Does only Rugby know.
We watched the empty platform wait
And sadly saw it go.'

The 5.15pm Nottingham-Marylebone service calls at Rugby Central on 20 May 1963 headed by 'Royal Scot' Class No 46143 *The South Staffordshire Regiment. CH Library, D. Smith*

The Nottingham shuttle DMU stands at the platform at Rugby Central waiting to return on 19 April 1969. *Roger Joanes*

BR Standard Class 4 No 75072 at the head of a northbound service passes the lower platform prior to reversal up the incline into the main-line upper station. *Roger Holmes*

70 TEMPLECOMBE LOWER
Always an awkward junction

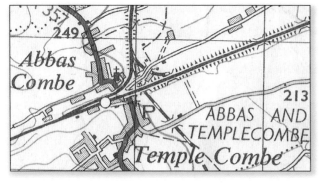

Always an awkward junction operationally, Templecombe witnessed some strange manoeuvres, as recalled by Gilbert Thomas in his poem 'Nostalgia':

'Did you keep slow company
With the "tanks" (royal) of the S. and D.,
That waited as it seemed, for crack of doom
(While they performed strange rites) at
Templecombe?'

These strange rites resulted from the failure of the Somerset & Dorset (S&D) and London & South Western (LSWR) companies to provide a logical interchange between the north/south route of the former and the east/west layout of the latter. The S&D passed beneath the LSWR but interchange was effected primarily by way of a spur leading up to the LSWR main line, which necessitated reversal in order to continue journeys either north or south on the S&D. A partial answer was provided by the lower platform situated between bridge No 152 Coomb Throop Lane and bridge No 153, carrying the LSWR main line. This was a very restricted site that could only accommodate a short platform of some two carriage lengths, quite insufficient for the long summer holiday through trains and inadequate even to cater for the three-coach locals that latterly plied the S&D. It would have been difficult to lengthen the platform, hemmed in as it was; what was really required here was a high level/low level platform interchange with the LSWR line in order to remove the necessity for the spur line and

Taken in July 1967, the year after closure of the S&D route, this is the view through the arch of Coombe Throop bridge looking south towards the LSWR main line bridge No 153 beyond the small lower platform on the right.

reversal procedures. However, one was never built and the time-consuming and operationally expensive reversals continued until the end of services in 1966.

The lower platform opened in 1887, taking over from the original lower station, which had been situated adjacent to the locomotive shed, and which was operational from 1862 to 1887. The platform was built on the up side but only a very few trains stopped here, although engine crews sometimes used it to change over on through workings that were not timetabled to stop at Templecombe Upper. In addition the platform famously served the last up train of the day from Bournemouth on Saturdays, the 10.00pm arriving at 11.17pm, thus enabling the locomotive to proceed to the shed without the need to traverse the spur to the Upper station. This arrangement lasted until 3 January 1966, when the 'emergency timetable' was brought in for the last few weeks of the line's life.

Back in the 1860s the directors of the S&D had agreed that their junction with the Salisbury & Yeovil Company at Templecombe was not a 'perfectly good junction'; they went on to say that it was 'the best which the circumstances would permit of', this being a reflection of the generally parlous state of finances that the company found itself enjoying for most of its existence.

No nameboard was ever provided for the information of the traveller, and just one light shining from a standard SR concrete post sufficed to illuminate the short platform, which had no buildings or seats. A short path led up to a wicket gate that gave access to the road and thence to the upper station. The 14.50 service from Bath called regularly for many years carrying mailbags for transfer to the main station. With the cooperation of railway staff it has been said that it was possible, should an intending traveller have missed his southbound train at the upper station, to race down the road and reach the lower platform in time to catch it, as it had in the interim been occupied in reversing down the spur line, with a pilot locomotive attached at the front, before proceeding towards Bournemouth.

Today the area has been transformed into a private sunken garden although there remains the possibility that a northward extension of the Gartell Light Railway could one day reach the lower platform at Templecombe.

A typical branch-line scene on the Hawkhurst line, a Wainwright 'H' Class tank has two coaches in tow. A solitary passenger alights at Goudhurst, indicative of the economics of this rural line.

71 GOUDHURST
Not nearly near enough

When railway routes were being planned it was often a case of following the contours to avoid expensive earthworks, particularly if the railway company was rather impecunious. This resulted in stations being sited in less than ideal locations, particularly if the settlement they purported to serve was on top of a hill. One thinks of Torrington station, situated at the foot of a mile-long 200-foot descent from the town, Semley, which was the closest the railway could come to the hilltop town of Shaftesbury, and Goudhurst, where the branch line to Hawkhurst skirted the town and was about a mile to the west and more than 250 feet below the rise on which the town was situated. In recognition of this, the station was originally named 'Hope Mill for Goudhurst & Lamberhurst', to which it was adjacent.

Obstacles such as climbing hills were not so much of a deterrent in the late 19th and early 20th centuries when walking considerable distances was common, but in the age of the motor car and bus travel the prospect of a long walk to a station to catch a train was sufficiently offputting to many would-be passengers. Indeed, the terminus of the line was also an inconvenient mile from Hawkhurst. The reverse was also true of course where the railway kept to the high ground and the settlement was in a valley bottom, for example Okehampton station, which is a long trudge up a steep hill from the town below, and Ilfracombe, perched 254 feet above sea level.

The appearance of the integral station house at Goudhurst, which was of a rather nondescript design, was not enhanced by the outsized dormer windows. A

Goudhurst awaits its fate of ultimate demolition in this view of 3 October 1964. *CH Library, L. Sandler*

signal box, which also controlled the adjacent level crossing, had sliding windows rather than the traditional SER sash type. This was the only passing place on the branch, and the station offices were contained in a corrugated-iron-clad building on the up side, the down side having a shelter that was demolished before the end of passenger services in 1961. By that time the locals preferred to catch the more convenient bus or to drive, and the traditional hop-pickers' specials that had brought Londoners into the country for a week's fresh air were becoming a thing of the past. At their peak, up to twenty-six hop-pickers' trains a day each brought 350 people into the area for the three-week picking season.

However, in its last year the line was carrying fewer than 200 passengers per day, many of them children attending schools in the area. The decision to transfer the school contracts to road was the final nail in the coffin for the line. Had the stations been more conveniently sited, passenger services might have lasted a little longer, but in the end the majority of rural branch lines were doomed. The track was removed in 1964 and the station offered for sale in 1967. It was eventually demolished and a house, appropriately named 'Haltwhistle', built on the site.

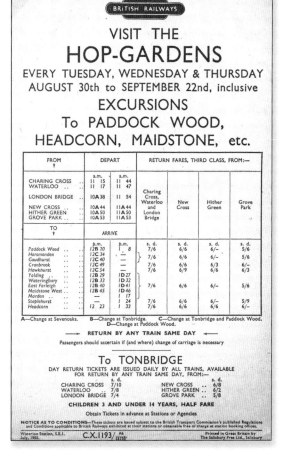

The rusting tracks testify to the former extensive layout at Seaton Junction. In this late-1960s view just a single through line of the route from Salisbury to Exeter continues through the closed station.

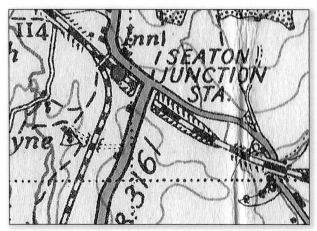

72 SEATON JUNCTION
Raison d'être gone

Across the country there were stations that owed their existence to the fact that they formed a junction with a branch line. Had it not been for this fact it is doubtful whether the localities would have been served by a station at all, and once the branch line had closed the raison d'être of the junction also disappeared, there being insufficient local population to justify retention of a station. Prime examples were Afon Wen on the Cambrian Coast line, junction for the line to Caernarvon, The Mound in Caithness, junction for the Dornoch branch, and Seaton Junction, interchange point on the LSWR's Waterloo-Exeter main line for the Devon coastal resort of Seaton.

Seaton Junction started life in 1860 as 'Colyton for Seaton', that is until the branch line opened in 1868, when it became Colyton Junction, not attaining its final name until July the following year. Its positioning was not ideal from an operating point of view, as it was placed at the foot of the fearsome 7 miles of the Honiton incline, much of it at 1 in 80 – quite a challenge for heavy westbound

trains starting from the junction. In 1898 the nearby Shute Arms Hotel opened its doors, but apart from a few houses there was little other habitation in the vicinity of the station.

A comprehensive rebuilding took place in 1927/28, retaining the original LSWR buildings but lengthening the platforms and providing two through running lines for non-stop trains, thus permitting overtaking. A new signal box was located on the down platform and a new curving branch platform was brought into use at a 45-degree angle to the main line, thus avoiding the previous problem of branch line trains having to reverse into the former down bay platform. Two footbridges were provided, products of the Exmouth Junction Concrete Works, one connecting the platforms and the other very long example carrying a footpath across the whole site.

A fateful 7 March 1966 saw the closure of many intermediate stations on the Salisbury-Exeter route, including Seaton Junction, whose services were no longer required with the closure of the branch to Seaton on the same day. Freight services were withdrawn from the yard here the following month, although coal deliveries and milk from the adjacent Express Dairies continued for a while longer, and a siding into the up platform was retained for some years after closure. Just one track was eventually utilised, the former up through road, and the station buildings were occupied by a variety of commercial users.

Although the Seaton branch has been given a new lease of life as the Seaton Tramway, this stops short at Colyton and there are no plans to extend it to the junction. Were such a scheme to take place, undoubtedly the case for reopening the junction as an interchange would be strengthened. However, the days of through coaches from Waterloo to Seaton and the shuffling branch-line train are now but echoes at the former Seaton Junction.

Looking west from the overbridge at the London end of the former platforms, telegraph poles now occupy the site of the former down tracks. The former up platform now serves only as a siding for the adjacent milk depot.

A DMU waits at the branch platform at Seaton Junction prior to returning to Seaton on 10 December 1965.
Roger Joanes

This June 1962 view shows the facilities at Bedford St Johns before severe rationalisation set in and prior to the ultimate relocation of the station on the spur line to the town's main-line station.
Ben Brooksbank

73 BEDFORD ST JOHNS
St John's worst – first in, first out

Although it was the first station to serve Bedford, rationalisation was to see St Johns downgraded, then ultimately closed while services were diverted to the third station to open in the town at a resited Bedford Midland Road. The LNWR arrived in the town first in 1846, with a branch from Bletchley to St Johns, followed by the Midland Railway in 1859 with its line to Hitchin from its original station at Midland Road; finally, the Midland's line to St Pancras, which opened in 1868, resulted in Midland Road station being resited 200 yards to the north of the original. The Hitchin line crossed the

Bedford-Bletchley line on the flat before a flyover was built in 1885 following a serious accident.

As originally constructed, St Johns was a terminus with a single low platform, which was later raised, and an overall roof. The main station buildings contained the usual offices including gentlemen's toilets, parcels office, parcels and cloak room, booking office, general waiting room, separate ladies' and gentlemen's waiting rooms, and ladies' toilets. A bookstall was located on the platform in front of the gentlemen's waiting room and a canopy at the front of the building provided protection from the weather for arriving

Seen from a passing Cambridge train in December 1967, it is just a week before the truncation of the 'Varsity Line', leaving just the middle section between Bletchley and Bedford. *Nick Catford*

This is Bedford St Johns in 2005 – minimal facilities on a basic platform. *Owen Dunn, Wikipedia*

passengers. The arrival of the Midland Railway's line to Hitchin saw that company's services make use of St Johns temporarily between 8 May 1857 and 1 February 1859 while its own station was being built at Midland Road; a petition for a joint station was not heeded, much to the chagrin of passengers who had to walk between the two to make connections. With the through route to London St Pancras in 1868 came a new Bedford Midland Road station (renamed Bedford Midland on 8 May 1978).

The role of St Johns diminished following the closure at the end of 1967 of the through 'Varsity Line', which linked Oxford with Cambridge, leaving Bedford at the end of a truncated route from Bletchley. The up platform trainshed at St Johns was removed in the late 1950s/early 1960s and replaced with a rather makeshift flat canopy supported on the girders that had once supported the more elaborate trainshed. By March 1971 the main station buildings and water tower had been demolished, leaving a rather unprepossessing terminus halt, which had been unstaffed since July 1968, to greet the arriving traveller.

On 14 May 1984 BR closed the original St Johns station and diverted services from Bletchley along a new chord to Bedford Midland, opening a new single-platform halt on the chord, also called St Johns. The new connection runs over the route of the Midland's former Hitchin line, which closed in 1964.

Currently the East West Rail Consortium is seeking to reinstate the entire Oxford-Cambridge route, which may include rebuilding St Johns on its original site. So although it might have been the first station on the Bedford railway map, and was the first to close, St Johns may one day rise again in another guise once more serving traffic between the two university cities that it helped to link for more than 100 years.

The passenger and staff facilities were minimal to say the least, as witnessed in this view of a departing passenger climbing past the ticket hut and waiting shelter.

74 SHOSCOMBE & SINGLE HILL HALT
By public demand

Railway companies generally took the lead in deciding the location of their stations. Some, sited for operational reasons, were often regarded as being inconvenient from the public's point of view, and requests for the provision of a station were often met with refusal or only grudging acceptance after a number of years had elapsed. The latter scenario was to be the case with Shoscombe & Single Hill Halt, located on the former Somerset & Dorset (S&D) line. When its Bath extension from Evercreech opened in 1874, no station was planned on the 4 miles of single line between Radstock and Wellow. This section was doubled as far as Midford between 1892 and 1894, but the impecunious concern turned down proposals for stations on either side of Devonshire Tunnel, to serve the expanding suburbs of Bath, and at Shoscombe. Although not a large settlement, containing fewer than 500 souls, the area around Shoscombe and Single Hill was isolated from the main road network with very narrow steep roads leading down to the village.

The concrete platforms and nameboards of Shoscombe & Single Hill Halt remained in situ for a while after track removal following closure of the S&D.

The locals continued to press for a station, as it must have be galling for them to see trains speeding through their village that could have delivered them into the centre of Bath in just 20 minutes, as well as providing them with travel opportunities as far afield as Bournemouth and the Midlands. For 55 years these voices went unheard by the railway.

However, by the 1920s it was becoming apparent that the railways were under threat from road competition in the shape of rural bus services. The situation was made worse by the effects of the economic depression towards the end of the decade, with declining rural milk traffic, the shift of roadstone haulage to motor lorries and colliery closures in the local Somerset coalfield. To meet this threat, no fewer than five halts were opened on the line between 1923 and 1929, to generate more passenger traffic, the final one being that at Shoscombe. No less a dignitary than the MP George Lansbury, who went on to lead the Labour Party in 1932-35, opened the simple halt to great celebration on 23 September 1929. Two products of the SR's concrete works at Exmouth Junction in the form of 'harp and slab construction' formed the two platforms, which were devoid of buildings, merely containing integral concrete nameboards and ornate oil lamps. A path leading up from the platforms to the village had a small booking office and waiting room situated at its top. No goods facilities were ever provided.

Staffing throughout its 36 years of existence was undertaken by two sisters – the Misses Tapper, later Mrs Beeho and Mrs Chivers – who, according to Michael Williams in his book *The Trains Now Departed*, 'were always ready for a chinwag in the booking office, which they ran like a community centre.' The latter company servant resided in a railway bungalow built on the bed of the old Somerset Coal Canal, whose formation the railway had partially used in constructing the line between Midford and Radstock. The bungalow was apparently located on the site of a former row of shacks occupied by navvies who had built the line. The provision of the halt turned out to be well-founded as the railway proved very popular with the local populace, the majority of local trains calling there. It also outlasted the other four halts opened on the line in the 1920s.

A few weeks prior to closure of the line in 1966 a spartan 'emergency train service' was introduced, which necessitated the provision of a supplementary minibus to take Shoscombe residents into Bath. Once the trains had been withdrawn, a minibus continued to operate for a while from the village to the main road to connect with buses to Bath and Radstock. The concrete platforms and nameboards of the halt survived for a time after the track was removed and today there is nothing to show that a station – however tardily provided – ever served the village. One bus a week now serves Shoscombe!

The exterior of the small building provided at Portsmouth Arms station represents a timeless scene that was once common at rural stations throughout the country. The half-open Booking Office door, the green SR signboard, timetable poster and red mailbox all add to the interest of the composition.

75 PORTSMOUTH ARMS
Local hostelry

Portsmouth Arms is one of those stations, such as Berney Arms in Norfolk, Bronwydd Arms in Carmarthenshire and Jolly Sailor (later Norwood Junction) on the London & Croydon Railway, whose name arose from the presence of a nearby public house – in the case of Portsmouth Arms, one situated a couple of hundred yards down the road from the station.

Portsmouth Arms is a tiny village with just four dwellings, a sawmill, railway station, cottage and farm, and an inn that has a good reputation for excellent food. When the Exeter-Barnstaple railway was built the line passed through the Earl of Portsmouth's estate, in return for which he reserved the right to stop trains for the convenience of himself or his guests at any time. The local

pub's name reflected the importance to the local community of the Earl and his Eggesford estate. The 4th Earl was instrumental in the construction of the turnpike road, now the A377, down the Taw valley. The station opened on 1 August 1854 together with the line from Exeter to Barnstaple.

A simple two-platform affair with a passing loop 138 yards long and capable of holding twenty wagons or eight coaches, Portsmouth Arms station had a stone-built station building on the down platform that was to a standard LSWR design with a separate stationmaster's house. The down platform was considerably shorter than the up, and housed a waiting shelter. A postbox was located on the road side of the building and this was

A Barnstaple-bound three-car DMU slows for the Portsmouth Arms stop, but as was all too common the platform appears devoid of custom. The passing loop together with the signal box were taken out of use in April 1966; however, the typical SR concrete running-in boards remain.

This is the current provision at Portsmouth Arms, which sees just two trains each way daily.

The eponymous pub and its signboard.

somewhat unusually cleared by the late-turn signalman who padlocked the mailbag and forwarded it by an up mail train, thus allowing a much later postal collection than would be normal in such a rural spot.

The goods yard with its single siding was provided with a 5-ton crane, but no goods shed, as this was located on the up platform just beyond the waiting room. In the 1920s 5,000 tickets were regularly being sold each year as the station acted as a useful railhead for several surrounding villages such as Beaford, Chittlehamholt, Roborough and High Bickington. The premier train of the day, the 'Atlantic Coast Express', was not booked to stop, but often the presence of several 1st Class passengers travelling to neighbouring country seats resulted in an unscheduled halt.

By 2014/15 the 'ACE' was 50 years in the past and the unstaffed halt saw fewer than five passengers daily. The ten-lever signal box dated from 1873 but was taken out of use, together with the passing loop, in April 1966, the goods siding, which contained cattle pens and a loading gauge,

having closed in July 1961. The former stationmaster's house is now in private ownership. Recalling the days when the 'Devon Belle' passed through, two vintage Pullman coaches were for a while located on a short isolated piece of track adjacent to Portsmouth Arms station undergoing restoration; 'Aries' was built in 1952 and 'Formosa' in 1921, but the former left for the KESR in 2012.

Not only has the station seen better days, but Eggesford House and the rest of the estate was put up for auction by the 6th Earl in 1913 when the whole comprised 3,277 acres; this included 700 acres of woodland, several large farms, the Fox and Hounds hotel, numerous smallholdings and 6 miles of salmon and trout fishing. The estate was sold to a syndicate, but a year later was put up for auction again. The house was withdrawn from the sale and left empty, a condition in which it was to remain apart from a period in 1917 when it housed German prisoners of war in the former servants' quarters. Today it is a ruin, having been stripped of all useful materials.

Although long closed to passengers, by the time of this 1970s view the station building at Kemp Town continued to be used as coal offices while the platform areas provided storage for a brewery. An industrial estate now occupies the site.

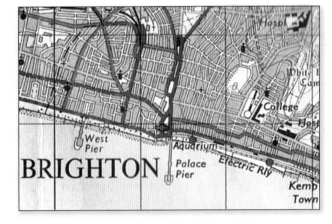

76 BRIGHTON KEMP TOWN
A casualty of bus competition

The closure of suburban stations with the rise of tram and bus services and of car ownership has been a common feature of railway services in many large towns and cities over the past 100 years. In some cases dedicated branch lines serving a city's suburbs were constructed, and these too have often suffered closure relatively early on in their existence. Such was the case with the Kemp Town branch serving the eastern side of the South Coast resort of Brighton.

Opened by the London, Brighton & South Coast Railway (LBSCR) in 1869, the 1 mile 32 chain branch involved acquiring some prime land, some expensive engineering works such as the fourteen-arch Lewes Road Viaduct, the three-arch Hartington Road Viaduct, embankments and a 1,024-yard tunnel. Costs for construction came to more than £100,000, a colossal sum for little over a mile of track.

A local entrepreneur and one-time joint Lord of the Manor, one Thomas Read Kemp, had promoted the development of the area named after him in the 1820s as a

London Brighton & South Coast Railway.

Newhaven Harbour to

Kemp Town

quality residential area laid out in the Regency style. Although building began in 1823, some houses remained untenanted 30 years later. Although on the face of it the railway company expressed a desire to serve this area and to promote tourist traffic, a significant factor in the construction of the branch was undoubtedly the wish by the LBSCR to keep out a competitive line endorsed by its rival, the London, Chatham & Dover Railway, which encouraged a local company to promote a route from Beckenham through East Grinstead into the heart of LBSCR territory at Kemp Town. This rivalry ensured that this fashionable suburb of Brighton received its very own terminus. Although close to the sea, the area did not develop a holiday trade of its own and most traffic was of a purely local nature into Brighton. An intensive push-pull service was provided that at its peak gave thirty-six trains daily.

A substantial terminus area was provided, with initially just one platform

Diesel shunter No D3669 was indulging in some shunting when captured on 3 April 1969. *CH Library, J. M. Tolson*

road, a short bay and run-round loop and four sidings in the goods yard, but there was scope to increase both the number of platforms and the area available for goods should traffic warrant. In the 1870s the surrounding area of chalk was excavated and additional sidings laid in, the majority of which lasted until the end of goods services 100 years later, together with a coal yard. The opening of two halts on the branch at Lewes Road and Hartington Road, the latter only operative between 1906 and 1911, did little to generate additional traffic and adversely affected journey times, which were already uncompetitive compared with the less circuitous route of the trams. Lasting damage to passenger numbers was done by the withdrawal of services temporarily as an economy measure during the First World War from January 1917 until September 1919. The former railway clientele having perforce transferred to trams found them more convenient for the relatively short distance involved.

Passenger services were withdrawn as early as January 1933, although Kemp Town continued to be served by goods trains until final closure in 1971. After closure to passengers the station terminal building served as a goods office, coal office and as residential accommodation. The whole site was subsequently redeveloped as an industrial estate, although the southern portal of what is now a bricked-up tunnel remains.

On 7 September 1955 Tidworth station plays host to '43xx' Class 2-6-0 No 5395, which is awaiting departure with its train of two coaches at the far end of the platform.
© www.railphotoprints.co.uk, Hugh Ballantyne

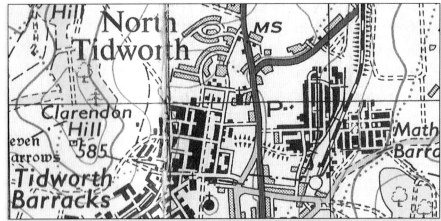

77 TIDWORTH
As you were!

Tidworth station and the 2½-mile branch to the Midland & South Western Junction Railway (MSWJR) main line at Ludgershall, comprising the Tidworth Camp Railway, were unusual in that they were built in 1900 by contractors working for the War Department. The workers travelled in what was optimistically known as the 'Workmen's Mail' consisting of open wagons hauled by contractors' small saddle tank locomotives.

Built originally as a military siding, it came into use in 1901 in response to the Boer War (1899-1901), conveying military stores, personnel and workers engaged in the construction of Tidworth Camp barracks. Tented summer camps had been held at Tidworth for up to 30,000 men prior to the building of permanent barracks. Bricks in their millions for the camp's construction came largely from Grafton, also on the MSWJR route.

The branch did not formally become a public railway until February 1903 when the MSWJR undertook to equip and operate the camp railway for public use on payment of rent to the War Department (WD). Such rent was set at 3% of the capital outlay, which worked out to some £1,400 per annum and was payable initially for a period of 14 years, although this was subsequently renewed at the end of this period. The branch was opened for goods traffic from July 1902 and for passengers the following October, remaining the property of the WD but in fact

As the county boundary runs through the platforms at Tidworth, this view from July 1963 is looking from Hampshire into Wiltshire, following track removal from the terminal portion of the station. The signal box and water columns remain in situ while adjacent to the goods shed is a line of wagons containing military vehicles. *Roger Holmes*

forming an integral part, and indeed the most profitable part, of the MSWJR. So profitable was it that Tidworth exceeded the takings from all other MSWJR stations combined. The line was double track from the junction at Ludgershall to the intermediate Perham signal box, and thence single track to the Tidworth terminus.

Gradients on the branch were gentle, with 1 in 90 being the steepest on the descent into Tidworth station, which sat astride the county boundary dividing Hampshire and Wiltshire. As at Ludgershall both of the platforms provided were very wide to assist in the embarkation and disembarkation of large numbers of troops. Water columns were sited on both platforms and a 26-lever signal box and goods shed and extensive sidings completed the facilities. These sidings could accommodate up to 290 wagons or ten twelve-coach trains. As might be expected, the branch was heavily used during both World Wars, and the annual Tidworth Tattoo was always popular and brought in many excursions. A further 2½ miles of track branched off from the line north

of the station into the camp, and this continued to be operated by the WD until closure in 1953.

September 1955 saw the withdrawal of passenger services over the branch, after which time the operation of the line to Ludgershall passed back into the hands of the WD, which continued to use it for military and goods traffic, although the final troop train ran in 1962. Final closure came to Tidworth in July 1963 and the line was cut back to Perham Yard.

A line is still operative today from the Defence Equipment & Support Rail & Container Terminal at MoD Ludgershall to Red Post Junction near Andover on the main line. Heavy equipment such as tanks is still occasionally conveyed for use on nearby Salisbury Plain. Town councillors from Andover and Ludgershall have recently proposed a £4 million scheme to reopen the Andover to Ludgershall rail line to serve the planned expansion of residential development in the area. Although Tidworth Camp continues in military use today, it is no longer served by its own branch railway.

Cliddesden is seen in 1938, six years after the final closure. The station building and level crossing gates remain in situ. *CH Library, S. Osborne*

78 CLIDDESDEN
Make up your mind!

Cliddesden was one of three intermediate stations on the route from Basingstoke to Alton, which opened in 1901. It had an uneventful existence for 15½ years until it closed at the end of 1916 as a wartime economy measure. The closure helped to overcome the shortage of staff on the LSWR caused by the wartime call-up and enabled the rails to be lifted for reuse on the Western Front in France. The LSWR provided a replacement lorry to cater for the district's goods traffic, mainly coal, milk and agricultural produce. Prior to closure the line had not been successful and had lost some £4,000 per annum.

In view of this, when the time came to review replacing the track in the post-war years, the Southern Railway, formed as part of the 1922 Grouping, was keen to avoid undertaking the task as it was felt that the losses would probably continue, or maybe escalate. A bill for abandonment was brought before Parliament in 1923. However, the SR had reckoned without strong opposition from local landowners, farmers, traders and public bodies, who organised a petition. The railway company was forced to relay the track, although this time without any passing loops or stationmaster posts, but it did manage to insert a provision that the continuation of services should be reviewed in 10 years' time. Reopening duly took place on 18 August 1924, but only three trains daily each way were provided, half of the 1914 level of service.

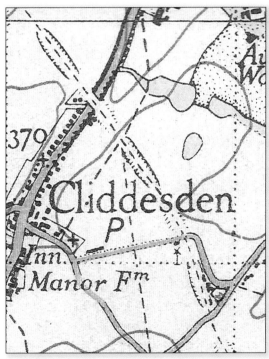

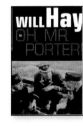

This passenger service lasted only eight years until September 1932, when it was withdrawn. Freight services continued on the section from Basingstoke to Bentworth, the penultimate station before Alton, until May 1936. The northern extremity of the line serving Thorneycroft's factory at Basingstoke remained in occasional use until 1967.

Cliddesden, a small village of fewer than 500 inhabitants, was served by a single-platform station with a building that was described disparagingly as 'most primitive, consisting of a little galvanised shanty divided into Booking Office and Waiting Room in neither of which is there room to swing a cat.' The residents of the

It is hard to believe that this overgrown platform is all that remains of Cliddesden (aka Buggleskelly).

village had made their views known at the enquiry into the provision of the line by the Light Railway Commissioners, stressing that they regarded a conveniently placed station as an indispensable condition of their assent to the application. In the event the railway company ignored their wishes and sited it 'at a point so distant from the village that it would be practically useless'. Although some slight adjustment in position was made, it was still far from ideal, being about 1½ miles from the village centre. As the *Hampshire Herald and Alton Gazette* of 8 June 1901 remarked:

> 'The man in the street expects to find the village somewhere near the station. But such little details do not trouble the promoters of railways who, if the station is somewhere in the parish named, are quite content to take the name which is generally associated with the village.'

The only dwellings near the station were houses for railway employees. A couple of sidings were provided and the level crossing gates were worked by hand, with ground frames for the points, there being no signal box.

A wind pump was sited adjacent to the line for pumping water to the station and cottages. Cliddesden station had at one time a telegraph office open to the public at train times, but this facility was discontinued upon initial closure of the line in 1916.

In the freight era just one train a day graced Cliddesden, which still had one staff member who featured in an article in the *Evening Standard* in 1932 when its reporter interviewed 'Lonely Bert of Cliddesden'. This was Bert White, who said, 'You are right – it's a dull life. No one to talk to, no tickets to clip, no trains to sing out the name of the station for.' A bus service was introduced shortly before passenger traffic ceased, but villagers had never seen their station as a useful means of travel, as witnessed by the fact that only three passengers had turned up to travel on the first train back in 1901.

Today, although it only served the travelling public for just 24 years, Cliddesden station lives on in the shape of 'Buggleskelly', for so it was named in the 1937 film 'Oh Mr Porter', the classic Will Hay comedy that featured the station prominently. Thus Cliddesden was an open and shut and open and shut case!

In 1936 it was decided to withdraw services north of Aylesbury. However, a limited service for war workers was reinstated in 1943, but this ceased in 1948. The track in the station remained in place as seen in this view of the former Metropolitan Railway platform at Verney Junction taken on 30 June 1963. *Ron Fisher*

79 VERNEY JUNCTION
Metropolitan outpost

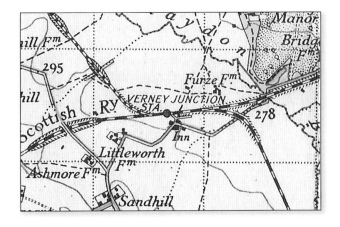

The first line to open on the site of what was later to become Verney Junction was that of the Buckinghamshire Railway, which opened a line from Bletchley to Banbury in 1850. This was followed by a line branching west to Oxford in 1851. No station opened at the meeting point of these two lines until 1868, when the single-track line of the Aylesbury & Buckingham Railway (A&BR) from Aylesbury reached the junction.

Verney Junction served a very remote spot with only a few dwellings nearby occupied by tenants of the Claydon House estate, owned by Sir Harry Verney, who was a major investor in, and sat on the board of, the A&BR. In the absence of a local settlement that could give its name to the station, it was decided to honour Sir Harry, who was later to have another nearby station, Calvert, named after him, having been born Harry Calvert.

Situated in the middle of a field with the only access being a narrow dirt track, traffic was initially virtually non-existent due to its isolated rural locality, but the Metropolitan Railway saw an opportunity for growth and absorbed the A&BR on 1 July 1891. Meanwhile Verney Junction became the largest intermediate station on the LNWR's Oxford-Bletchley line, boasting two platforms, one of which was an island. Initially there was merely a small building on the up platform with nothing provided on the island. After rebuilding, the station was given new longer platforms spanned by a lattice footbridge. The

outer face of the island was used by trains arriving from Quainton Road and London. A goods yard was also provided to the west of the station on the down side consisting of three sidings, one of which served a cattle dock and pens. A second signal box to the east of the station controlled access to the yard. Reflecting the railway company's optimism, even a station hotel was built nearby.

This was as far north as the dream of 'Metroland' – the marketing ploy developed by the Metropolitan Railway, which was able to buy large swathes of land for residential development adjoining its railway routes – would ever get. However, with the arrival of the Great Central Railway's London Extension at Quainton Road in 1899, Verney Junction's importance seemed to be enhanced.

A lingering reminder of the days when one could journey to town from the depths of rural Buckinghamshire.
Ron Fisher

The view from the front of a DMU coming off the Buckingham line and approaching Verney Junction in January 1964. *Ron Fisher*

The Metropolitan introduced a service of through trains between this rural Buckinghamshire outpost and Baker Street, perhaps more in expectation than in response to actual traffic requirements. A new Pullman service was even introduced in 1910 as part of a drive to attract 1st Class passengers. However, just three years after the absorption of the route into London Transport in 1933, the LPTB decided to discontinue its service beyond Aylesbury and in consequence passenger trains between Quainton Road and Verney Junction ceased on 6 July 1936. The line was then singled, with freight services continuing until 1947, when the route closed altogether. Verney Junction then relapsed into relative obscurity, being served only by trains on the 'Varsity Line' between Oxford and Cambridge until the section from Oxford to Bletchley closed in 1968. The track was then singled and 'mothballed', but one disused set of rails has remained through the overgrown platforms of the former station, whose buildings were demolished.

Even if the planned reopening of the Oxford-Bletchley route goes ahead, the isolated location of Verney Junction militates against the reopening of the station. The hopes of establishing the Metroland idyll in this outpost unfortunately came to nothing, but as John Betjeman remarked when closing his *Metroland* TV film of 1973, gazing over a deserted trackbed, 'Grass triumphs. And I must say I'm rather glad.'

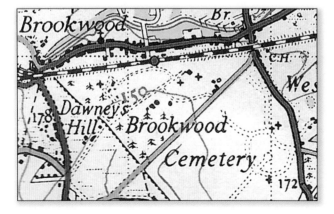

80 BROOKWOOD NECROPOLIS
A dead end

One of the more bizarre reasons for the provision of a railway station was in order to serve a burial ground. Such was the thinking behind the London Necropolis Company (LNC), which was established by Act of Parliament in 1852 as a reaction to the crisis caused by the banning of new burials in London's overcrowded graveyards the previous year. The LNC, which intended to establish a single cemetery large enough to accommodate all of London's future burials for the foreseeable future, recognised that the recent innovation of railway travel raised the possibility of conducting burials at some remove from heavily populated areas. The company therefore purchased a very large site at Brookwood in

The exterior of Brookwood station is seen in 2012.
Antony McCallum, licensed under the Wikipedia Creative Commons Attribution Share-alike Licence

Surrey, some 25 miles from the capital. When the cemetery opened in 1854 the nearest railway station was at Woking, 4 miles away; the tardy LSWR did not open its own station, Brookwood Necropolis on the main line adjacent to the cemetery, until almost ten years later in spite of previous verbal assurances.

The LNC ran its own trains from a terminus adjacent to Waterloo station using the LSWR main line as far as Brookwood where, after reversal, a track three-quarters of a mile in length branched off to the south-east to serve dedicated stations located within the cemetery. To prevent any abuse of monopoly power, an Act bound the LSWR to carry corpses and mourners to the cemetery in perpetuity and set a maximum tariff that could be levied on funeral traffic.

No 121 Westminster Bridge Road, near Waterloo station, is all that remains of the London terminus of the London Necropolis Railway station, whose platforms were bombed during the London Blitz and never reopened.
Wikipedia, licensed under GNU Free Documentation Licence

The Brotherhood House of St Edward the Martyr Monastery incorporates the remains of the South railway station within the cemetery. *Iridescent, licensed under the Wikipedia Creative Commons Attribution Share-alike Licence*

Two separate stations of similar design were provided within the cemetery itself, North station serving the Nonconformist section of the cemetery and South station the Anglican section. Each station consisted of a range of single-storey buildings constructed around a square courtyard, with the side adjacent to the railway left open. Two wings extended parallel to the platform edge with a large roof overhang on the platform side. Although platform faces were built of brick, as were the chimneys and foundations, the station buildings themselves were only of battened wood construction as it was felt that the company should gain experience of the most suitable type of accommodation to be provided before committing itself to anything more permanent. In fact, the buildings were never replaced.

Each station had 1st Class and ordinary reception rooms for mourners, a 1st Class and an ordinary refreshment room, a set of apartments for LNC staff and a chaplain's room. Somewhat surprisingly, both cemetery stations included licensed premises, and visitors to these bars would see notices stating 'Spirits served here'! To enhance the view for visitors arriving by train, the areas around the stations and their associated chapels were planted with attractive groves of trees and bushes. A dip in the platform edge facilitated the unloading of coffins from hearse vans. A siding adjacent to the LNC masonry works was laid in together with an unloading platform and a water tower to enable locomotives to replenish their supply before returning to the capital. Trains ran once daily, assuming funerals were booked to take place, but after about 1900 they operated largely on an 'as required' basis.

By the 1930s the trains were running only a couple of times a week, the volume of burials never having reached the expected levels. The London terminus of the LNC, which had relocated a couple of times from its original site adjacent to Waterloo station, was severely damaged by bombing during the Second World War. After the war the LNC decided that the service was no longer viable and the track in the cemetery, the condition of which was giving concern, having been laid on the very sandy soil of the area and providing a poor foundation for the ballast, was removed in about 1947/48. Both stations were converted to bars to serve visiting mourners, although North station was demolished in the 1960s due to dry rot, and South station survived until it was closed in about 1967. Much of the building burned down in September 1972 and although there were hopes of restoration the remainder was subsequently demolished. However, the platforms and funeral chapels associated with both stations still survive today.

The land for the LSWR's Brookwood Necropolis station was provided by the LNC, which also built the stationmaster's house and the station approach roads. The LSWR constructed the station building, goods yard and a new siding into the cemetery, which included a run-round loop. Opening on 1 June 1864, the station building was extended in 1900 and a footbridge added. With the quadrupling of the main line in 1903, the down platform was demolished and the short-lived footbridge removed to make way for a new down platform with waiting room. A subway replaced the footbridge and the buildings on the up platform were also extended. In the early 1900s a short siding, known as Masonry Works siding, for the reception of tombstones and memorials, was added halfway along the cemetery branch.

Pneumatic signalling between Woking and Basingstoke was provided between 1904 and 1907, and a new signal box opened to replace the previous Brookwood East manual signal box. Today plain Brookwood station, the 'Necropolis' suffix having been dropped probably in the 1920s, lies in the heart of commuterland and many of the million or so passengers who rush through its doors annually are doubtless unaware of its rather more sedate history.

81 FARRINGTON GURNEY
A pie, a pint and a ticket

There was nothing too remarkable about this small halt on the Frome-Bristol line until you considered its rather unusual ticket office. Other small halts often had their own idiosyncratic ticket facilities, such as Dilton Marsh near Westbury, where signs directed intending passengers to 'Holmdale, seventh house up the hill' where a Mrs H. Roberts had sold tickets from her home on a commission basis since 1947. At Appleford near Oxford, tickets could be obtained from the local Post Office. At Farrington Gurney Halt, which was never staffed and had opened in 1927 in response to local demand, the adjacent pub The Miners Arms had a small window underneath a water tank at the rear of the pub displaying the notice: 'GWR Farrington Gurney. Passengers requiring Tickets up to 7.0pm on Weekdays are requested to Ring the Bell. After that time, and on Sundays, Passengers without Tickets should notify the Guard on joining the Train.' Whether the pub did a good trade in beverage sales to intending passengers is not recorded, but it was certainly an opportunity to buy a ticket, a pie and a pint as there was often a long interval between the sparse service offered on this route! In BR days the wording on the sign remained the same but 'GWR' was replaced by 'British Railways'. The 7.00pm limit was not dictated so much by the fact that the pub would undoubtedly be busier in the evening and therefore the landlord would be less inclined to serve rail passengers, but more by the timetable reality that it was only on Saturdays that there was a train scheduled after that time.

The platform only contained a seat, a small wooden shelter and a nameboard, although after closure to passengers in 1959 these items disappeared and the line played host to freight traffic only until it was breached by flooding near Pensford in July 1968. Following closure to freight the track was removed together with the overbridge to the north of the former halt; the road was straightened and the cutting infilled in the mid-1970s, so covering all traces of the platform.

Today The Miners Arms trades as Spice Dunes, an Indian restaurant, so I suppose if the railway had still been running one might have had a lager, a 'Ruby Murray' and a ticket! The small window in the side of building remains, having been restored in 1985 as part of the 'GWR 150' celebrations, although the sign is a reproduction of the original.

BRITISH RAILWAYS.
(FARRINGTON GURNEY.)
Passengers requiring Tickets
up to 7·0 P.M. on Weekdays,
are requested to Ring the Bell.
After that time, and on
Sundays, Passengers without
Tickets should notify the Guard
on joining the Train.

Farrington Gurney Halt is seen in June 1959, looking south-east. *Rail Photoprints*

There are still some unusual ticket offices on the network today, for example that at Ledbury, where ticket sales are done privately from a wooden chalet by the station entrance. Action for Rail has drawn attention to the current Government thinking that in future the majority of travellers will either buy tickets online or at automatic ticket machines, thus the plan is to close or greatly reduce the opening hours of up to 50% of the current number of offices.

Opposite: The famous noticeboard at Farrington Gurney attached to the side of The Miners Arms public house adjacent to the halt. *Rail Photoprints*

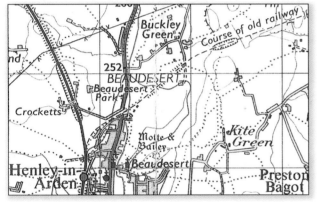

82 HENLEY-IN-ARDEN
A better proposition

The attractive station at Henley-in-Arden is complete with its running-in board in GWR colours and decorative flower borders.

In 1908 a completely new link was constructed from Bearley Junction near Stratford-upon-Avon to Birmingham. Known as the North Warwickshire line, it was part of the GWR's route from Birmingham to Cheltenham, Bristol and the South West, and rendered Henley-in-Arden's original railway, a branch line from Rowington Junction 1 mile south of Lapworth on the GWR's main line from London to Birmingham, somewhat superfluous. A direct train was always going to be preferable to the alternative of taking a branch-line train, with the necessity of changing at the junction.

Plans for a branch line to Henley were laid as far back as 1860, when construction began, but it was to take another 34 years before the single-platform terminus at Henley opened in 1894. It was to have a relatively short life, being closed to passengers with the opening of the new line when services were diverted into the new station via a 50-chain spur line connecting the two railways. However, services from Lapworth continued for several years, routed into the new station, until withdrawal of trains in March 1915; goods traffic continued until the following year, and formal closure of the branch came in January 1917. Track was lifted that year and was destined for the battlefields of France; however, it never got there as the ship carrying the rails was sunk in the Channel. The original terminus station was converted into accommodation for the stationmaster, while the goods yard and shed continued to be used as the town's goods depot until 1962, being accessed from the new line.

The new station at Henley, one of the more prestigious buildings on the line, had three platforms, one of which was for trains terminating from Birmingham and, for a short period, terminating services from the old branch line. Today the station is unstaffed with only two of the three platforms in use. Although the original station building with canopy remains in situ on one platform, it is now boarded up. The footbridge originally provided was dismantled, being replaced by a modern lift-equipped structure; the old bridge was donated to the preserved Gloucestershire Warwickshire Steam Railway for its Broadway extension. However, the old-style running-in boards have been retained and the platforms adorned with floral displays to brighten up the scene.

Trains currently run from Stratford to Stourbridge Junction at generally hourly intervals. This is a far cry from the heady days of the 1950s when three or four through

The nameboard in GWR colours together with the roses climbing the fence make for an attractive scene.

expresses passed through Henley from the Midlands to the South West, the main one being the daily 'Cornishman' from Wolverhampton to Penzance. At least the line has survived, with closure attempts having been made in the 1960s and again in the 1980s, and it is now marketed as the 'Shakespeare Route'.

The first station to serve Henley subsequently served in a goods-only capacity. In this undated view vegetation is slowly taking over, although there is evidence of activity at the goods shed in the distance. *CH Library*

83 MARGATE SANDS
On the beach

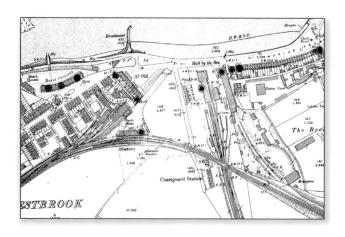

It is unusual to find a railway station situated virtually on the beach of a seaside town, but this is what happened in the case of the popular Kent resort of Margate. Between 1846 and 1863 it was to be the only railway serving the town, whose firm smooth sands had transformed the small fishing village into a resort particularly favoured by Cockneys. By the middle of the 19th century Londoners were pouring into the town in their thousands by both train and by coastal steamer. Although eclipsed by Ramsgate, which prided itself on catering for the more discerning visitor, Margate continued to supply a demand from the working classes.

The single-track South Eastern Railway (SER) branch from Ramsgate was not doubled until 1863, when a triangular junction at St Lawrence was also completed, thus removing the need for Margate trains to reverse at Ramsgate. The Kent Coast Railway, which although nominally independent was in fact worked by the London, Chatham & Dover Railway (LC&DR), reached the town from Herne Bay in 1863.

The impressive SER station building, which faced onto Marine Parade, had an overall roof spanning the two tracks and platforms with arched side walls. There was also a bay platform and goods shed to one side, and in 1893 a cattle dock and siding were added. Originally known as plain 'Margate', the suffix 'Sands' was added in 1899 soon after the SER and LC&DR combined to form the South Eastern & Chatham Railway. Not content with one station on the beach, a second, albeit short-lived, terminus was opened by the Kent Coast Railway when its Ramsgate line opened. It left the line east of the main Margate KCR station, later to be named 'West', terminating on the seafront, with the SER terminus immediately to the west.

However, it seems to have been something of a white elephant and the decision was taken to concentrate attention on the main KCR station built on the through line to Ramsgate. Royal Assent to commence the running of

scheduled services along the short spur into the enclosed LC&DR terminus was not given, the track was quickly lifted and the embankment became a feature of Margate's Pleasure Gardens, while the station building became a dance hall and restaurant known as 'The Hall by the Sea', both of which became part of the Dreamland complex, the station building being replaced by the Dreamland Cinema in the 1930s.

At the Grouping the Southern Railway, inheriting two lines serving Margate, decided to rationalise the situation and the Sands branch closed in 1926. This was a logical step as Sands station was little more than 200 yards from Margate West station, and in any event lay at the end of a rather circuitous route from London via Ramsgate. Even though the triangle had been installed at St Lawrence, it was in fact lightly used by passenger services as Margate was an important intermediate traffic centre and warranted the stopping of the majority of services to and from the seaside town. The area leading to the Sands station became a car park, although the station building survived as a cafe and Casino Ballroom for many years, being in a prime location on the seafront. A section of the branch remained to serve as a loop and headshunt for the new goods yard developed on part of the formation and this remained operative until November 1972, being latterly used only for coal traffic. The former station site was redeveloped in the 1960s with flats and an amusement arcade.

This postcard view of the Lifeboatman's Monument at Margate conveniently shows the former Margate Sands station in the background.

84 BOX
Stopping the stoppers

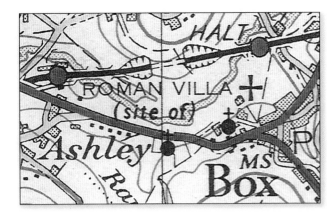

The small village of Box just to the east of Bath could boast two railway facilities, Box station itself, which opened with the line in 1841, together with the small halt of Mill Lane, which was more convenient for the village and opened in 1930. Both were located near the famous Box Tunnel, 1.83 miles (2.95km) in length, which opened in 1841. It had been considered an impossible and dangerous engineering project due to its length and the difficult underlying strata being Great Oolite at the surface with Fuller's earth, Inferior Oolite and Bridport sand beneath, a combination dreaded by tunnellers at the time. At the Box end was a grand classical portal designed by Brunel. The Rev W. Awdry, of 'Thomas the Tank Engine' fame, lived for a time in the 1920s at 'Journey's End', a house just 200 yards from the mouth of the tunnel, and the sound of locomotives working hard and whistling codes to each other no doubt inspired his writing. Recently the track level has been lowered to enable wiring to be installed for the London-Bristol-South Wales electrification project.

The main station building, which was originally of timber construction, was replaced in about 1855 by one in stone in the Brunellian 'chalet style' with a hipped roof. This was located on the down platform at Box as most of the traffic was towards Bath. A shelter was subsequently added to the up platform and a covered footbridge was provided; a single-road engine shed was also located here until closure in February 1919, together with banking engines to assist heavy freight trains up the gradient into the tunnel. A goods shed and 6-ton crane were provided in the goods yard, which closed in June 1963. In years gone by some intriguing items were shipped in and out of Box, including tennis balls from Price's rubber works, and bicycles for the use of staff at the nearby RAF Colerne, where they were used by aircraft crews to reach the dispersal areas. The signal box carried the rather apt name 'Box Signal Box' and was in use from 1898 until 1964.

Closure to passengers came on 4 January 1965 when local stopping services between Bath and Swindon were withdrawn, resulting in the closure of not only the two Box stations but also Bathford, Corsham, Christian Malford and Wootton Bassett stations. As late as 1960 some nine people were still employed in the Traffic Department of the railway here, either at the station, goods shed or in the signal box, and more than 13,000 passengers were using the station annually.

A major strand of the Beeching Report was not merely branch-line closures, which tended to grab the headlines, but the withdrawal of local stopping trains, which were considered to be big loss-makers. Such withdrawals resulted in the closure of many wayside stations on lines that remained open for faster limited-stop services. A frequent bus service from Box into Bath, which had begun in 1905, helped to seal the fate of the rail service here, which by 1964 was down to just six trains daily into Bath, generally at commuter times, with a similar number to Chippenham and/or Swindon. Box was thus typical of many less well-patronised wayside stations that suffered from the drastic cuts following the publication of the Beeching Report in 1963.

On the penultimate day of local trains serving intermediate stations between Bristol and Swindon, 1 January 1965, a Class 116 DMU forming the 10.15 Swindon-Bristol local service slows to pick up the sole passenger from Box station. © www.railphotoprints.co.uk, Hugh Ballantyne

Ivatt Class 2 2-6-0 No 46506 passes Westmoor Flag Station with the 12.42pm Hereford-Three Cocks Junction service on 6 June 1960.
© *www.railphotoprints.co.uk, Hugh Ballantyne*

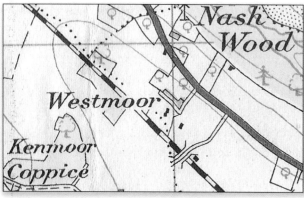

85 WESTMOOR FLAG STATION
Flagging down the train

The necessity of signalling trains to stop at minor stations was a not uncommon feature on the early railway system. On the Hereford, Hay and Brecon route, opened to Brecon in 1864, Moorhampton and Westmoor stations were both located on the Foxley estate of the Davenport family. Moorhampton served the village and catered for the estate's goods traffic, while Westmoor served as a private station for the Davenport family and

the adjacent hotel. In view of its prestigious position, Westmoor was the only brick-built station on the line between Hereford and Three Cocks, the others being constructed of timber, and it later became referred to as a 'flag station'. When a train was required to stop at Westmoor the stationmaster hung a flag in a prominent position in order that the locomotive crew could see it in time for them to stop at the short platform provided.

The diarist Francis Kilvert was a frequent traveller on the line from Hereford to Hay. He entered the Anglican church and became a rural curate working primarily in the local area, and is perhaps best known as the author of his voluminous diaries describing rural life. In 1877 he became vicar of Bredwardine, moving in the social circle of the Palmers of Eardisley, the Cornewalls of Moccas and the Davenports of Foxley. No doubt he would have used Westmoor on occasion when visiting the Davenports. The pages of his diary are full of 'squarsons', that peculiarly English combination of parson and squire.

Westmoor flag station and station house were constructed in about 1863 from brick with a tiled roof. It is listed Grade II and described in the listing as follows:

'The house is irregular in plan and aligned roughly north-west to south-east. The building is of two storeys. The south-west elevation has two round-headed glazing bar sashes to the left in front of which is a loggia with three round arches and imposts. Behind the arches are more sashes and an entrance. To the right of the loggia is an advanced two-storey block with a two-light sash under cambered head to the ground floor, blind first floor opening, two plat bands and mono-pitched roof with panelled stack. The platform to front is ramped to either side and rock-faced in coursed sandstone.'

Located at 6 miles 66 chains from Hereford, the station was served by only a handful of trains daily as passengers were never particularly numerous on the line, through freight being the mainstay of the traffic. One of the more unusual items passing through towards the end of goods services were tanks of liquid ammonia from Dowlais to Haverton Hill, worked over the Brecon & Merthyr line. Latterly only two stations on the line had stationmasters, Eardisley and Hay, the remainder being staffed by porters under their supervision.

After nationalisation this former Midland Railway line remained under the Midland Region, but control passed to the Western Region in April 1950. The station did not appear in the public timetable.

Foxley had been home to Sir Uvedale Price (1747-1829), a leading proponent of the 'picturesque' vogue in landscape design, and the surrounding wooded valley landscape was modified to reflect his views, being much visited and admired. In 1855 the Foxley estate was sold to John Davenport of Westwood (Staffs), elder son of a china manufacturing family. He died in 1862 and was succeeded by his second son, the Rev George Horatio Davenport MA JP, who was involved in the local railway developments. He was also Lord of the Manor of Yazor and twice vicar of Yazor and vicar of Mansell Lacy. A US/Canadian camp was located in the grounds of Foxley during the Second World War, and two American hospitals were based there.

The stately home was sadly demolished in 1949, but the station house at Westmoor Flag Station lives on in residential use, although the trains are long gone, the line having closed at the end of 1962.

86 ALTNABREAC
In the middle of nowhere

The question most often asked about this station is why is it there at all. Altnabreac, derived from the Gaelic Allt nam Breac, is an extremely small settlement lying within the former county of Caithness in the far north of Scotland in what is today the Highland council region. The settlement, whose main claim to fame lies in its remoteness, consists merely of the railway station, a former school that had but one teacher and closed in 1986 to be converted into a dwelling the following year, a former gamekeeper's house adjacent to the school house and station, and a couple of deserted cottages now used as barns. The school once provided some regular railway customers in the form of pupils travelling by train.

During the 1980s peat banks were worked to provide fuel for residents who were regularly cut off from the nearest sizeable town, Thurso, during the winter months. Even today the settlement, such as it is, can only be approached by train or along unsurfaced Forestry Commission roads from Westerdale, the nearest village, some 12 miles distant.

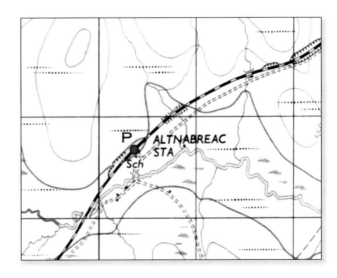

Altnabreac station is situated on the Far North line some 9 miles from Scotscalder station to the north and 8¼ miles from Forsinard station to the south. The station was opened by the Sutherland & Caithness Railway in July 1874, which was later absorbed by the Highland Railway. Looking at the map one can appreciate its isolation, which begs the question why have a station here at all serving

The lonely stopping place of Altnabreac is seen on 27 May 1979, with a water tank, bagless water crane and a solitary van. *RCTS photographic archive*

such a miniscule local population? It might be thought that its provision was a concession to a local landowner to allow him and his guests access to the Lochdhu Hotel, located a mile to the south; however, this theory does not stand up as the hotel was not constructed until 1895, 21 years after the station. At one time the owner of the Lochdhu estate was none other than Sir Archibald Sinclair, 1st Viscount Thurso, and Secretary of State for Air during the Second World War and commemorated in the name of Bulleid 'Pacific' locomotive No 34059.

The answer may lie in the distances between the neighbouring stations, leading one to speculate that the purpose of the station was purely operational, breaking up as it did a long section of single track. Altnabreac did originally have two platforms, a passing loop, a signal box, sidings and a water tower for replenishing the tenders of thirsty locomotives toiling over the line's gradients. Station staff included a stationmaster, porter and several permanent way men who were based here. The passing loop has since been removed, as have the

signal box and station staff, and today just one platform is in use and all services, of which there are four northbound and three southbound daily and one on Sundays each way, pick up or set down on request. However, the station does boast a newly constructed shelter, a seat, cycle rack, help point, and a public telephone together with a useful Onward Travel information board that tells the traveller that the nearest taxi rank is in Halkirk – what it omits to say is that this is a mere 16 miles away!

Some years ago there was a proposal that could have seen nuclear waste trains coming to Altnabreac, which, because of its isolation, was being considered as a final repository for the UK's nuclear waste. After exposure by a national newspaper, the plan was hastily abandoned and today Altnabreac slumbers on, visited by the occasional cyclist, hiker and of course hordes of midges in the season. Passenger figures for 2014/15 revealed that 240 passengers used the station in that period.

87 FAWLEY
Oiling the wheels of industry

A long time in its gestation, the branch line from Totton to Fawley alongside Southampton Water needed the impetus provided by the establishment of an oil refinery to see plans turned into reality. The first scheme for a railway in the area dated from as far back as 1860, but it was to take 65 years before Fawley finally saw a train when the line opened for business in July 1925 under the terms of a Light Railway Order, which had been sought some 22 years before.

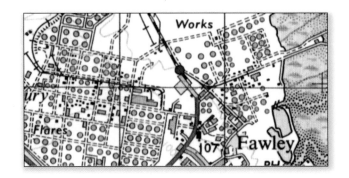

After withdrawal of the passenger service, the station and signal box remained intact for some time before demolition. They are seen here in the 1970s.

In the 19th century there had been plans for a railway line to Stone Point, situated south of Fawley, to link up with a proposed Solent Tunnel joining the mainland to the Isle of Wight. This scheme faded away and by the early 20th century it appeared that a railway-operated bus service might be sufficient for local transport needs to this largely agricultural area, but even this suffered from poor patronage and had been withdrawn by 1908. However, construction of an oil refinery in 1920/21 by the Anglo Gulf West Indies Petroleum Corporation Ltd was to change the Fawley area forever and to make the viability of a railway much more attractive. Even so, once more passenger traffic was to prove disappointingly light and it was to be oil traffic that proved to be not only the spur for the opening of the route but the reason for its long-term survival into the 21st century, 50 years after passenger services were withdrawn.

Although not slated for closure in the Beeching Report, proposals were put forward by the Southern Region to close the line to passengers, which it duly did in February 1966. By the end there were only two services daily southbound and three northbound, mainly for the benefit of oil refinery workers and commuters into Southampton. Withdrawal of goods services followed in January 1967, leaving only oil trains operating along the 9½-mile branch.

A clinker-surfaced single platform sufficed at Fawley with a pebble-dashed station building. A signal box and

goods shed and a 'parachute' water tank supplied locomotives' needs. An extensive layout of sidings was provided to serve the refinery, which is the largest facility of its type in the UK.

Concrete running-in boards and the platform are all that survive at the location today, which has been subsumed into the refinery complex. This does militate against any reopening of the line to passengers as a new station would have to be built outside the refinery limits. Such a reopening was seriously mooted back in 2009 when ATOC (Association of Train Operating Companies) published a report indicating that the reopening of the branch certainly as far as Hythe, to serve the village of the same name north of Fawley, would be viable. Any extension south of Hythe would not be part of the initial proposal, but could form part of any subsequent plans. However, in January 2014 Hampshire County Council decided against progressing the project, citing a perceived poor value for money business case together with concerns that the costs required to support the rail link might result in the reduction of support for the existing Southampton to Hythe ferry and for local bus services.

Thus the line south of Marchwood, which saw occasional freight trains until recent years, lies in limbo and Fawley station slumbers on awaiting a reawakening that may now never come. Rail-borne oil traffic is also now dead, the last outgoing train, comprising empty tanker wagons, having run on 5 September 2016.

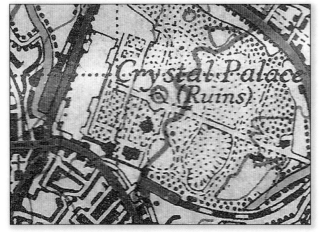

88 CRYSTAL PALACE HIGH LEVEL
Not such a great exhibition

The transfer of Joseph Paxton's Crystal Palace, erected in Hyde Park for the 1851 Great Exhibition, to a site in Penge took place in 1854. The West End of London & Crystal Palace Railway (WEL&CPR) wasted no time in opening a line to take advantage of the crowds that were anticipated to visit the relocated Palace. August 1865 saw a second route opened, courtesy of the Crystal Palace & South London Junction Railway (CPSLJR). To differentiate between the two stations, the earlier one, which became part of the LBSCR empire, became known as Low Level while the later facility, which was absorbed into the SECR, the great rival of the LBSCR, became High Level.

The CPSLJR obviously felt that a suitably impressive station building was called for, to complement the

There are EMUs aplenty in this 29 April 1969 view of the High Level station at Crystal Palace. *CH Library, J. Scrace*

architectural splendour of the adjacent Crystal Palace, and some £100,000 was spent on the splendid terminus. It was a classic example of Victorian architecture with lofty terracotta and red brick end and side walls and a lofty glass and iron trainshed roof. Square towers topped with four short spires were added at each corner and the station was divided longitudinally by a series of brick arches with a passenger concourse above the tracks at each end. It was estimated that some 7,000-8,000 passengers per hour could be handled.

Four tracks entered the station through narrow openings at the north end and these were served by two wooden platforms in each half of the station. The two inner lines had platform faces on both sides to speed the loading and unloading of the expected crowds. At the far end the tracks passed through the end walls via a second series of narrow openings to a turntable, allowing locomotives to run round speedily and thus avoid delays. One half of the station was intended for the exclusive use of 1st Class passengers, who were given segregated access at the north end with the benefit of a refreshment room at first-floor level. A subway consisting of a wide vaulted and tiled chamber under Crystal Palace Parade linked the station directly with the Palace. This subway, apparently built by Italian crypt-builders, was on a similar grand scale to the station with its roof being supported by a series of octagonal pillars of red and cream brick interlaced with stone ribs. Nine sidings were provided to cater for expected goods traffic and to stable additional locomotives and carriages that could be called upon when required to move large crowds away from the station after special events.

After initially attracting the crowds, unfortunately in the longer term the line never fulfilled its potential; although the opening of the Palace had encouraged the development of the local area as a quality middle-class suburb, the Palace itself was very much in decline. In 1866 a fire destroyed the north transept and it was never rebuilt; strong opposition to Sunday opening further damaged its commercial prospects. By 1900 it was viewed very much as yesterday's attraction, with extensive repairs being required, and it even suffered the indignity of being divided up into booths and stalls, making the whole place look down-at-heel.

A renaming of the station in 1898 to Crystal Palace High Level & Upper Norwood did little to address the decline in passenger numbers, nor did subsequent electrification in July 1925. Periods of closure of the line during both World Wars did little to encourage continuity of travel habits, and after 1945 the station took on a very run-down appearance, as much of the glass trainshed roof, which had been damaged during bombing raids on the capital, was never repaired. Consequently rain gained easy access to the station below and badly affected the timber platforms, which were soon covered with mould and vegetation, and there was an accompanying rat infestation. By the end only one platform was in use; the northern stairs, concourse and booking office had all being abandoned to the weather, while those at the other and were little used outside peak hours. Safety nets were draped from the roof to protect passengers from falling debris.

The finale, one of the very few examples of an electrified line in the London area being closed, came in September 1954 and at a time when off-peak trains were only carrying an average of four passengers. This once fine terminus thus met a sad end, with demolition in 1961. Housing now covers much of the site, but the glorious subway still exists and is occasionally open for viewing.

The provision of a second station was always questionable on purely economic grounds, and traffic on the new High Level line never lived up to expectations, for once the Crystal Palace had been destroyed by fire in 1936 the unnecessary duplication of a rail facility became even more obvious. Although the station was better sited than its rival, the branch had really come too late to compete with the LBSCR station, which remains open today. In 2013 a Chinese developer hoped to rebuild the Crystal Palace, but his exclusivity agreement with Bromley Council to develop his plans was cancelled when it expired in February 2015, so a renaissance now seems unlikely.

89 THE HAWTHORNS
Up the Baggies!

There were several railway stations that originated to serve sporting venues throughout the country, with their fortunes as mixed as the clubs they served. One thinks of Ashton Gate Platform, now closed, which once served fans of Bristol City FC, Old Trafford Halt, also known as Manchester United FC Halt for the club of the same name, and Ramsline Halt, previously known as Baseball Ground Halt, which was a single-platform station opened in 1990 to serve the former home of Derby County FC. The station cost £26,000 to build, but in 1997 Derby County moved to a new stadium and the halt closed. Exeter's Lion's Holt Halt opened in 1906 but changed its name to St James Park in 1946, that being the name of Exeter City FC's adjacent ground. The club has since adopted the station under the community railways scheme and today contributes to its upkeep. Curiously, furious sports fans have been banned from using Coventry City's new £5 million Ricoh Arena railway station ostensibly because the trains serving it are too small, the hourly service only being capable of carrying 75 passengers. Thus the station has been ordered to shut for 60 minutes after matches finish due to safety concerns. Boothferry Park served Hull FC's ground and provided a dedicated match day service until it closed for safety reasons in 1986.

However, one station serving a football ground that has seen a rebirth in recent years is The Hawthorns next to West Bromwich Albion FC's ground. The Hawthorns, which has been the home of the club since 1900, was sited on the old Hawthorns Estate; apparently hawthorn bushes had grown there in the past, and the name stuck.

The Hawthorns Halt was a late-comer to the region's rail scene, not opening until 1931 on the former GWR line from Birmingham Snow Hill to Wolverhampton Low Level. Catering for football specials, it had minimal facilities and consisted of three wooden platforms. It closed in 1968 although a skeletal passenger service continued to pass through until 1972, when trains between Birmingham Snow Hill, Wolverhampton Low Level and Langley Green were withdrawn. The line subsequently remained open for the occasional freight train to Coopers Metals scrapyard at Handsworth. Albright & Wilson's chemical works and Blue Circle Cement, both at Handsworth, were also served. However, it looked as though this had effectively disappeared as a passenger route for ever.

The present station, which opened in 1995 as part of the 'Jewellery Line' project to restore services to Snow Hill station and to relieve congestion at New Street, was built partly on the site of the old halt. This time, however, it opened as a fully fledged station with regular services on the cross-city Snow Hill lines, and in 1999 the Midland Metro tram line opened between Birmingham and Wolverhampton, adding two tram platforms alongside the two railway platforms. The current service frequency is approximately every 10 minutes, with extra trains laid on for match days. The trams operate every 6 to 8 minutes, thus giving The Hawthorns by far the best service it has ever enjoyed.

Following the 1995 reopening of the line, providing a service between Birmingham's regenerated Snow Hill station and the Kidderminster line, the Midland Metro arrived in 1999 with a tram service between Birmingham and Wolverhampton, the tram stop being visible in the foreground. *Stephen McKay, licensed under the Wikipedia Creative Commons Attribution Share-alike Licence*

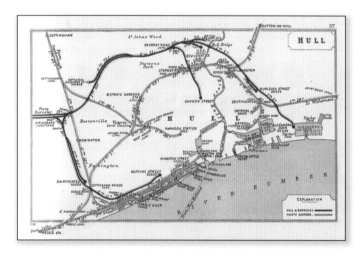

90 HULL CORPORATION PIER

A station without trains

Like its more famous counterpart at Dartmouth, Hull's Corporation Pier station was one of the very few in Britain where you could purchase a railway ticket but where there were no trains. An intervening stretch of water was the reason for the lack of railway tracks in both cases. The River Dart separates Dartmouth station from its nearest railway, situated on the opposite bank of the river at Kingswear, while in the case of Hull the River Humber separated the town from the railway station on the south bank at New Holland Pier.

Kingston-upon-Hull's railway system was pretty well sewn up by the North Eastern Railway and the Hull & Barnsley Railway, whose plethora of lines are shown on the accompanying railway junction diagram. The forerunner of the Great Central Railway, the Manchester, Sheffield & Lincolnshire Railway, was unable to gain access to Hull, but saw an opportunity to serve the city by the back door via its line from Grimsby to New Holland Pier, which opened in March 1848. This dovetailed with a ferry service from New Holland Pier to Hull Corporation Pier using the MS&LR's own fleet of steamers. Corporation Pier station acted as a booking office and waiting room for the ferry service. The first MS&LR offices in Hull, at Walkington's Lodgings, were purchased in January 1849 for £850. The company's offices moved in August that year to 7 Nelson Street, a building that also contained the living quarters for the clerk in charge. These offices expanded into the adjacent building in May 1854 and both were enlarged in 1880 to form the present building.

Following a visit by Queen Victoria in October 1854, during which she sailed from Corporation Pier to Grimsby, the pier was renamed Hull Victoria Pier in her honour; although the new name was generally applied to the pier, it never found favour with the locals, and was always known as Corporation Pier station. The ferry service continued in railway ownership, passing to the LNER and thence to BR, under the Sealink banner, and details of the ferry were included in the railway timetable headed 'Cleethorpes, Grimsby, New Holland & Hull'.

A floating pontoon was added to the pier in 1877 and replaced in the 1930s. The station building itself and maps, tickets and timetables always referred to it as Corporation Pier until its closure and withdrawal of the ferry service, which took place on 25 June 1981 after more than a century of service, consequent upon the

The frontage of Hull's Corporation Pier station is seen in October 1974. *George Woods*

The PS *Lincoln Castle* was a long-term resident on the River Humber ferry crossing from Hull to Barton-on-Humber. She was the last coal-fired paddle steamer still in regular service in the UK when withdrawn from the route in 1978. *George Woods*

opening of the Humber road bridge. The ferries were one of the last bastions of the paddle steamer, several being used including the PS *Lincoln Castle* and PS *Wingfield Castle*. In 1968 there was a brief ferry service from Grimsby to Hull using hovercraft, but they were unable to cope with the vagaries of the River Humber.

Following closure, the station stood empty for many years but was subsequently converted into apartments. The MS&LR trefoil device and construction date are still in place at the top of the building, but the stone band above the lower windows that originally carried the

lettering 'MANCHESTER, SHEFFIELD & LINCOLNSHIRE RAILWAY' in relief was removed many years ago. A blue plaque commemorates the Humber Ferry, stating that:

'A ferry between Hull and Lincolnshire was first recorded in 1315. The Humber ferry operated between here and New Holland from 1825 (prior to the coming of the railway to that town) until the completion of the Humber Bridge in 1981.'

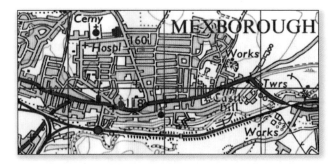

91 MEXBOROUGH
Moving along

The former mining town of Mexborough in South Yorkshire saw its original station move some 600 metres east as the original station located at Mexborough Junction, opened by the South Yorkshire Railway in January 1850, did not serve the line to Rotherham and Sheffield when this opened in 1871. The old station, which was some distance from the town centre, was replaced by a new structure immediately on the Doncaster side of the junction, approximately halfway between the old junction station and the halt located at Mexborough (Ferry Boat); this new station was in a much better position to serve the town centre. In June 1874 the third side of the triangle was installed, which allowed trains to work from the Sheffield line direct to Barnsley without the need for reversal.

Mexborough station is a Grade II-listed building and was constructed in 1871 for the Manchester, Sheffield & Lincolnshire Railway, later to become the Great Central Railway. Thinly coursed dressed sandstone with ashlar dressings and a Welsh slate roof characterise the attractive station building, which comprises an elongated single-storey range incorporating parcels office, ticket office and waiting rooms, with a two-storey house at its east end. A noteworthy feature, and once fairly common at stations where a number of railwaymen from the local area, or from one local railway company, served in global conflicts, is a wall monument to the Great Central railwaymen of Mexborough who gave their lives in the First World War.

Mexborough once had a third platform, which turned the Sheffield-bound platform into a virtual island. This was used occasionally for regular passenger services travelling via the Great Central line to Sheffield, but more often by excursion trains to East Coast resorts such as Scarborough, Bridlington and Cleethorpes. This platform face ceased to be used in the late 1970s but can still be seen.

As part of the South Yorkshire Passenger Transport Executive's four-year plan for upgrading the railways in the county, Mexborough received an improved waiting area and ticket office, completed in May 1989. Further improvements took place in 2009/10 when help points, an updated public address system, refurbished toilets and booking office area, additional shelters and CCTV, information screens and improved access for the disabled were all provided. Indeed, in 2011 Mexborough won the 'Station of the Year (Small)' category at the National Rail Awards.

Mexborough's railway routes have declined over the years. The Barnsley to Doncaster local passenger service was withdrawn on 29 June 1959 and in 1966 all passenger

Mexborough station is seen in September 1977.
George Woods

Class 37 No 37120 trundles through Mexborough on 9 June 1977 with a loaded coal train. *George Woods*

The Great Central Railway war memorial at Mexborough station. *George Woods*

trains to Sheffield were routed to the city's Midland station, initially via the Swinton curve until its closure in January 1968, and thereafter via the Great Central route through the closed Kilnhurst Central. Services today to Sheffield are generally half-hourly with some continuing to Worksop, Gainsborough and Lincoln. Eastbound services serve Doncaster with some continuing to Scunthorpe, Goole and Hull. On Sundays there is an eastbound service from Manchester Airport to Cleethorpes in the morning, although there is no return service westbound.

A Metropolitan-Cammell Class 101 DMU set led by coach No NE50226 leaves Alnwick with a local service for Newcastle on 28 May 1965. © *www.railphotoprints.co.uk, Chris Davies*

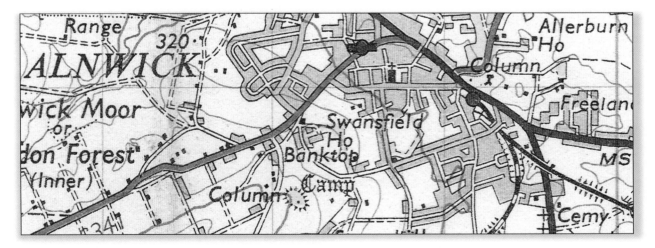

92 ALNWICK
A wizard terminus

Alnwick, the principal market town of central Northumberland and at one time the county town, which held a strategic position on the Great North Road, is located 3 miles west of the nearest railway, the East Coast Main Line (ECML). Had the grounds of Alnwick Castle, ancestral seat of the Dukes of Northumberland, not extended across any potential north-south route that might have served the town directly, Alnwick today would

surely still have a train service. Like much of the aristocracy in mid-19th-century England, animosity towards railways intruding upon their acreage meant that any proposal to route the ECML via Alnwick was probably a non-starter. In any event, the local topography of the area, which would have required expensive earthworks to maintain an easy gradient for the limited power of the steam locomotives of the period, mitigated against a route closer to Alnwick.

Alnwick's fine terminus is shorn of its tracks and with loading ramps in place of platforms in this mid-1970s view prior to restoration.

Table 53

ALNMOUTH and ALNWICK

WEEKDAYS ONLY

Miles			D am	am	am	From Newcastle (dep 8.42 am) (Table 2)	SO am	From Newcastle (dep 8.45 am) (Table 2)	SX am	SX am	SO am	SO pm	SX pm	From Newcastle (dep 12.32pm) (Table 2)	SO pm	SO pm
—	ALNMOUTH	dep	7 7	7 58	8 28		9 37		9 40	10 10	10 10	12 2	1 0		1 27	2 10
3	ALNWICK	arr	7 12	8 5	8 35	9 43	9 46		9 46	10 15	10 17	12 9	1 7	1 33	1 33	2 15

WEEKDAYS ONLY—continued

		From Newcastle (dep 2.20 pm) (Table 2)	SX pm	SO pm	SX pm	SO pm	From Newcastle (dep 5.7 pm) (Table 2)	SX pm	From Newcastle (dep 5.55 pm) (Table 2)	SO pm	SX pm	SO pm	pm	From Newcastle (dep 10.30 pm) (Table 2)	pm	
ALNMOUTH	dep		3 17	3 25	5 30	5 40		6 2		6 50	7 25	8 36	10 17		11 28	....
ALNWICK	arr		3 23	3 30	5 37	5 47		6 8		6 56	7 30	8 43	10 24		11 34	..

WEEKDAYS ONLY

Miles			To Newcastle (arr 8.34 am) (Table 2)	D am	am	am	SX am	To Newcastle (arr 11 am) (Table 2)	SO am	To Newcastle (arr 11.26 am) (Table 2)	SX am	SO am	SX pm	SO pm	SO pm	SO pm
—	ALNWICK	dep		7 32	7 45	8 14	10 0		10 0		10 25	11 46	12 45	1 10	1 56	3 13
3	ALNMOUTH	arr	7 37	7 51	8 20	10 5		10 5		10 30	11 52	12 51	1 16	2 1	3 18	

WEEKDAYS ONLY—continued

		To Newcastle (arr 4.40 pm) (Table 2)	SX pm	To Newcastle (arr 5.3 pm) (Table 2)	SO pm	SX pm	SO pm	SX pm	To Newcastle (arr 8.41 am) (Table 2)	pm	SO pm	pm	D pm			
ALNWICK	dep		3 40		4 3	4 34	5 11	7 13		7 42	8 19	10 0	11 40	......	..	..
ALNMOUTH	arr	3 45		4 8	4 40	5 17	7 18		7 47	8 25	10 6	11 45	..	..	..	..

D—Diesel Train. | **SO**—Saturdays only | **SX**—Saturdays excepted.

Two rival proposals to close the gap between the valleys of the Tweed and the Tyne came before Parliament in 1844. Brunel proposed that the Northumberland Railway should pass inland through Morpeth, Widdrington, Embleton and Chathill using his ill-fated atmospheric system of propulsion. Fortunately the other proposal, drawn up by the Newcastle & Berwick Railway and backed by the 'Railway King' George Hudson with technical support from George Stephenson, was successful in obtaining the Royal Assent on 21 July 1845. However, this did mean that Alnwick would have to rely on a branch line, which opened in 1850 from Alnmouth on the ECML to a terminus on the outskirts of the town. Not only did this mean the inconvenience of having to change trains, thereby increasing journey times (although some through trains to Newcastle were provided), but also in later years the very existence of often increasingly uneconomic branch-line services was viewed as anathema to the modern railway and came under severe threat, particularly in the early 1960s, although Alnwick was omitted from the Beeching proposals.

One benefit of the presence of Alnwick Castle and of the Duke, who numbered royalty among his visitors, was the provision of a suitably architecturally splendid stone terminus station covering some 32,000sq ft, with a double overall roof span. It was constructed in 1887 upon the opening of the Cornhill line to Coldstream, where connection could be made with the Waverley Route and to Tweedmouth. The station was a fitting addition to the numerous attractive buildings that had earned the town the soubriquet 'Windsor of the North'.

Although the Coldstream line was an early casualty, closing in 1930, a frequent shuttle service linked Alnwick with the ECML until withdrawal in January 1968. Despite the platforms being removed after closure, the impressive terminus at Alnwick survived demolition and after use by an agricultural merchant was restored and currently houses one of the largest second-hand bookshops in the country.

The Aln Valley Railway is planning to restore services to Alnmouth, but to a new station on the outskirts of the town for, as has happened in so many cases, a bypass road and other commercial development precludes access to the original terminus. Like Alnwick Castle, which has played a prominent role in the 'Harry Potter' films, the former station, once a 'wizard' terminus of two lines, lives on.

93 KELSO
Will ye no come back again?

Stations originally planned as the terminus of a branch line have, on occasion, taken on a new role as through stations when another branch line has arrived to serve the same town from another direction, taking the opportunity to join up with the original route. Such is the case with Kelso in the Scottish Borders, which welcomed its first trains in 1851. A year prior to that rails had actually reached a temporary terminus at Wallace Nick, sited a little to the west of the town, when the North British Railway route from St Boswells, on the Waverley Route, opened in January 1850. The line was extended into Kelso station, situated at Maxwellheugh, south of the town, the following year, while the Newcastle & Berwick Railway (N&BR) was constructing its route into Kelso from Tweedmouth, near Berwick-upon-Tweed. By July 1849 the N&BR was within 2 miles of the town, but the gap was not closed for a further two years until 1 June 1851, when Kelso became a through station on a 23-mile inland route that was to become a useful diversion should the ECML ever become blocked. Such a situation occurred during the floods of 1948 when the main line to Scotland north of Tweedmouth was impassable for three months and Anglo-Scottish expresses such as the 'Flying Scotsman' travelled by way of Kelso. 1954 saw a further instance of flooding with diverted traffic again taking the Kelso route. Although originally double track throughout, the line from Kelso to St Boswells was singled in the 1930s, making use of the line as a diversionary route more difficult, with speed on this section being limited to 25mph.

Kelso station had three platforms, an engine shed, a goods shed and several sidings. The main station building was 'L'-shaped with two storeys in the Tudor style, containing the booking office on the ground floor and a flat for the stationmaster on the first floor. A single-storey wooden building sited in the angle of the main building contained the waiting rooms.

All intermediate stations between Tweedmouth and Kelso were closed to passengers on 4 July 1955, except for Coldstream and Norham, which remained open until all

A scene from yesteryear as Class 'D30' 'Superheated Scott' 4-4-0 No 62440 *Wandering Willie*, named after a story rather than a character from the Walter Scott novel *Redgauntlet*, calls at Kelso with a St Boswells service on 25 September 1954. *CH Library*

passenger services were withdrawn. Notwithstanding the fact that the arrival of trains at Kelso had been in two stages, services were withdrawn at a stroke when all passenger trains along the whole route between St Boswells and Tweedmouth ceased in June 1964, by which time there were only two trains each way on weekdays. Freight traffic between Kelso and Tweedmouth finished in March 1965, while that to St Boswells carried on until 1968, after which time the track was removed and Kelso station was left to decay until it was later demolished. Nothing tangible remains at the site today, apart from the name Station Road, as part of the trackbed was used for a bypass road.

Kelso station is seen in the 1970s shortly before demolition. Will trains ever return here following the successful reopening of part of the Waverley Route?

Table 54

BERWICK-UPON-TWEED and KELSO

Miles		Through Train—Berwick to St. Boswells	am 6 55	SO pm 4M40	Through Train—Berwick to St. Boswells	SX pm 4M25	....	Miles			Through Train—St. Boswells to Berwick	am 8 25	Through Train—St. Boswells to Berwick	pm 4 0	..	..	..	..
	2 Newcastle .. dep		6 55	4M40		4M25	....	—	St. Boswells dep			8 25		4 0	..	..	..	..
	2 Edinburgh (Wav.) .. ,,		8G30	5 8		5 8	..	—	KELSO ...... dep			8 50		4 40	....			
—	BERWICK-upon-TWEED .... dep		9 56	6 33		6 37	....	10	Coldstream .. ,,			9 9		5 4	....			
1¼	Tweedmouth { arr		9 59	6 36		6 40	....	15¾	Norham ...... ,,			9 19		5 14	....			
	{ dep		10 6	6 43		6 47	....	22¼	Tweedmouth { arr			9 30		5 25	....			
7¾	Norham .. ,,		10 17	6‡54		6‡58	....	23½	{ dep			9 37		5 34	....			
13½	Coldstream .. ,,		10 27	7 7		7 11	....	23½	BERWICK-upon-TWEED arr			9 40		5 37	..	..	..	..
23½	KELSO .. arr		10 43	7 24		7 28	....											
								81	2 Edinburgh arr			12D30		9F 0	....			
35	St. Boswells .. arr		11 8	8 0		8 0	....	90½	2 Newcastle ,,			1L22		7E34	..	..	..	..

For other trains between Berwick-upon-Tweed and Tweedmouth, see Table 2.

D—On Mondays to Fridays from 16th July to 24th August arrives Edinburgh 11.46 am. On Saturdays from 30th June to 18th August arrives Edinburgh 11.38 am.
E—Arrives Newcastle 7.21 pm on Fridays and Saturdays.
F—On Saturdays arrives Edinburgh 8.54 pm.
G—On Saturdays also on Monday, 6th August, departs Edinburgh 6.50 am.
L—On Saturdays arrives Newcastle 12.50 pm (11.42 am from 30th June to 28th July).
M—Connection at Tweedmouth.
SO—Saturdays only.
SX—Saturdays excepted.
‡—No staff in attendance.

However, the success of the recently revived Waverley Route between Edinburgh and Tweedbank bodes well for a possible future extension south to St Boswells, Hawick and maybe even Carlisle one day, undoing the closure of the route in 1969. There has been a suggestion that any expansion of the new Borders Railway should include consideration of reopening the line to Kelso and on to Berwick-upon-Tweed. The Scottish Borders Council leader has agreed that it is an idea that might be worth at least exploring in the next phase of feasibility work for the Borders Railway, with a study looking at connecting Tweedbank with Hawick and Carlisle. He has also said that,

'Tweedbank to St Boswells, Kelso and Berwick may seem ambitious and impossible, but in 2015 the Borders delivered the longest domestic railway to be built in 100 years. So the impossible can be achieved.' Perhaps the words of the Scots poem 'Bonnie Charlie', commemorating the Jacobite rebellion that ended at the Battle of Culloden in 1745, may well be apposite here:

'Will ye no' come back again?
Will ye no' come back again?
Better lo'ed ye canna be
Will ye no' come back again?'

94 POYLE ESTATE HALT
What about the workers?

As we have seen in the case of Acrow Halt (No. 46), halts were provided for individual factories. On occasions they were also built to serve whole industrial estates and this was the case with two halts on the Staines West branch sited at Poyle Estate and Colnbrook Estate.

Poyle Estate Halt opened in January 1954 in response to the establishment of factories beside the railway between Colnbrook and Poyle, which had resulted from the opening of Heathrow Airport in 1946. The basic halt consisted of a 50-foot prefabricated concrete platform just long enough for the normal train on the branch at that time, a single-car diesel railcar. It was provided with a concrete awning in the centre, for weather protection for intending passengers, together with concrete lamp posts at each end, although that at the north never seems to have been graced with the luxury of a lamp. Access was along a short path from the factories that lined the

A single-car DMU pauses at Poyle Estate Halt on 26 March 1965.
Colour-Rail

adjacent road and up a concrete ramp at the south end of the platform, the ramp at the north end being steeper and of wooden construction. Two WR totems were provided, one under the awning and the other attached to the lamp post at the southern end. In 1960, consequent upon the introduction of two-car DMUs to the branch, the platform was lengthened by a further 50 feet.

As might be expected, trains were only scheduled to stop at the halt in the morning and afternoon peak hours coinciding with the arrival and departure of the factory workers; in 1963, for example, there were four morning stopping trains in each direction and three in the afternoon. There was a footnote in the timetable to the effect that passengers wishing to alight at the halt at other times, availing themselves of the other ten services provided on the branch not scheduled to stop, should notify the guard at West Drayton or Staines West, and that those wanting to join a train were required to give an appropriate hand signal to the driver. Trains departed from Poyle Estate Halt 2 minutes after leaving Colnbrook or Poyle stations.

The other halt provided, which served an industrial estate at Colnbrook, was governed by similar instructions and its opening in May 1961 meant that there were no fewer than four stations or halts in a little over a mile. Poyle Estate Halt closed on 29 March 1965, after some 11 years of life, when passenger services along the branch were withdrawn. The journey from Staines to London for commuters via the branch was rather indirect, while the competitive route via the SR electrified service was preferred as the more convenient way to travel to town. The halt remained intact for a number of years after passenger closure, but by the early 1970s it had been demolished.

Poyle Estate Halt is seen again looking north in August 1968 after closure to passengers.
Nick Catford

The eastern end of Temple Meads is seen in the 1970s with a couple of Brush Type 4s on view. The water tank is a relic from steam days and the Royal Mail trolleys for use with mailbags are also a thing of the past now that mail no longer goes by rail.

95 BRISTOL TEMPLE MEADS
A co-operative venture

In its early days Temple Meads played host to three railway companies. The Great Western arrived in August 1840 and was accommodated in a magnificent Brunel building that featured a mock hammer beam roof that, when constructed, was the largest timber beam roof in the country. Next to arrive was the Bristol & Exeter Railway (B&ER) in 1841; it initially used the Brunel terminus, but this was not particularly suitable for trains departing towards the South West as it involved reversals to gain access to and from the terminus. The B&ER put up with this until 1845, when it was accommodated in a considerably less salubrious but more operationally efficient station, which was described by observers as 'a simple makeshift structure' and 'a cowshed' set at right-angles to the GWR building. Finally, the Bristol & Gloucester Railway, later part of the Midland Railway, began running into the GWR station from 1844.

The original Brunel station with its impressive hammer beam roof can be seen beyond the Digby Wyatt 1870s extension, during its period of relegation to a car park. Note the wall-mounted signal cabin on the right of this view, which remained in use until September 1965.

In this modern view of the refurbished station, it is playing host to a Virgin Trains CrossCountry service with unit No 220018 in charge on 1 March 2008. *George Woods*

This atmospheric night view shows the magnificent curved overall roof with a 'Warship' diesel and a DMU in evidence.

To relieve congestion at both stations with the increase in traffic in the 1850s and 1860s, it was decided to build a new joint facility on the site of the B&ER station, which after delays formally opened in January 1878, and apart from various platform extensions this is basically the station we see today. Pride of place must go to the vast curved trainshed roof, 500 feet long with a span of 125 feet, although not far behind is the central block and clock tower built in perpendicular Gothic style. A fine building constructed by the B&ER as its headquarters remains in the shape of the Jacobean-style structure now known as Bristol & Exeter House. In 2014/15 Temple Meads handled more than 10 million passengers annually, many of whom used it as an interchange point between north/south and east/west services.

After a period as a car park, the original Brunel wooden-roofed section has been refurbished as an events centre available for hire for weddings, conferences, corporate hospitality, etc. Temple Meads is a good example of cooperation between railway companies, which in this case produced one of the finest railway stations in the country.

Bristol is among just a handful of large cities that have not had a plethora of competing stations for, apart from the small MR terminus at St Philips, traffic has always been concentrated at Temple Meads. Manchester and Glasgow both had four central stations, while Leeds, Liverpool, Leicester, Plymouth and Nottingham had three and Birmingham, Sheffield, Edinburgh, Bradford and even Bath had two.

A quintessential timeless Southern Electric scene is captured at Caterham during the 1960s. The green enamel running-in board, the totem on the concrete lamp post with its typical SR octagonal shade, plus of course the semaphore signals on their bracket together with the adjacent signal box and 10mph speed restriction signs, all add to the period charm of the view. Human interest is added by the figure of the signalman seen outside his box with watering can in hand attending to the display of colourful blooms and climbers rambling up the signal box steps. It is quite probably his motorised velocipede parked at the platform's end.

96 CATERHAM
A difficult birth

The long-held animosity between the South Eastern Railway (SER) and the London, Brighton & South Coast Railway (LBSCR) finally broke out into the open with the battle over the Caterham Railway. June 1854 saw the incorporation of the Caterham Railway to build a 4¾-mile single-track branch from Godstone Road (later Purley) on the joint SER/LBSCR London-Redhill route to the then relatively obscure village of Caterham on the cusp of becoming a dormitory suburb for the metropolis. Trouble began right away, for although the line was clearly within the SER sphere of influence the company had no right to stop at Godstone Road on the LBSCR-owned section of the joint line. A complicating factor was

that Godstone Road had been in any event closed since 1847, the Brighton company claiming that it could not be reopened 'in the interest of public safety', a phrase strangely redolent of today.

By contrast, the rather soulless modern image has a Class 455 electric unit arriving at Caterham on 25 August 2008.
Wikipedia, Sunil060902

Although ready for opening in September 1855, neither company was willing to allow the other to lease or work the line. Services finally began in August 1856 through the expedient of the Caterham Railway hiring a set of coaches and locomotive from the LBSCR. In November Godstone Road miraculously reopened as Caterham Junction, but not before the Caterham Railway had sued the LBSCR for its delaying tactics. The LBSCR retaliated by creating difficulties over the continued hiring of stock, as income was below that anticipated and the company as unable to pay the hiring charges in full. This, together with other financial problems, led to the small company becoming bankrupt and, after failed negotiations with the LBSCR, the SER duly stepped in and took over the Caterham Railway for less than half the cost of its construction.

The inter-company problems continued with the LBSCR denying the use of East Croydon station to the SER, insisting that all passengers from the Caterham line to Croydon should hold LBSCR tickets; however, trains departed from the junction before passengers for Croydon could possibly rebook. Attempts were also made to prevent Caterham passengers from entering SER main-line trains at Caterham Junction. Following letters to *The Times* and editorials emanating from the 'Thunderer', sanity was restored and peace prevailed for the Caterham branch.

Caterham station opened with just one very short platform. The line was doubled between 1897 and 1899 and an enlarged station consisting of an island platform with loops, locomotive release crossovers and a turntable dated from 1900. The station frontage containing the offices was at road level and a sloping covered ramp led down to the platforms. Electrification came to the line in March 1928. Although initially some 1 mile from the village centre, Caterham soon grew outwards towards the station and today it is in a very central location. The population grew from less than 1,000 in 1861 to 7,000 in the 1880s. By 1921 it was up to 12,000 and had reached 30,000 in 1951. The Brighton Works 'Terrier' locomotive was used on special trains in 1956 to mark the centenary of the opening, and a plaque was unveiled in 2011 to mark the 150th anniversary.

Freight traffic was withdrawn in 1964, there was rationalisation of the track layout at the terminus, and considerable areas of railway land were sold off for development. The end of semaphore signalling in the area came with the closure of the signal box in September 1983, when it came under the control of Purley, which in turn closed in January 1984 when the Three Bridges Signalling Centre took control of signalling of the Brighton line south of Anerley and Thornton Heath, including both the Caterham and Tattenham Corner branches.

Today the station and all trains serving it are operated by the Southern TOC, the branch having a line speed of 60mph. It continues to have a single island platform with a single-storey ticket office, and there is a carriage siding on the up side. Caterham enjoys an off-peak service of four trains per hour to East Croydon, two of which continue to London Bridge with two going on to Victoria. In 2014/15 Caterham station was used by some 1.065 million passengers per annum, the majority of whom are regular commuters to the capital. After a difficult birth Caterham is now truly catering for the commuter.

The small station building at Hemyock terminus is seen during its freight-only days, with a number of milk tank wagons, the lifeblood of the line, in the yard.

97 HEMYOCK
No milk today

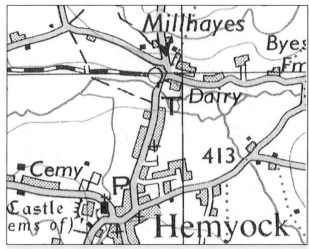

Milk was once an important traffic for the railways, until abandoned by BR in 1980, often beginning its journey to the metropolis from dairies and creameries on country branch lines that made connection at junction stations with main-line express freight trains. A number of stations in Wales and the West Country became identified with the carriage of this commodity, and one thinks of Semley, Seaton Junction, Chard Junction, Bason Bridge, Bailey Gate, Torrington, Lapford, Saltash, Totnes, St Erth, Lifton, Lostwithiel and Felin Fach in this context. One of the smaller operations was that on the former Culm Valley route, a very rural branch line running from a junction with the main line at Tiverton Junction to its terminus at Hemyock.

Opening in 1876, it had been planned as a low-cost line under the provisions of the Light Railway Act. However, by the time of opening it had cost more than twice the originally anticipated budget and took more than two years to complete rather than the projected six months. Operated by the GWR from its inception, and purchased by that company in 1880, it proved to be a loss-maker, taking just £4 per week in receipts, and very underutilised until Culm Valley Dairies began production in 1884, moving to premises close to Hemyock station in 1890. United Dairies took over the operation in 1916 with output from this facility becoming the dominant traffic and outlasting withdrawal of passenger facilities, which occurred in 1963, by some twelve years.

One interesting fact from the last years of passenger service was the use of a gas-lit coach on passenger services, likely the last of the type in regular use. This arose simply from the short distance travelled by services between Tiverton Junction and Hemyock, which would have been insufficient to charge the batteries of a conventional electrically lit coach fitted with a dynamo. Even at its height, annual passenger numbers only just exceeded 4,000, partly owing to the rather sparse service but more a reflection of the lack of appreciable local population along the route. Although the line had been strengthened latterly to take larger diesel locomotive types, the arrival of the M5 near the junction together with a decline in milk traffic spelled the end for this bucolic route in 1975, the final traffic being only fuel oil for the dairy.

Hemyock station was a single-platform affair with a loop and two sidings, one serving a cattle dock on the south side of the station and the other running behind the station. Two additional sidings gave access to a goods shed and an engine shed. Although it was so termed until

In this view of the track leading over the road into the dairy, note the signboard indicating that BR locomotives were not permitted to pass this point, necessitating shunting of wagons into and out of the dairy by hand.

An April 1963 view of the pleasant setting of Hemyock station some five months before closure to passengers. *John Thorn, licensed under the Wikipedia Creative Commons Attribution Share-alike Licence*

extended into the dairy. As locomotives were not allowed over the road crossing, milk tanks for the dairy had to be propelled over the road by utilising a length of empty wagons placed in front of the locomotive. The factory also had a winch for pulling wagons into the premises.

A rather ugly concrete block extension was made to the station building and this served as a waiting room. It is hard to believe, but in an effort to attract tourists a refreshment room had been opened in 1878. The expected influx failed to materialise in any numbers and after just one season the refreshment room promptly shut its doors, becoming a carriage shed, village club room and subsequently a poultry store. Today nothing remains of the station, the area being used as a car park, and the dairy has been demolished and replaced with housing.

1925, the 'signal box' was in fact only a seven-lever covered ground frame housed on the platform to control access to the goods yard. In the early 1930s a major refurbishment of the site was undertaken when the original goods shed and engine shed were demolished and the sidings removed. The siding serving the cattle dock was extended over a crossing into the dairy and a second siding to the north of the station was also

This view of the pier from the west side shows its position on the exposed shingle shore, which during the winter months was prey to south-westerly gales that hampered the operation of a regular ferry service at that time of year.

On the pier itself there was rickety wooden decking, an overall roof at the seaward end and a single platform. The Admiralty supplied a couple of cranes for offloading supplies on either side of the pier.

98 STOKES BAY
Hopes torpedoed

Opening on 6 April 1863, predating the opening of its future competitor Portsmouth Harbour station in 1876, Stokes Bay pier was constructed by a local company primarily for the conveyance of ferry passengers to and from the increasingly popular holiday destination of the Isle of Wight. A terminal station was constructed entirely on the pier, being 600 feet in length with two wooden platforms and an overall roof. Waiting rooms and offices were housed at the seaward end of the platforms with ramps leading down on either side of the pier berths, of which there were four, for the use of waiting steamers. Although the station was equipped to handle goods traffic, little was generated with only the occasional goods wagon being attached to passenger trains. A routine examination of the pier supports in 1895 forced the closure of the pier for repairs to be undertaken the following year at a cost of £6,000. During that period a temporary platform was built on land to the north of the pier.

At the start there was considerable opposition from existing ferry operators, but this was dropped when the new company agreed to let other operators use its pier. Initially reversal at Gosport was required as the Stokes Bay branch was only accessible from a trailing connection into the main line from Fareham, but a new east curve was opened on 1 June 1865 giving direct access from the Fareham direction.

The Stokes Bay Railway & Pier Company sold out to the LSWR in 1875, who were keen to improve the service as it provided the shortest and most convenient route to the Isle of Wight. Although the actual ferry crossing was quicker than that from Portsmouth, at just 15 minutes, the lack of through trains from London rendered the route less popular than the LBSCR route via Portsmouth. The Stokes Bay service was really only anything like busy

Looking landward, the rusting single track finishes at a chain-link fence. Redundant steelwork, lifting tackle and assorted ironmongery heighten the poignancy of this scene, which the promoters in the 1860s doubtless hoped would become a hive of activity.

during the summer, and from 1902 the ferry service was suspended during the winter months. In any event there had always been problems during the winter with docking at the exposed pier on the Solent.

The opening of a new route in 1903 allowing through services between Waterloo and Stokes Bay, via the recently opened Meon Valley Line, should have improved matters, but it failed to bring the expected increase in passenger numbers and the through service was withdrawn in 1914.

The steamer service to the Isle of Wight was suspended at the start of the First World War and was never reinstated. Despite the absence of the ferry, the rail service was perversely still running in the summer of 1915, but unsurprisingly was little used and Stokes Bay closed for the duration of the war as from 1 November of that year. This closure proved to be permanent as the pier was leased to the Admiralty for the transportation of munitions and fuel during the conflict. After the war the LSWR did not reopen the line to passengers and in 1922 sold the pier and the line south of the main line to the Admiralty, which proceeded to convert the pier into a torpedo station.

The pier was rebuilt with a complex of buildings to form the Torpedo Experimental Station, part of HMS *Vernon*, and the structure and its cranes were used for the preparation of torpedoes for test runs. By the early 1930s the waters of Stokes Bay were used for air-dropped torpedo tests and the pier used for recovering the missiles. In June 1944 the pier was a mooring point for landing craft and motor launches involved in the D-Day landings. By 1946 it was part of the Aircraft Torpedo Development Unit (ATDU) with combined RAF and RN staff quartered in Fort Grange, which was part of the Royal Naval Air Station HMS *Siskin*. The final military use of the pier was by the Royal Naval degaussing service (ADGE) until it moved to Fort Rowner.

The railway track back to the main line was lifted in stages. The buildings on the pier were removed in the 1960s and the pier demolished in stages between 1972 and 1976, leaving just the piles remaining. However, it was not until 1985 that the supports were finally destroyed by the Royal Engineers' diving establishment at Marchwood, who removed the 90 piles and two crane bases. Today just a slipway at the end of Military Road indicates its former position.

As an aside, there has always been some debate about whether Queen Victoria ever used the pier to journey to Osborne House on the Isle of Wight. A newspaper article dated 7 February 1880 would tend to lend credence to the stories:

> 'Owing to the dense fog which prevailed the ordinary route from Cowes to Clarence Yard (Gosport) had to be abandoned and the Stokes Bay route substituted. The Queen and suite embarked shortly after eleven o'clock on board *Alberta*, Staff-Captain Alfred Balliston and Captain Thomson of the Royal Yacht *Victoria and Albert* being also on board. The *Alberta* proceeded at a very slow rate of speed piloted by the *Elfin*, and the steam whistle was kept continually blowing, while a steam whistle on Stokes Bay Pier was blown at frequent intervals to indicate its position.'

This is also supported by an entry in the Queen's own journal in which she was obviously somewhat unimpressed with the station facilities at Stokes Bay:

> '...it was decided we should go but very slowly crossing to Stokes Bay ... our crossing was very disagreeable as we literally crawled across blowing the fog horn constantly, the *Elfin* answering by bells and unable to see anything but a few yards all around though occasionally it was a little better. We had some difficulty in finding the pier and a man called out, "I am Stokes Bay Pier." ...we stepped on to the pier and at once entered the train. There was no station only a covered shed.'

Of course, her final sad journey back to the mainland, after her death at Osborne in 1901, was made via the confines of the Royal station located in the Admiralty's Clarence Yard at Gosport.

99 SAVERNAKE
Highs and lows

There were many locations where two lines served the same location without necessarily approaching each other or physically connecting and where the suffixes High Level and Low Level were appended to the station name. One thinks perhaps of Tamworth on the West Coast Main Line, Builth Road in mid-Wales, Crianlarich in Scotland, and several locations in the Welsh valleys such as Blaenavon and Quakers Yard. The terms 'High' and 'Low' were relative and seldom reached the topographical extremes of Crumlin, where the High Level and Low Level stations were separated by a vertical distance of some 200 feet.

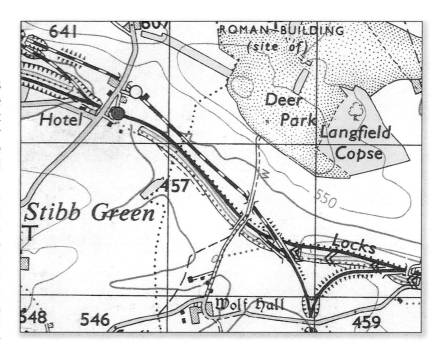

Such stations were often in sparsely populated locations, their position being dictated by the vagaries of railway geography rather than proximity to settlements.

Such was the case with Savernake to the south of Marlborough. First on the scene was the GWR station, opened in 1862 as part of the Berks & Hants extension line through Devizes. A branch to Marlborough opened from Savernake in 1864. Having endured the bottleneck of Savernake for a number of years since the opening of its line from Andover through to Marlborough in 1881, the Midland & South Western Junction Railway (MSWJR) decided to provide its own route bypassing the GWR station and create its own station some little way to the north in 1898.

When the GWR's Reading–Taunton through line was created and the Westbury cut-off opened in 1900, the platforms at Savernake were lengthened, the footbridge roofed and brick waiting rooms provided on the down platform. On 1 July 1924 the station was renamed Savernake Low Level, the nearby station on the former MSWJR line becoming High Level. The WR station was renamed Savernake for Marlborough in September 1961 when the High Level station officially closed, although the small number of MSWJR trains running by that time had used Low Level since September 1958 due to the state of weak underline bridges on that route. MSWJR trains ceased in September 1961, then Low Level station closed on 18 April 1966. While the remains of Low Level were demolished in 1968, trains still pass through today, whereas at High Level the opposite is true, with much of the station infrastructure remaining although trains have been absent for nearly 60 years.

The attractive brickwork of the Low Level station is apparent in this view looking west in September 1966, some five months after closure to passengers. *CH Library, Andrew Muckley*

The Low Level station is in the course of demolition as a 'Western' Class diesel-hydraulic powers through the closed station in the late 1960s.

The remains of the MSWJR High Level station are seen in the 1970s. Remarkably the signal box and water tank have survived.

The High Level station boasted a private waiting room for the Marquis of Ailesbury, who had leased land in Savernake Forest to the MSWJR. The main station building is now in use as a residence and the water tower still stands, although cloaked in ivy. At Low Level a bay platform was provided for the shuttle service to Marlborough. Savernake provided a useful interchange point between north-south traffic coming from the Midlands to Southampton and east-west traffic from the West Country to London.

100 ST ANNE'S PARK
Dual role

Although situated on the GWR main line from London to Bristol, which opened in 1840, it was to be another 58 years before a station at St Anne's Park, just 1¼ miles east of Temple Meads, welcomed passengers. It was situated near to the boating resort of Conham on the River Avon, which was a summer favourite with Bristolians, and was close to St Anne's Wood, a popular beauty spot. The reason for constructing a station here was twofold, to deliver the citizens to the open space of the countryside and to open up the area to residential development and thus generate traffic into the city and elsewhere.

The handsome station building was constructed of local stone with a booking office and parcels office, and boasting ladies and general waiting rooms on each of the two platforms, which were connected by a covered footbridge. Passengers entered and left the station at first-floor level, which connected with the footbridge. No fewer than eight staff were based here at one time, from stationmaster to lad porter, although with the closure of

the nearby signal box in 1909, when it was amalgamated with Temple Meads' East Depot box, the three signalmen formerly based here were no longer required. Small flower beds adorned the platforms at one time surrounded by the usual whitewashed stones. Although no goods yard was provided, which was unsurprising in view of its proximity to Bristol and its East Depot yard, the station did handle parcels traffic.

With the rise of the motor car, the attractions of journeying by rail to local beauty spots faded and the station settled into a primary role as a facility for commuters into Bristol and Bath. In the 1930s the not inconsiderable volume of such traffic topped 72,000

The down morning 'Bristol Pullman' leaves a miniature snowstorm behind it as it races towards its westerly destination on 8 December 1967. On board was the Duchess of Kent, whose planned flight to Bristol had been cancelled due to the weather conditions. She was visiting the city for an opening ceremony and tour of a local hospital. *CH Library, P. J. Fowler*

Pictured in 1968, a couple of years before closure, St Anne's Park has already taken on a rather forlorn air following the withdrawal of staff the previous year.

tickets per annum. In the summer of 1964, for example, there were fifteen services daily into Bristol with a similar number to Bath. However, traffic fell away over the years and following the destaffing of the station in 1967 in an effort to reduce costs the inevitable end came in March 1970 when Saltford, also served by local Bristol-Bath trains, closed together with St Anne's Park. Although not one of the casualties of the cull of suburban services that took place in the Bristol area in the 1960s, St Anne's Park only just survived into the new decade. Today no lineside trace remains of this attractive station, a most impressive structure for a modest suburban location.

The new Cranbrook station has a starkly utilitarian look. In the absence of staff, vandal-proof fittings, remote help points, ticket machines and CCTV are the order of the day.

101 CRANBROOK (DEVON)
New town – new station

Cranbrook is a new town being developed in East Devon, initially consisting of 2,900 residential properties rising to more than 6,500 by 2027. It is located 9 kilometres (5.6 miles) east north-east of the centre of Exeter just north of the village of Rockbeare between the B3174 London road and the former LSWR West of England main line. The requirement to build extra housing in this area was identified in Devon's 2001-16 Structure Plan, with the first houses being completed in 2012.

By March 2015 Cranbrook's population was estimated at 2,200 with nearly 1,000 homes occupied. Designed as an environmentally friendly 'eco-town', Cranbrook is powered by an energy plant that will eventually run on sustainable wood fuel. The scheme seeks to encourage commuters to opt for public rather than private transport, and to this end a new station was opened on 13 December 2015, after lengthy delays due to the original contractor pulling out and to drainage problems. It cost £5 million, funded by Devon CC and Cranbrook New Community Partners. An hourly service to Exeter (less than 10 minutes' journey time) and Waterloo is provided.

Although the facilities at this single-track platform are fairly basic, and of course it is unstaffed, it does boast a large car park, currently with 135 spaces and with land for further expansion for the eventual numbers that it is hoped will use it. The platform has a useable length of 150 metres, sufficient for the three- or six-car trains that generally operate on the route. Basic waiting shelters and seating

One nod to contemporary design is evident in this curved glazed cycle shed.

together with an automatic ticket machine and indicator train displays complete the ensemble. The site has been developed with the potential to reinstate the original double-track formation that was so short-sightedly removed in the 1960s. Eventually a half-hourly service between Exeter and Axminster is envisaged, although this would almost certainly require the provision of an additional passing loop somewhere in the Whimple/Cranbrook area.

Although nothing to write home about architecturally, one of the most striking features of the new station is the secure sheltered cycle parking facility with its semi-circular Perspex roof. The station is within reasonable walking and cycling distance for local residents, although the bus stop sited at the station currently sees no services. Even though Exeter Airport is only 2½ miles away, there is currently no linking bus service from the station, although this facility may well follow in the future, possibly using electric vehicles, thus promoting rail-air passenger transfer.

Index

Personalities & *Films*

Titles by the Same Author

**Impermanent Ways Vol 3
the Closed Lines of Britain – Wiltshire**
ISBN: 9781906419721
Paperback, 104 pages
Price: £11.95

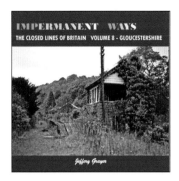

**Impermanent Ways Vol 8
the Closed Lines of Britain – Gloucester**
ISBN: 9781909328143
Paperback, 104 pages
Price: £11.95

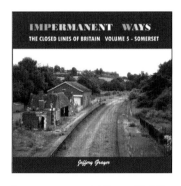

**Impermanent Ways Vol 5
the Closed Lines of Britain – Somerset**
ISBN: 9781906419981
Paperback, 104 pages
Price: £11.95

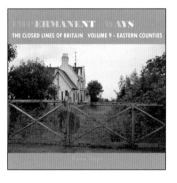

**Impermanent Ways Vol 9
the Closed Lines of Britain – Eastern Counties**
ISBN: 9781909328280
Paperback, 104 pages
Price: £12.95

**Impermanent Ways Vol 7
the Closed Lines of Britain – Dorset**
ISBN: 9781909328129
Paperback, 104 pages
Price: £11.95

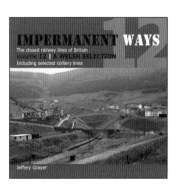

**Impermanent Ways Vol 12
– Wales**
ISBN: 9781909328563
Paperback, 104 pages
Price: £12.95

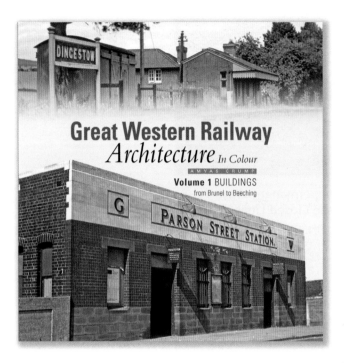

Great Western Railway Architecture

Amyas Crump

Great Western Railway Architecture is the first volume in a two-part survey by Amyas Crump looking at the architecture of the Great Western Railway.

This first volume presents a variety of structures encompassing both classic standard GWR designs and the non-standard contributions of many engineers and architects who worked for companies which were subsequently absorbed by the GWR.

Stations, depots and wayside halts, goods sheds, signal boxes and other fixed structures are examined showing how designs changed over the decades. From the sublime architectural gems of the nineteenth century to the mundane yet attractive Pagoda style shelters and corrugated iron buildings used across the vast GWR estate in the last century, the book covers a magnificent tapestry of structures.

Great Western Railway Architecture is a must have for all those interested in the GWR, its history and legacy and for the many who are active in recreating, researching or modelling this fine railway.

ISBN: 9781909328662
Price: £25
172 pages

Volume 2
Grouping, Signalling, Sheds and Miscellany
ISBN: 9781909328846
Price: £25
160 pages

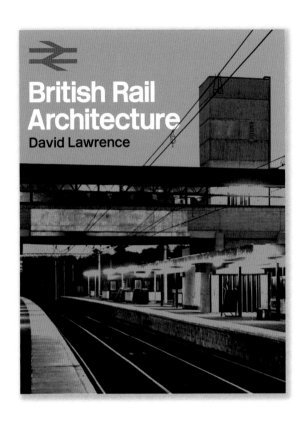

British Rail Architecture

David Lawrence

British railway stations were finally brought into the mainstream of modern architecture in the twentieth century.

Focusing on the architectural legacy of British Rail and how it pursued innovation and experimentation in its field *British Rail Architecture* explores not just the buildings and their designers, but styles, materials, furniture, colours, artworks and the unexpected links to distant places that inspired these changing design idioms.

The ambitious ideas conceived during the 1930s with inspiration from mainland Europe couple with post Second World War reconstruction and form a precursor to the considerable innovation of the 1950s and 1960s. New design ideas also appeared in the railway environment during the 1970s together with considerable investments in comprehensive reconstruction and new station projects in the 1980s and 90s.

This profusely illustrated book together with its companion volume *British Rail Designed 1948-1997* form a detailed historical insight into the appearance of British railway architecture.

Price: £35.00
ISBN: 9780860936855
240 pages

Atlas of Railway Station Closures

It is often said that it was Dr Richard Beeching, Chairman of British Railways in the 1960s, who was responsible for scrapping the vast majority of the UK rail network. However, closures, replacements, re-alignments and modifications to the network had been taking place from the very earliest days of the railways. This exhaustively researched and original work deals with all the closures which were made throughout the railway age in Britain.

A valuable new work of railway reference, the *Atlas of Railway Station Closures* maps all the standard gauge railway lines built in Britain and lists the dates when each line and every station on those lines was closed. The company, BR Region or later organisation owning the station at the time of the closure is listed, as well as the last pre-grouping owner. The name of the station used is, in every instance, that applied at the time of its closure.

Encompassing a wealth of invaluable information organised and presented in an easily accessible format, the *Atlas of Railway Station Closures* includes comprehensive cartographic mapping of the entire railway network of Britain showing its railway station closures; a complete easy to use index and gazetteer listing the date of each closure; and a photographic section illustrating some of these lost stations. An invaluable and comprehensive record and a fascinating insight into the history and development of Britain's railway network, the *Atlas of Railway Station Closures* is a must have reference for the bookshelves of any railway enthusiast, local historian and anyone with an interest in Britain's industrial heritage.

ISBN: 9780860936770
Price: £25.00
160 pages

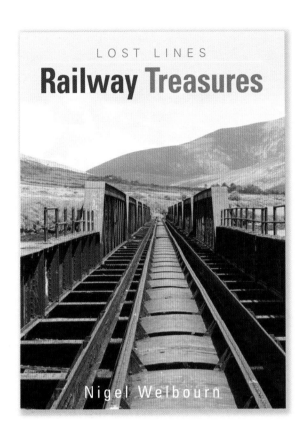

Lost Lines Railway Treasures

Nigel Welbourn

Many readers will be familiar with this author's long-running and best-selling *Lost Lines* series in 15 volumes, each covering a part of the country.

In this brand new book, he takes an overview of what has been lost from a national perspective. The book spans a period from the temporary closure of the Oystermouth Railway in the 1820s – to the Folkestone Harbour branch closure in 2014.

Nigel Welbourn takes us on a journey through a huge variety of closed lines, including those abandoned by the 'Big Four' post-1923, as well as those lost in the savage cuts of the Beeching era. It offers an intriguing perspective on what remains of many lines and stations, from the largest structures to tiny relics of past glories.

Most of the book's 400 colour photographs have never been published before. Over 200 stations and halts, 75 tunnels and viaducts, and 40 docks, ports, quays and harbours are included, as well as a treasure trove of maps, tickets and other items of railway ephemera. This book will delight not only railway enthusiasts, but will appeal to a much wider cadre of readers with an interest in the British countryside and our transport and industrial heritage.

ISBN: 9780860936916
Price: £25
224 pages

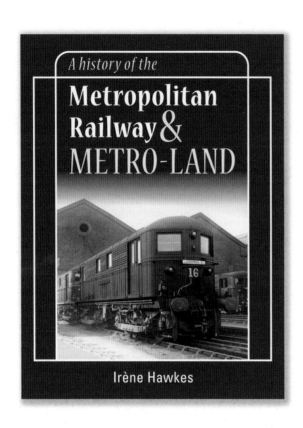

A History of the Metropolitan Railway & Metro-land

Irene Hawke

It was in London on the 10th January 1863 the world's first metro was opened – the Metropolitan Railway. The rapid growth in the population and wealth of the largest city in the world at that time had been achieved by expanding outwards, facilitated by the development of the railways but creating its own huge transport problems. People and goods were crammed onto inadequate roads and congestion threatened to bring London to a halt. The answer was a new railway that would travel underground into inner London.

The first section was built between Paddington and Farringdon, but over the next 40 years the Metropolitan Railway extended into East London and to the northwest beyond the boundaries of the city. Led by the ambitious Sir Edward Watkin, the Metropolitan Railway intended to generate income by developing the land along the railway and building housing, extending the urbanisation of London and creating new customers at the same time. This new outer suburbia became known as 'Metro-land'.

Irene Hawke's story of the Metropolitan Railway and the development of Metro-land examines how these two ambitious plans were pursued until the railway was first taken into the London Passenger Board in 1933, then nationalised in 1948. The fascinating text is accompanied by over 200 photographs, illustrations, diagrams and advertisements to bring the full story of the rise of the Metropolitan Railway and Metro-land to a wider audience for the first time.

ISBN: 9780860936749

Price: £30.00

160 pages